Qing-Yun Jiang

Court Delay and Law Enforcement in China

GABLER EDITION WISSENSCHAFT

Ökonomische Analyse des Rechts

Herausgegeben von
Professor Dr. Peter Behrens
Professor Dr. Manfred Holler
Professor Dr. Claus Ott
Professor Dr. Hans-Bernd Schäfer (schriftführend)
Professor Dr. Rainer Walz
Universität Hamburg, Fachbereich Rechtswissenschaft II

Die ökonomische Analyse des Rechts untersucht Rechtsnormen auf ihre gesellschaftlichen Folgewirkungen und bedient sich dabei des methodischen Instrumentariums der Wirtschaftswissenschaften, insbesondere der Mikroökonomie, der Neuen Institutionen- und Konstitutionenökonomie. Sie ist ein interdisziplinäres Forschungsgebiet, in dem sowohl Rechtswissenschaftler als auch Wirtschaftswissenschaftler tätig sind und das zu wesentlichen neuen Erkenntnissen über Funktion und Wirkungen von Rechtsnormen geführt hat.

Die Schriftenreihe enthält Monographien zu verschiedenen Rechtsgebieten und Rechtsentwicklungen. Sie behandelt Fragestellungen aus den Bereichen Wirtschaftsrecht, Vertragsrecht, Haftungsrecht, Sachenrecht und verwaltungsrechtliche Regulierung.

Qing-Yun Jiang

Court Delay and Law Enforcement in China

Civil process and economic perspective

With a foreword by Prof. Dr. Hans-Bernd Schäfer

Deutscher Universitäts-Verlag

Bibliografische Information Der Deutschen Bibliothek
Die Deutsche Bibliothek verzeichnet diese Publikation in der Deutschen Nationalbibliografie; detaillierte bibliografische Daten sind im Internet über <http://dnb.ddb.de> abrufbar.

Dissertation Universität Hamburg, 2005

1. Auflage Januar 2006

Lektorat: Brigitte Siegel / Sabine Schöller

Der Deutsche Universitäts-Verlag ist ein Unternehmen von Springer Science+Business Media.
www.duv.de

Umschlaggestaltung: Regine Zimmer, Dipl.-Designerin, Frankfurt/Main
Druck und Buchbinder: Rosch-Buch, Scheßlitz
Gedruckt auf säurefreiem und chlorfrei gebleichtem Papier
Printed in Germany

ISBN 3-8350-0082-9

Foreword

Qing-Yun Jiang was born in Fujian, China. He studied International Business Administration at the Shanghai Institute of Foreign Trade in Shanghai, where he graduated with a Bachelor of Economics. In 1997, he started studying at the University of Hamburg. After his Master study and his successful completion of the necessary law examinations, he was admitted as a doctoral student in the law faculty in 2001. In addition to his study of German civil, criminal and administrative laws, Jiang demonstrated an increasing interest in law and economics, especially in the relationship between law and economic development.

It is now a well-established fact that the rule of law, the protection of property rights and a swift and timely resolution to conflicts are corner stones of economic development and long-term economic growth. In many developing countries court delays are a major shortcoming of the legal system. This is true for countries in Latin America and in many Asian countries. Empirical findings show a 15 year length of civil procedure from the first filing of the case to the Supreme Court decision. This leads to court crises in the sense that private disputes are not brought to the court. Private parties attempt to circumvent the official legal system all together. When making contracts they resort to self enforcing contracts, to self help and, if available, to private alternative dispute settlement. In his thesis, Jiang presents an empirical study of court delays in China. He collected around 600 court files from various courts and sources in China on the district level, the provincial level and the high court level. It is an encouraging sign that Jiang could collect this data for scientific purposes and for the purpose of completing his dissertation thesis. Not long ago this would probably have been very difficult, if not impossible.

The most interesting finding in his thesis is that court delays are not a prime factor for the problems of the legal system in China. Due to the time bound program of the courts at the district level, more than ninety percent of the cases in the sample are discharged within half a year. The Supreme Court decision seldom takes more than five years from the date of the first filing. These figures are roughly equivalent to those in Western countries, such as Germany. Therefore, court delays in China seem not to be the main problem unlike in a large number of other developing countries. One weakness of the Chinese legal system is the low level of training received by lower courts judges. Some years ago less than sixty percent of all judges had a bachelor's degree in law and less than one percent had a master degree. This has lead to a very high quota of appeals. According to opinion polls, judges have admitted that they are not independent – even in their own view. They are often subject to interference, especially from the local political parties and other state organizations. These weaknesses, along with the problem of corruption, are now widely discussed within China. Another weakness of the legal system, which Jiang describes in his thesis, is sluggish enforcement of court decisions. Again, it seems that quite often court decisions are not properly enforced because of local partisan interference.

However, unlike in many Latin American countries, private demand for court services in civil law has grown rapidly in China. The number of civil cases filed has more than tripled over the last 13 years, with more than four million cases filed per year. This shows that private individuals in China have an increasing demand for court services. This is an encouraging sign for the development of the Chinese market economy.

Jiang's dissertation is a very valuable contribution toward the understanding of the civil law system in China, particularly of its strengths and weaknesses. It is a scholarly work, which substantially adds to the discussion about the development of the legal system in China. Moreover, it is a contribution to the overall legal and economic debates on the interrelationship between the economic system and the rule of law. This book can be readily recommended to everyone interested in the development of the legal system in China and to scholars who are interested in the more general consequences of the law in developing countries.

Prof. Dr. Hans-Bernd Schäfer

Preface

This study aims to touch on the concern of court delay and its, both monetary and social, costs in the Chinese judiciary. As the work of inquiry proceeded, it was revealed to me that reform of the judicial system in China is a keen task to accommodate the vast social and economic changes over the past 20 years. Such reform, which China is now undergoing, demonstrates that lawmakers are aware of the importance of speedy judgment in the courts and a well-functioning judiciary is an assurance of social justice, and economic efficiency.

This study will be of value to lawyers, judges and others concerned with the problem of court delay and law enforcement, in assisting in a solution for what is increasingly a practical problem. The application of statistical method in measurement and quantification of court delay is very useful to help find the relationship between court delay and the costs incurred in civil litigation.

As court delay is a worldwide problem facing not only developing countries, this study will not ignore the experiences of other countries in ways of coping with this practical problem. Some comparisons are made with the legal systems in the Western countries, especially referring to the US and Germany, with respect to court delay and costs in litigation.

Throughout this study, I have had tremendous assistance from the many people named below, without their guidance and help this thesis would not have been possible. My gratitude is extended to all of them.

I am extremely thankful to Prof. H. B. Schäfer of the Law Faculty of the University of Hamburg (Fachbereich Rechtswissenshaft, Universität Hamburg) who was my supervisor and who has extended much assistance in designing the inquiry, recommended materials in this field, structuring of the thesis and discussions throughout this study. I have benefited a lot from his distinguished knowledge of law and economics. I also want to thank Prof. Eger, my second supervisor, for all his guidance and kindness.

I am grateful to Judge Assistant Ah Yang in the District Court of Huli, Xiamen, China, who collected useful first-hand data from the courts and from whom I have also benefited quite a lot through discussions on specific issues concerning court delay and its costs, as well as enforcement of judgments in China. Judge D.S. Zhang of the Intermediate Court of Xiamen City has also extended many of his views to the reform of the judicial system in China. I am also grateful to Mrs. Wang, Yan Bin, from the Judicial Statistics Department of the Supreme People's Court, who provided me with very useful materials and information for this study. Furthermore, I have benefited a lot from the discussion with her on the issue of court delay in China.

Many thanks are extended to lawyer Lin, Jian Xin and his colleagues for providing data collected from his law firm, which made the sampling of data diversified and more reasonable and convincible.

Special thanks also are extended to Prof. Qi, Shu Jie of the law school at the University of Xiamen, China, who specializes in the research of Civil Procedure Law and who gave me useful advice about data-collection and current judicial reform in China. Thanks are also extended to Prof. Fang, Liu Fang of China Politics and Law University who instructed me to read some of the latest publications in the field. I am also thankful to Prof. R. Cooter, Berkeley Law School, University of California (US), who gave me useful advice during his workshop on Law and Economics of Development at the University of Hamburg.

Great thanks also extend to Susan Schneider (Ohio/the US), who spent her precious time to check the language and provide some useful comments.

Many judges, lawyers and friends spent their time to discuss and argue with me and help me on various points. I regret that I cannot thank each of them individually.

Qing-Yun Jiang

Contents

List of Charts and Graphs

Charts

Graphs

List of Tables

Introduction

Many countries, especially developing countries, have experienced the difficulty of the functioning of the judiciary systems and have come to the awareness of the importance of reforming the court system.[1] Obviously, delays, backlogs and uncertainty associated with unexpected court outcomes have diminished the quality of justice.[2] The Chinese courts system, as well known publicly, faces the same problems as many other developing counties. Court congestion and delay, corruption in the judiciary, and miscarriage of justice, have been heavily criticized by the public, as well as the difficulties in law enforcement.[3]

In this context, this thesis will focus on the problem of court delay and its costs in China with an empirical study and a comparative, as well as an economic, perspective. The thesis will first address the problem of court delay and judiciaries in developing countries and in China. Afterwards, it will apply quantification to survey the current duration and costs of the courts in China, as well the enforcement of judgment. Furthermore, the thesis is an effort to aid in resolution of the problems by providing a detailed study of court delay, costs and law enforcement.

Court Delay in Developing Countries

An efficient judicial system shall provide speedy redressal and less expensive court services to the parties involved. In an efficient judicial system, basic elements include: relatively predictable outcomes within the courts; accessibility to the courts by the population regardless of income level; reasonable time to disposition; adequate court-provided remedies. Court delay and congestion diminish the quality of justice and bring to the entire court system a loss of public confidence, respect and lack of pride in the judiciary. This problem is much more serious in developing countries, as courts in developing countries usually lack human capital and face difficulties in judicial independence, budget autonomy and judicial

[1] Adrian A.S. Zuckerman (ed.), Civil Justice in Crisis, Oxford University Press, 1999, p. 12.
[2] Buscaglia, Edgardo, Law and Economics of Development, Encyclopedia of Law and Economics, Vol. II, de Geest and B. Boukkaert (eds.), 1999, pp. 582-583; Also see homepage (http://encyclo.findlaw.com/).
[3] In a poll made by China Commercial Press just before the assembly of the People's Congress in Dec. 2002, 91% of the interviewed replied that they were not confident in the judiciary and were pessimistic about 'access to justice'.

administration etc.; meanwhile, the problem of corruption and incompatibility of laws affect and diminish the functioning capability of the courts. All these factors lead to a dysfunctional court system and cause civil crisis.[4] For example, in Latin America, some judicial systems failed to provide remedies to the parties in the 1980's when filings in the courts continued to decline under the absence of legally enforced alternative dispute resolution mechanisms, like arbitration or mediation.[5]

Court Delay and Litigation Costs in China: an Empirical Study

In order to have a critical evaluation of the functioning of the court system with respect to court delay, decisions on cases and enforcement of court orders/decisions, primary data with categorized filings were collected from the District Court, Huli and Intermediate People's Court in Xiamen City.

The secondary data in respect to filings and dispositions by the High People's Court and the Supreme People's Court is collected from the publications of the Supreme People's Courts, mainly from case books and China Law Year Books. The study of filings and dispositions in these higher courts will cover all of the 4 judicial hierarchies in the court system.

The opinions of court users, judges, and lawyers were collected through interviews and questionnaires to assist in further analysis and evaluation of the functioning of the court system. The addressing of ADR is to evaluate whether or not the current legal system can be reformed to reduce the caseload of the courts and achieve a higher efficiency within the court system.

The analysis of litigation costs, which has a strong impact on 'access to justice', will be based on the current laws and regulations. Furthermore, the analysis of the operational cost of the courts is based on data available from the High People's Court of Jiang Xi Province.

The Problem of Law Enforcement in China

Another important aspect of this study is the investigation of enforcement of judgments in China. As law enforcement currently is at a bottleneck in the judiciary in China, this study

[4] Ditto. Specifically, a judicial crisis begins at the point when backlogs, delay and payoffs increase the cost (implicit or explicit) of accessing the system.

[5] Buscaglia, Edgardo, Law and Economics of Development, Encyclopedia of Law and Economics, Vol. II, de Geest and B. Boukkaert (eds.), 1999, p. 584; Also see homepage (http://encyclo.findlaw.com/).

will therefore extend special investigation into law enforcement and trys to find out the reasons behind it. Due to the lack of systematic records of statistics in this regard the study of law enforcement is based on fragmentary sources of information and on my own collection of data from different Chinese courts at various court levels.

The Main Goal of the Study

In the past 20 years, court delays, backlogs and miscarriage of justice has admittedly been seen as serious problems facing the judiciary in the 1990's as society showed its' frustration with the judiciary. Reform in recent years has been a response to the people's demand for an efficient judicial system which can provide justice and due remedy. Therefore, this thesis attempts to answer the question: What is the problem of court delay in the Chinese judiciary today? There are different opinions in China: according to a research report of the High People's Court of Chongqing City,[6] the problem of court delay in China could be divided into 3 phases: i) Before 1999, due to the dim view of law among the judges and many procedural defects, there were many cases delayed in the courts and the public was very dissatisfied and frustrated with court services; ii) from 1999 to April 2002, due to the effects of *the Five Year Reform Outline of the Supreme People's Court* and *the Regulation on Strict Implementation of Time Limit (2000)*, court delay was reduced sharply; iii) after April 2002, due to the procedural reform and regulations on time limit for evidence-collection, the problem of court delay is not seen as 'serious' anymore.[7] Furthermore, the statistics collected by the Supreme People's Court indicates that most of the dispositions were within the time limit. Less than 10 % of the dispositions have over run the time limit;[8] whereas many reports and literature still regard court delays and backlogs as a serious problem in the judiciary, though no empirical study has been conducted. Thus, this empirical study is to answer the question of the current status of the problem of court delay facing the judiciary in China.

Another main task of the study in this thesis is to address the problem in enforcement of judgments in China, as the difficulties in law enforcement have become the main obstacle of

[6] Unpublished internal investigation report provided by the Supreme People's Court.

[7] See the internal report conducted by the research team of the High People's Court of Chong Qing City in 2002, p.2. The investigation was assigned by the Supreme People's Court to analyze the problem of court delay.

[8] See Huang, Shuang You, judge of the Supreme People's Court, Efficiency Analysis of Judicial Work, in: People's Judiciary (11) 2001, p. 21.

legal construction and functioning of the legal system.[9] Law enforcement has become an imminent task for the judiciary nowadays. For example, in the first half of 1998, only 39.5% of the court orders were enforced,[10] as 'a right without remedy is not a right', failure in enforcement not only deprives the rights of the parties, but also hampers the efficient functioning of a market economy. The reasons come not only from the internal organization of the courts, which are responsible both adjudication and law enforcement,[11] but also from the external social and economic environment, the attitude of the general public towards the rule of law, the economic system, especially the corporate system, and the development of the economy. Therefore, the existing difficulties in law enforcement not only concerns the reform of court organization, but also reform in politics, administration and the economic systems, such as banking and taxation, corporate, etc., and further deterrence to administrative interference, localism and corruption.

Judicial Reform and Suggestions

The procedural reform being undertaken in the courts[12] may be a reflection of part of judicial reform aimed at enhancing efficiency and pursuing justice. The internal impetus of the judicial reform not only originates from court delay, backlogs, high litigation costs, and difficulties in enforcement of judgments, but also originates from the difficulties and problems arising from the old and backward judicial system and its dysfunctions. For example, the spread of localism (regionalism) in the judiciary affects uniform rule of law and the authority of the state, low productivity of the courts due to the current backward judicial administration, low quality of judges in general and non-adaptation to the professionization requirement of the judiciary, the problem of corruption and inequality in judgment lead to distrust by the public and has damaged judicial authority. Further, the administrative pattern[13]

---

[9] See Wan, Fei Hong, judge of the Supreme People's Court, Report about the action to clear up backlogs in law enforcement, People's Judiciary (9) 1998, p. 4.

[10] The figure is even lower as mentioned by some lawyers in interviews. Many said that less than 20% of the court orders/decisions were duly enforced in their cases.

[11] Art. 207, Section 3 (Enforcement Procedure), Civil Procedure Code.

[12] The judicial reform in China starts from the reform of the pattern of trial with respect to evidence, inquiry, judgment and the responsibility of judges and collegial panel. The trial reform was first put forward in the 14th meeting of the courts in China in 1989. As a result, Civil Procedure Code (1979) was amended in 1991, the amendments reflected the experiences especially in the burden of collecting evidence, public hearing and voluntary mediation etc..

[13] It refers to the absence of arbitrariness of judges in making his own judgment in individual case, as the opinions have to be reported to each higher hierarchical level, from presiding judges to the president of the court, for final decision. Under such pattern of trial, the duration is longer and uncertainty of judgment is more likely, as the officers of higher hierarchy do not involve in the original trial and enjoy the discretion of decision.

in disposition of cases seriously affects the functional capability of the courts; backward facilities and low salary especially in lower courts hamper the capability of the courts. External force from the transition to market economy and the demand for rule of law as stated in the constitution requires the legal system to adapt to social and economic change.

If the judiciary is to provide equality and efficiency, it cannot simply deal with the symptoms of court delay, backlogs, failure in enforcement of court orders or decrees, corruption, etc.; it must also touch on 'the root political, economical and legal causes of an inefficient and inequitable judiciary'. 'Basic elements of judicial reform must include improvements in the administration of the courts and case management practices; the redefinition and/or expansion of legal education programs and training for students, lawyers and judges; the enhancement of public access to justice through legal aid programs and legal education aimed at fomenting public awareness of their rights and obligations in the courts, the availability of ADR mechanisms, such as arbitration, mediation and conciliation: the existence of judicial independence (that is, budget autonomy, transparency of the appointment process and job security) coupled with a transparent disciplinary system for court officers; and the adoption of procedural reform'.[14] As reform of the judicial system cannot be completed in a short time, each component forms an integral part of the reform. Such reform concerns the readjustment of judicial thinking, repositioning of judicial function, judicial administration and the modernization of the judicial system in China.[15]

Structure of the Thesis

This thesis is structured as follows: Chapter 1 addresses the legal system in developing countries and the importance of a well-functioning judicial system to foster social and economic development. Specifically, the shortcomings of the legal system in developing countries will be discussed. Furthermore, this chapter serves as an introduction to the central issue in this paper: the problem of court delay and its costs to the judicial system in China. Chapter 2 will first present an introduction to the judicial system in China, and further discuss the civil process and the problems facing the judiciary in China. Chapter 3 is the core of the

[14] Buscaglia, Edgardo, Law and Economics of Development, Encyclopedia of Law and Economics , Vol. II, de Geest and B. Boukkaert (eds.), 1999, p. 586; Also see homepage (http://encyclo.findlaw.com/).
[15] Qi, Shu Jie, Research on Reform of Civil Procedure Law, Xiamen University Press, 2000, p. 11.

thesis in which empirical study is conducted. This chapter first applies the data available from 1989 to 2000 in all of the courts to make an analysis of the nationwide courts' productivity and efficiency. An empirical study is presented based on random samples from the District Courts, Intermediate People's Court in Xiamen City and the High Courts, as well as the Supreme People's Court, serves as an investigation of the duration of disposition of cases in each hierarchical level of courts. Furthermore, critical evaluation and assessment of the functioning of the court system will be made. Chapter 4 demonstrates the problems of litigation costs and accessibility of justice stressing the importance of budget autonomy for the courts. In connection with the study, a data-based analysis will be made to discuss how important it is that the state should subsidize the judicial system so as to promote economic development. In Chapter 5, a thorough analysis of the difficulties of law enforcement will be made, since enforcement of judgment has been the toughest task facing the judiciary for quite a long time. This chapter will also discuss the current social and economic environment of law enforcement, and its reasons as well as the measures, which should be taken to enhance law enforcement. Chapter 6 summarizes the findings and provides policy recommendations and stresses the importance of the reform program aimed at a well-functioning judicial system.

The study has some obvious limitations. The content would be enriched if it had more samples and data from courts in other regions and provinces. The reason for such limitations is due to the difficulties in obtaining first-hand information from the courts, which are reluctant to disclose inside information under the current internal administration, and the high cost of collecting the information from courts in other provinces due to the limitations of contacts and travel. However, this empirical study is an endeavor to conduct an investigation on the duration of civil procedure and litigation costs, as well as law enforcement in China based on statistical data and samples from the courts.

Chapter 1

Special Problems of the Judicial System in Developing Countries

The legal framework in a country is as vital for economic development as for political and social development. Creating wealth through the cumulative commitment of human, technological and capital resources depends greatly on a set of rules securing property rights, governing civil and commercial behavior, and limiting the power of the state... The legal framework also affects the lives of the poor and, as such, has become an important dimension of strategies for poverty alleviation. In the struggle against discrimination, in the protection of the socially weak, and in the distribution of opportunities in society, the law can make an important contribution to a just and equitable society and thus to prospects for social development and poverty alleviation. (World Bank, 1994)[16]

I. Introduction

A well functioning judiciary is a central element of civil society.[17] The judicial system, as indicated by the World Bank, is considered to be among the top ten significant constraints to private sector development.[18] The quality and availability of court services will affect private investment decisions and economic behavior at large, from domestic partnerships to foreign investment. However, basic elements that constitute an efficient judicial system are missing in developing countries.[19] These elements are: relatively predictable outcomes within the courts; accessibility of the courts by the population regardless of income level; reasonable time to disposition; and adequate court-provided remedies. In developing countries generally, the judicial systems do not come close to the goals of the judiciary, which should be capable of applying and enforcing laws equitably and efficiently, and laws often are not subject to predictable interpretation. The lack of access to a predictably impartial and efficient judicial

[16] World Bank, Governance: The World Bank's Experience (Washington DC: The World Bank, 1994).
[17] Sir Jacob, The Reform of Civil Procedural Law, in: The Reform of Civil Procedural Law and Other Essays in Civil Procedure, London, 1982, p. 1.
[18] World Bank, Ecuador: Constraints to Private Sector Development, Washington, DC, The World Bank, Trade, Finance and Private Sector Development Division, LAC Country Department IV, 1993.
[19] Buscaglia, Edgardo, Law and Economics of Development, Encyclopedia of Law and Economics, Vol. II, de Geest and B. Boukkaert (eds.), 1999, p. 582; Also see homepage (http://encyclo.findlaw.com/).

system creates uncertainties that hamper completion of new transactions, particularly those involving previously unfamiliar parties and small or start-up businesses. This uncertainty, which is closely related to rapidly increasing backlogs, delays, and corruption, has generated a broad distrust of the system by the private sector and the general public and even increasing concern within the system itself.[20]

The legal systems in developing countries are mostly established through legal transplantation by adopting Western civil law. Most African countries, countries in Latin America, and East Asia (China, Japan, and South Korea) transplanted Western civil code into its legal system. The adoption of a civil code, as proposed, would "assure as quickly as possible a minimal security of social relations".[21] Although the codification of civil law has helped many developing countries establish their legal systems in shorter time, in practice the rights of the general public are frequently ignored and violated due to the traditionally dim view of law and the dysfunctional judicial system. Even the best legislation is meaningless without an effective and efficient judicial system to enforce the law. Without the judicial system, the law is only written on paper and its goals cannot be realized. Another concern is the compatibility of the laws enacted by the parliaments in developing counties to the social norms followed by the people and businesses in their daily life.[22] The cost of complying and enforcement will be high if the law lacks compatibility to the social norms and customs.

Developing countries are fully aware of the importance of a well functioning judicial system in establishing a market economy and to its economic development. A well functioning judicial system with easy access to the courts and swift law enforcement would lead to "comparatively low costs in using the market",[23] whereas in an economy with a weak judicial system, the costs of using the market would be comparatively high, and even the growth of GDP would be restrained to 2.6 percent.[24] "Judicial reform is on the modernization

[20] Buscaglia, Edgardo Jr., Dakolias, Maria and Ratliff, Willam, Judicial Reform in Latin America: A Framework for National Development, Stanford University 1995, p. 2.
[21] Rene, David, A Civil Code for Ethiopia: Consideration on the Codification of the Civil Law in African Countries, Tulane Law Review, Vol. 37, 1963, p. 189.
[22]. Buscaglia, Edgardo Jr, Law & Economics of Development, 1999, in: Encyclopedia of Law & Economics, p. 566. Also see homepage (http://encyclo.findlaw.com).
[23] Schaefer, H.-B., The Significance of a Well-functioning Civil Law in the Process of Development, Paper presented at the Conference of the Latin Americans Law and Economics Association in Quito (Ecuador) June 15th to June 17th 1998, Manuscript, 1998, p. 4.
[24] Sherwood, Robert M, Shepherd, Geoffrey and De Souza, Celso Marcos, "Judicial Reform and Economic Performance",

agenda of many countries. Demands for reform, however, are not founded on an acknowledgement that a more effective judicial process is needed to facilitate economic performance. The rationale for reform needs to be strengthened in order to sustain reform efforts in the face of strongly entrenched interests which will oppose all but superficial reform".[25] The economic reforms give rise to the modernization of legal systems in many developing countries. In Latin America, China and South-East Asia, judicial reform is one of the top national agendas for fostering economic growth. The need for a well functioning judiciary becomes increasingly evident. Democratization, urbanization and the adoption of market reforms have all created additional demands for court services.[26] The current undergoing legal reform in China reflects this tendency and shows that judicial reform in this country is aiming to safeguard the economic reform, to facilitate trade and transaction, and define property rights.

II. The Judicial System in Developing Countries

Most developing countries and countries in transition adopted Western civil law into its legal system. The Civil Code was transplanted into the French colonies and the Common Law was taken over by the English colonies. The German Civil Code, (Buergliches Gesetzbuch – BGB) or at least parts of it, have been exported to Japan, Korea, Taiwan, China and countries in South America.[27] Today, the formal socialist countries in Eastern Europe and China have slowly shifted from a socialist legal system[28] characterized by the production of centralized regulations to pre-revolutionary private civil law. The second phase of transplantation of Western laws into the reforming countries of Eastern Europe and Asia (especially China) is still ongoing, especially in the field of trade-related law, such as commercial law, bankruptcy

in: The Quarterly Review of Economics and Finance, Vol. 34, 1994, p. 101.

[25] Ibid.

[26] Buscaglia, Edgardo Jr. and Domingo, Pilar, "Political and Economic Impediments to Judicial Reform in Latin America", in: Buscaglia, Edgardo, Ratliff, Willam and Cooter, Robert (eds), Law and Economics of Development, JAI Press, 1996.

[27] See Schaefer, H.-B., The Significance of a Well-Functioning Civil Law in the Process of Development, Paper presented at the Conference of the Latin Americans Law and Economics Association in Quito (Ecuador(June 15th to June 17th 1998, Manuscript, 1998, p. 16.

[28] There are four legal traditions in the 20th century, namely civil law, common law, administrative law and socialist law. Civil Law or Code Law is mainly rooted in the Continental Europe and some of the colonial countries in Africa, in Latin America and in some Asian Countries; Common Law or judge-made law based on stare decisis is applied in the US, UK and the Common Wealth Countries; Administrative law is regarded as the framework to establish the rules to be followed in the relationship between the state and private individuals, and it has been the byproduct of the expansion of the government role in Western countries; Socialist Law was applied in the Eastern Bloc.

law, contract law, property law etc. Through legal integration and by adapting the law and its enforcement mechanisms to a modern economy, developing countries try to build up a sound judicial system and foster economic growth.

However, access to justice is the central issue in the judicial systems nowadays in developing countries. When individuals, or in some cases groups of people, are aware of their legal rights, the judicial system shall enable them to obtain legal services to invoke these rights. The rights of the people can only be effectively protected when the court system is functioning effectively to secure access to justice and provide court remedies without delay. But in most developing countries, the judiciary still faces many problems ranging from lack of public confidence and accessibility of justice due to court congestion and long delays in the courts, as well as the perception and reality of severe problems with corruption. In this context, judicial reform shall not only deal with symptoms, but also a profound reform in judiciaries.

III. The Problems facing the Judicial System in Developing Countries

Any reform shall first identify the existing problems. In the judiciary, lack of confidence of the general public in judicial system and difficulty in 'access to justice' are the main problems of the judiciaries in developing countries. According to the study done by Buscaglia, "the majority of people in Latin America lack confidence in the judicial system for many reasons. Surveys conducted in Argentina, Brazil, Ecuador, and Peru show that between 55 percent and 75 percent of the public manifests a very low opinion of the judicial sector. More specifically, in Argentina 46 percent of the people surveyed perceived the judicial sector as inaccessible. The same attitudes prevail in Brazil, Ecuador, and Venezuela, where the percentages are 56 percent, 47 percent, and 67 percent, respectively". Furthermore, "In Brazil, some 76.9% percent of the judges interviewed think there is some sort of crisis in the judiciary. This crisis is due to the fact that the efficiency of the courts has declined markedly, driving litigants to make every effort to avoid using the courts at all".[29]

The reasons for a lack of confidence by the general public in access to justice are attributed to the lengthy disposition of cases, inequality of judgment, high cost of litigation and corruption

[29] Buscaglia, Edgardo Jr., Dakolias, Maria and Ratliff, Willam, Judicial Reform in Latin America: A Framework for National Development, Stanford University 1995, p. 5.

etc., and this added cost is perceived as an increase in the price of using court services and consequently impedes the accessibility of justice.

1. Court Delay

The consequence of court delay has a negative effect on the society. Frequently, court delay causes deterioration of evidence due to the lapse of time and makes it less likely that justice will be done when the judgment is finally made; court delay affects social trust in the credibility of the judiciary, and in the meantime causes society to incur a high cost. As a consequence, court delay deprives citizens of a basic public service.[30] Court delay leads to a loss of public confidence and respect in the overall court system. Moreover, court congestion and delay not only causes an overload of work and tiredness of the judges, but also severely harms the parties involved in the case as well as the society as a whole.

In civil litigation, however, a prompt trial is merely a desirable objective and the litigants themselves have no means of compelling their case to be handled more quickly. On the one hand, to keep the quality of the judgment, the judge must look carefully into the cases and consequently may need more time, which may cause a delay, thus the parties involved may have 'delayed justice'; on the other hand, if the judges want to speed up the judgment, the quality of the disposition could be diminished and the parties may only receive "rough justice". Beside the lower quality of judgment, the trial court will consequently cause more appeals and burden to the appellate courts. Furthermore, the long duration of litigation may result in a departure from legal ethics, as lawyers find it necessary to provide financial support for indigent clients over the long interval between the filing of the lawsuit and the trial. A delayed calendar creates another new issue for the courts: whether some cases should be given preference and tried ahead of others. Any reform to improve efficiency may cause new enactment or regulation, as court congestion is not happening just for a short time, it cannot be solved overnight. It requires judicial reform and implementation of new regulations in order to find a solution. Moreover, the administration of the court is not simply the administration of a business; too frequent use of the summary judgment procedure may create

---

[30] Zeisel, Hans, Kalven, Harry, Jr. and Buchholz, Berhard, Delay in the Court, Little, Brown and Company, 1959, p. xxii, Introduction.

other problems, such as miscarriage of justice. Consequently, "rough justice", a result from a speedy judgment, denies the value of the judicial system.

Judiciaries in many developing countries suffer from increasing backlogs, delay and corruption, and this has generated complete distrust of the system by the private sector and the public in general. Lack of access to an equitable and efficient judicial system creates added uncertainty and hampers the realization of beneficial transactions.[31]

Through a study on the judicial system in Latin American countries by Buscaglia, it indicates that increasing delays, backlogs and the uncertainty associated with expected court outcomes have diminished the quality of justice throughout the region. The judiciary is faced with several obstacles, including a dysfunctional administration of justice, lack of transparency and a perception of corruption.[32]

The effectiveness of the law depends, to a large extent, on the rapidity of the proceedings. Court delay increases costs to the parties involved, in return decreasing the use of the court as a means for dispute resolution and will result in inaccessibility to the courts. In many countries in Latin America, the duration of proceedings has increased dramatically between 1983 – 1993,[33] which led to a court crisis and the collapse of the judiciaries as the demand for services of the civil courts decreased under the complete absence of legally enforced alternative dispute resolution mechanisms (i.e. arbitration or mediation). The results of polls in Latin America showed that 47 to 67% of the populations consider the civil law court system as "not accessible".[34] In India some cases even took up to 15 years for a court filing to receive a supreme court decision; according to a World Bank report, in the trial courts in Brazil and Ecuador proceedings take an average of 1500 days. Conversely, in France the average proceedings take 100 days.[35]

Delays encountered in litigation before the courts in South and South-east Asia create a barrier to economic success. For example, in 1987 the Supreme Court of India noted that

---

[31] Buscaglia, Edgardo J, Law and Economics of Development, 1999, in: Encyclopedia of Law and Economics, p. 581 ff. (http://encyclo.findlaw.com).

[32] Ditto.

[33] In Argentinean 47.8%, in Brazil 39.1 %, in Chile 11.1%, in Columbia 27.8% and in Venezuela 48.3%. Compared with Buscaglia, Edgardo, and Maria Dakolias. Judicial reform in Latin American Courts: The Experience in Argentina and Ecuador, 1996, World Bank Technical Paper No. 350, World Bank, Washington D.C.

[34] Buscaglia, Edgardo Jr., Judicial Reform and Corruption in Latin America, Paper presented at the International Workshop on Law and Economics, Ghent, February 1996, p. 8.

[35] World Development Report 1997, p. 100; also in: Schaefer, H.-B., Die Bedeutung des Zivilrechts fuer den Entwicklungsprozess, Sonderdruck aus Braunschweigische Wissenschaftliche Gesellschaft 2001, S. 1.

even if no new cases were subsequently filed, it would take 15 years to dispose of all pending cases.[36] In 1993 it took between 12 and 15 years for a case to be tried before the Bombay High Court, with an additional period of 10 to 12 years before all appeals were exhausted.

The problem of court delay in China is also considered to be serious, especially before the year 1999.[37] The judicial capacity is not competent enough to deal with the increase in the filing of cases; delays, backlogs and low quality of judgments damaged the confidence of the general public toward the judiciary. Some cases took more than 10 years because of the complicated procedures for filing, trial and appeals, and complaints to the Supreme People's Court.[38] In a poll conducted before the People's Congress was held in Dec. of 2002, 91% of those interviewed replied that they were not confident in the judiciary and were pessimistic about the accessibility of justice and that court remedies were difficult to be realized due to the problem of law enforcement.[39]

2. *Difficulty in Judicial Independence*

Judicial independence requires the judges to follow the law only in civil process and that the courts shall be free from any interference in the course of jurisdiction. Judges shall choose, interpret and apply the law in a suitable and correct way, and not subject to any outside influences and/or pressures, which may affect the result of the judgment.[40] The courts can only be a neutral third party and are not inclined to any other party in the judgment, otherwise the litigation process will be an unfair "two against one" game, and justice is not possible in such a situation.[41] If the judiciary cannot be independent and the law cannot be enforced, the rule of law will not be materialized. Hence, judicial independence is regarded as one of the most important principles of the rule of law.[42] Judicial independence is commonly accepted

---

36 P.N. Kumar v. Municipal Corporation of Dehli, 1987, 4 SCC 609, 610.

37 See the internal research report conducted by the High People's Court of Chongqing City, 2001, p. 2.

38 In an interview with a big state trading house in Xiamen (Xiamen International Trade Inc.), it was told by the law consultant of the company that one case concerning contract dispute has consumed already more than 10 years and it hasn't been finally settled since the company held that the final judgment made by the appellate court could not justify the facts and that the application of law was in question. The company appealed to the Supreme People's Court and applied for retrial procedure.

39 Source from Chinese Commercial Press, in Nov. 2002.

40 Redishs, Martin H., Federal Judicial Independence, 46 Mercr Law Review, 1995, p. 707.

41 Shapiro, Martin, Courts: A Comparative and Political Analysis, the University of Chicago Press, 1981, p. 8; also see Larkings, Christoper M., Judicial Independence and Democratization, in: 44 American Journal of Comparative Law, Fall, 1996, p. 605.

42 It is defined in the Dehli Declaration during the International Legal Scholars Conference in 1959: Judicial Independence

by all countries based on the rule of law, namely, the judiciary shall be separated from executive, legislature and free from any arbitrary interference and impediment.

In reality, however, it is very difficult for judges and the courts to be independent from the executive branch of the government, although judicial independence is written into the Constitution and the relevant laws. "More than 55 percent of judges interviewed in Argentina, Brazil, Chile, Ecuador, and Venezuela said that lack of independence was one of the main barriers to justice".[43] In an investigation of 288 judges in China, it shows that none of the judges interviewed regarded the jurisdiction of the courts as completely independent pursuant to the stipulation in the Constitution, and 43.1% regarded judicial independence in China as not realized.[44]

There are several obstacles which must be overcome in order for judicial independence to be realized in developing countries. Unlike in Western countries, where the judicial system is established on the basis of separation of power in the legislature, executive and judiciary; judiciaries in developing countries are not significant institutional counter forces to legislative and executive abuses of power for several reasons. Despite formal structural independence which is "guaranteed" by national constitutions, judiciaries face difficulties and are less active in asserting their powers vis-à-vis the other branches of government. This is due to the historical roots of the colonial legal systems, which are characterized by the deep involvement of executive power in the process of interpreting the law.[45] In China, the institutional arrangement gives rise to easy intervention of the executive and legislative branches since the Constitution allows the ruling party to enjoy power in all branches of the state. "Intervention by the legislative and executive branches destroys public confidence and trust in the judicial system and forces judges to be even more dependent on the other branches of government".[46] Moreover, in many developing countries, judges are financially

---

is a Principle of Rule of Law. In the Black Law Dictionary, "The Rule of Law is regarded as the most important principle of law, it requires the judges to make judgment only in accordance with the current principle or law, and avoid any arbitrary interference and impediment". See Black Law Dictionary, p. 1196.

[43] Buscaglia, Edgardo Jr., Dakolias, Maria and Ratliff, Willam, Judicial Reform in Latin America: A Framework for National Development, Stanford University 1995, p. 12.

[44] Jiang, Hui Ling, The Condition and Ways to Realize Independent Jurisdiction in China, in: People's Judiciary, (3) 1998, p. 16.

[45] In the Colonial territories, king's representatives – the viceroys, held a permanent seat in a superior judicial body (Consejo) throughout Latin America during the sixteenth and seventeenth centuries. See Alejo Carpentoeros M., Historia Judicial de Latinamerica (Caracas: editorial Cruz, 1978), pp. 15 , 16, also in: Buscaglia, Edgardo Jr., Dakolias, Maria and Ratliff, Willam, Judicial Reform in Latin America: A Framework for National Development, Stanford University 1995, p. 12.

[46] Buscaglia, Edgardo Jr., Dakolias, Maria and Ratliff, Willam, Judicial Reform in Latin America: A Framework for National Development, Stanford University 1995, p. 13.

dependent on the local governments who provide salary, pension, and housing etc. Under such circumstances, the principles of judicial independence are often violated since it is easy for the administrative authorities to intervene in the decisions made by the judges in specific cases. Delay always occurs when the local government interferes with these cases. Weak job security and budget autonomy force the courts and judges to be reluctant to resist the intervention of the local governments and the administrations, because the local governmental administrations have strong discretionary power in personnel management and budget supply. In most developing countries, due to the shortage of state appropriation, local courts rely heavily on the budget supply from the local governments. It is therefore not surprising to see that judges can be easily influenced by the executive branch when they fear for their job security and positions, as well as the necessary budget for the operation of the courts. Uncertainty related to court outcomes is generally more common in a system where jurist doctrine is subject to significant levels of partisan interference and pressure groups. The finality of law is therefore vulnerable when the ruling party and its administrations very often interfere into the court's decisions.

3. Non-adapted Civil Law

Many developing countries have transplanted parts of Western civil law into their own to modernize its legal system. The centralization and 'modernization' of the laws through transplanting was proposed by the first law and development movement during the 1960s and 1970s, such comprehensive, centralized and 'top-down' legislative reform aimed at modernizing of the public and private dimensions of law was sponsored by Galanter, Seidman, Trubek.[47] The latest development in the economic analysis of efficiency-enhancing substantive legal reform in developing countries was initiated by Cooter who argues that efficiency is enhanced by a 'bottom up' process of capturing social norms that are already in place as 'informally' relevant in human interaction.[48] 'Good Law' in this respect is formed as a spontaneous order and as already existing in trade or salesman customs before the legal

[47] Galanter, Michael, 'Why haves' Come Out Ahead: Speculation on the Limits of Legal Change, in 9 Law and Society Review, 95 ff., 1974; Seidman, Robert B., State, Law and Development, New York, St Martin's Press 1978; Tubek, E., Towards a Social Theory of Law: ' An Essay on the Study of Law and Development', 82 Yale Law Journal, 1 ff., 1972.

[48] Cooter, Robert, Decentralized Law for a Complex Economy: The Structural Approach to Adjudicating the New Law Merchant, in: 144 University of Pennsylvania Law Review 1996, pp. 1643-1696.

system defined them as binding laws, following this perspective, the costs of complying and enforcing the law become higher if the codified laws and regulations are not in conformity with the social norms followed by people and businesses in daily life, in other words, the laws or regulations are not compatible with the social norms or business customs. The dysfunction of the civil law system leads to high cost, for instance, if late delivery were not sanctioned, firms would produce the products by themselves rather than buying from the market so to avoid risks, even it is costly to do so.[49] On the contrary, "existence of enforceable contractual entitlements in Western countries has reduced stocks and often even replaced them by just-in-time delivery".[50] As mentioned by De Soto, under these so called 'bad law' systems, the transaction costs will be high when the law does not comply with the social norms. It is observable that in many developing countries many newly enacted laws can not be implemented, as in China, the so called 'policy from the top, game playing in the bottom' sometimes refers to the difficulty in implementation of those new regulations for specific purposes since the majority of the people resist following the rules due to the high cost of compliance.[51]

4. Absence of Arbitrariness in Judgments

The intervention of the higher courts and governments into the judiciary could deteriorate the problem of delays and impede fairness of judgments, since judges cannot make their judgments according to their will based on the law in due process. The absence of arbitrariness of the law leads to inequality of the judgments, as judges cannot be effectively protected against partisan and political influences. Very often judges cannot be independent of the influences of the higher courts, which should only be authorized to revise the decisions made by the judges in the lower courts during the appeal procedure.[52] In China, the

---

[49] Schaefer, H.-B., Enforcement of Contracts, Comment given at the Workshop on Institutional Foundations of a Market Economy, World Development Report, 23 -25, Feb 2000 Berlin, Manuscript, p. 3

[50] Ditto.

[51] To make the law attractive to the people, the new law should be designed to induce people to follow so that it can be adapted to the national culture. In economic terms, the law can only be adapted and accepted by the general public when the expected benefits – B (or cost reduction) is larger than the cost incurred in the adaptation (learning cost – C1, investment in learning) plus the losses – C2 due to the abolishment of the old law (benefits from the old law): $\int (B_t' - C_{1t}' - C_{2t}')e^{-rt}.dt > 0$

[52] Schaefer, H.-B., The Significance of a Well-Functioning Civil Law in the Process of Development, Paper presented at the Conference of the Latin Americans Lawn and Economics Association in Quito (Ecuador), June 15th to June 17th 1998, Manuscript, p. 14.

hierarchical relationship of the higher and lower courts has deviated from a supervisory function to, to some extent, an administrative relationship. It is a common practice in the Chinese jurisdiction for the lower courts to ask for instructions from the higher courts with respect to substantive and procedural questions.[53] In the process, the lower courts normally ask higher courts or the Supreme People's Court to reply on how to deal with some complicated cases.[54] Although the guidance of the higher courts helps the lower courts in solving some complicated cases especially when the human capital in the lower courts is low. However, such an instruction system is often used to conduct ex-ante communication between the courts and deprive the right of appeal (since the result of appeal will be most likely the same when the two-tier courts have already reach a consent on the trial of the case), or are used by the higher courts to influence the result of the judgments in the name of instruction..

5. Corruption

In many developing countries, vague legal standards provide an opportunity for the courts to be used as rent-seeking mechanisms. Judges thus can have discretionary power and broad latitude to decide cases.[55] Administrative deficiencies, like poor computer data processing allow judges and lawyers to conduct irregularities and corrupt practice. Furthermore, poorly trained judges in an already overburdened legal system are also susceptible to corrupt influences and create an environment where the rule of law cannot be guaranteed.[56] In most developing countries, communication is permitted between the judges and the lawyers; such communication creates an incentive for corrupt behaviors.[57] Under a corrupt legal system, each party tries their best to influence the judges so that he/she can win the case. According to the game theory, parties will pay the judge when the expected benefit of winning the case will be larger than not paying. This, however, in the end will increase the litigation cost of both

[53] The so-called "Instruction System" in the jurisdiction is not stipulated in relevant law and regulation, but it is accepted by the judicial interpretation. See Jing, Han Chao, Reform of the Pattern of Trial, People's Court publication, 1997, p. 63.
[54] From the publication of the Supreme People's Court, it is very common to see the reply of the Supreme People's Court on how to apply the law with regard to specific cases which are filed at the lower courts.
[55] Schaefer, H.-B., Die Bedeutung des Zivilrechts fuer den Entwicklungsprozess, Sonderdruck aus Braunschweigische Wissenschaftliche Gesellschaft, J. Carmer Verlag 2001, Sonderdruck, S. 143.
[56] .Buscaglia, Edgardo Jr., Law and Economics of Development, 1999, in: Encyclopedia of Law and Economics, p. 588.
[57] Ditto.

parties and lead to a lengthy process.

Further procedural elements contributing to the existence of corruption have to do with the lack of standards applied to times of disposition. As addressed by Buscaglia, "Lack of explicit standards coupled with court delay allows court personnel to charge a price for speeding the procedure".[58] Besides procedural defects, organizational arrangement in the court system also creates corrupt behavior of the judges when they enjoy a large discretion over planning, management of personnel, resources administration, budget and adjudication of cases.[59]

In this context, legal reform should narrow or diminish the playroom of the judges so as to reduce the opportunity to conduct corruptive behavior, and it is better for developing countries to choose rules rather than standards[60]. Standards may have lower initial 'specification costs' but they have higher enforcement and compliance costs than rules.[61] For example, if a legal norm regulates that all consumption of toxic substances should be forbidden; such imprecise standards would give room for the judges to engage in corruptive conduct since the judges may decide by himself/herself what a toxic substance is. Although the generating cost of such legal norm is low, the cost for enforcement and compliance will be higher since the parties would disagree with the judgment by their own definitions; whereas a legal norm, which provides a list of toxic substances, will prevent or control the corrupt behavior of the judges.[62]

The effects of corruption in the civil law are more difficult to analyze compared to criminal or public law, since in a civil law process, both the litigants and the defendants can bribe the judges to win the case,[63] it is difficult to decide whether the rules are violated by the judge or

---

[58] Ditto.

[59] Ditto.

[60] Rules are more precise legal norms, for example, 'a violation of speed limit would be fined for 50 Euro', is a clear definition of the legal consequence if a person breaches the regulation; whereas standards are more vague and flexible legal norms, for example, 'a violation of careful driving would be fined for 50 Euro', extends discretion to the judges and the playroom for him to decide what is the due level of care in driving. The generating cost of rules will be higher than that of standards, since it needs more careful investigation to find out the optimal amount of fine so that such rules will generate best legal effects; obviously, rules incur lower enforcement and compliance costs due to its clear definition. Furthermore, considering the lack of human capital in developing countries, rules would help to reduce the problem of lengthy procedures. Compare: Schaefer, H.-B., Enforcement of Contracts, Comment given at the Workshop on Institutional Foundations of a Market Economy, World Development Report, 23 -25, Feb 2000 Berlin, Manuscript, pp. 3, 4.

[61] Ditto.

[62] Schaefer, H.-B., Die Bedeutung des Zivilrechts fuer den Entwicklungsprozess, Sonderdruck aus Braunschweigische Wissenschaftliche Gesellschaft, J. Carmer Verlag 2001, Sonderdruck, S. 144; compare: Louis Kaplow, General Characteristics of Rules, in G. de Geest / B. Boukkaert, International Encyclopedia of Law and Economics, Internet Homepage.

[63] In criminal and public law, the judge will be bribed by only one party to a better and favorable judgment, whereas in civil law both parties can use their influence to make the judgment in their favor by bribing the judges. For example, 2 opponents fight for a sum of money of 100 and both expect with a probability of 60% to win the process. The judge could make a fair

not, especially when the standards are not precise enough. Thus, though precise rules may have higher generating costs, it will deter judges from taking time to figure out whether the standards are violated or not, thus avoiding the delay and corruption by speeding up the process.

6. Law's Enforcement

Law's enforcement constitutes another problem nowadays. The effectiveness of law enforcement does not only depend on the decision of the courts, but also on the behavior of the law enforcing authorities, like land registries or enforcement officers. In some countries, law enforcement bodies are under administrative authorities.[64] Law enforcing authorities in most of countries are subordinate to the courts.[65] In many developing countries, the court decisions or orders are difficult to enforce due to the following reasons: first, the enforcing officers have weak discretion in dealing with the cases involving local interest and lack of arbitrariness in enforcing the law, this has again much to do with the independence of judiciary when the local governments or parties can influence the executors; secondly, it is very common that the court's decisions or court's orders are difficult to enforce when the respondents are out of the territorial limit of the original courts, the coordination of the courts is weak in such situation. In China, crisis in enforcement occurred when the pending cases for enforcement in 1998 reached a historical high.[66] This forced the Supreme People's Court to shift the judicial work to law enforcement, and within three months in 1998 from September to December, the number of cases with court orders enforced or settled amounted to 1,200,000, but there were still around 530,000 pending cases for enforcement at the end of 1998.[67] The size of the backlog for law enforcement amounted to 850,000 at the end of June

decision if he is either not bribed or if both parties offer him the same sum of money. In the later scenario, parties are put in a game to keep their chance for a fair decision, the result is the increase of courts cost and demand for using court services will be reduced. See Schaefer, H.-B., The Significance of a Well-Functioning Civil Law in the Process of Development, Paper presented at the Conference of the Latin Americans Law and Economics Association in Quito (Ecuador(June 15th to June 17th 1998, Manuscript, 1998, p. 15.

[64] For example, America, Canada, France set up the law enforcing bodies outside of the court, whereas most of the countries like Germany, Japan, Taiwan and developing countries subordinate the enforcing bodies within the court systems.

[65] It is perceived that the enforcing authorities are better to be subordinated to the courts rather than the administrative authorities on the account of better coordination, since the bureaucracy will have the discretion to decide whether in certain cases property has to be transferred, orders of attachment have to be enforced or courts decisions have to be executed.

[66] The estimated number could be around 2 million cases. Also see statistics in: People's Judiciary, 1998, 1999, 2000.

[67] Tan, Shi Gui, Research on Judicial Reform in China, China Law Press, 2000, p. 284.

1999.[68] The difficulties in law enforcement in China mainly can be attributed to bureaucracy and the political motivation of the government in many cases; furthermore, a rough definition of relevant law and regulations make law enforcement more difficult.[69] From 1990 –1999, around 70% of all courts decisions were enforced; this quota is even lower concerning cases of economic issues, only around 50% of the cases were settled under enforcement procedure.[70] The same situation occurs in other developing countries, for example, in 1993 and 1994, only 50% of all court decisions were enforced in Poland and in Vietnam the quota was even lower, around 40%.[71]

The inability to enforce court orders and decisions create the same problem as court delay, as the general public foresee the lower probability of law enforcement, they lose confidence in judiciary and distrust redress of suffering by the courts, consequently the demand for courts services diminishes and settling the disputes out of the court often substitutes the courts resolution.

Summary of the Problems of the Judicial System in Developing Countries

Generally speaking, increasing delays, backlogs and the uncertainty associated with expected court outcomes have diminished the quality of justice; the judiciary is faced with several obstacles, which include a dysfunctional administration of justice, lack of transparency and a perception of corruption. All of these problems increase the costs to the parties using the court services. People will react to this added cost by reducing their filings in the courts and seek to solve the disputes out of the courts by ADR, by mediation or arbitration. Judicial reform should therefore promote uniformity of law and enhance efficiency in jurisdiction, and further enhance transparency and accountability in the process of enforcing laws. In a transition economy, judicial reform is urgent and necessary to foster economic growth and serve the long-term benefits of the people.

---

[68] Ditto.

[69] The stipulations in the Civil Procedure Code and the relevant regulations contain many gaps, which are often used by the respondents as excuses for not following the court orders; some regulations are too abstract or not logical enough to be applied in practice. See Qi, Shu Jie, Research on Reform of Civil Procedure Law, Xiamen University Press, 2000, pp. 257, 258.

[70] It is based on the statistics issued by the Supreme People's Court in 1990 – 1999, the quota could even be lower in reality as some of the pending cases were considered to be 'settled' due to long delay.

[71] Compare World Development Report, 1997, p. 100.

IV. The Impetus of Judicial Reform

Court delay impedes economic development due to lack of legal protection to the people in general, and impedes the private economy as well as the functioning market. Civil crisis in many countries reveals that in a dysfunctional judicial system justice are unavailable; therefore, civil crisis is regarded in the same terms as the justice crisis. The crisis arises only when judiciary deviates from the designed framework of justice. Thus, judicial reform shall be aimed to improve the accessibility of justice and establish a well-functioning judicial system to enhance the efficiency of the courts, in a way to foster the economic reform and economic growth.

1. Access to Justice: Internal Impetus

The evaluation of civil process is based on: litigation cost, time needed for dispute resolution, and the fact finding and application of law by the judiciary system.[72] Civil crisis mainly arises from a dysfunctional civil procedure and from structural problems in the civil procedure, which result in court delay, a high litigation cost, and inequality in the judgment, which hinders "access to justice". Civil crisis in many developing countries is attributed to the structural and organizational problems originating from the division of power in legislation, executive, judiciary, the political system, for example, the problem of interference by the administration, corruption etc., is different from the nature of reforms undertaken by Western countries which are aimed at improving the functioning capacity of the judicial system, since civil crisis in these countries is much related to the design of the civil procedure and the operation of court system. For example, in America the regulation of evidence results in court delays and a waste of judicial resources, thus the reform focuses mainly on procedural aspects so as to improve court efficiency. Whereas the judicial reform in developing countries is much more complicated since these countries not only have to revise and modernize the laws but also have to undertake political and economic reform, which may cause some losers during the process of reform; moreover, the government officials may use

[72] Leubsdorf, John, The Myth of Civil Procedural Reform, in Civil Justice in Crisis, ed. by Adrian A.S. Zuckerman, Oxford University Press, 1999, p.55.

the courts as rent-seeking mechanisms in the reform process.[73]

The reform efforts made by developing countries focus on revision of civil procedure mainly within the time limit of disposition, pre-trial preparation, readiness of certificate, enhancing judicial independence by budget autonomy and reducing influence by local governments etc. The judicial reform which China is undergoing focuses mainly on civil procedural reform with respect to the burden of evidence, judges' competence in the trial, jurisdiction system and the litigation system. The reform concerning the trial system shall be regarded as part of the judicial reform in China.

Judicial reform in China is much more complicated compared to the reform in industrialized countries. It originates not only from the necessity to enhance "access to justice" and tackle the problem of court delay, high litigation cost and enforcement of law, but also the necessity to establish an impartial court system in which judicial independence can be guaranteed. The reform faces great challenge since the problem of localism has damaged the uniform rules of law and the authority of the judicial system, and the incompetence of judicial personnel lead to low quality of judgment. The problem of interference and corruption has frustrated the confidence of the general public. The functioning of the court is heavily affected by the backward judicial administration and the insufficient budget supply to the courts; especially the local courts are affected in their daily operations. All these problems indicate the complexity of judicial reform in China.

As mentioned above, court delay is a common phenomenon in the world, especially in many developing countries. In China, after more than 20 years of construction of legal system, the country has improved greatly in modernizing of its judicial system, but problems like court delay, piling of cases, poor administration, and corruption are still the obstacles for legal reform. This thesis will focus on the reform of the legal system, specifically focusing on the problem of court delay and its cost in China through an empirical study and comparative analysis.

---

[73] Buscaglia, Edgardo Jr., Law and Economics of Development, 1999, in: Encyclopedia of Law and Economics, p. 588. (http://encyclo.findlaw.com/)

2. Well-Functioning Legal System for Market Economy: External Force

A well-functioning legal system will enhance economic efficiency, since a modern market economy requires laws to be able to constantly redefine rights and market relationship when new forms of corporate structure emerges and provides ever-changing determinations of contractual obligations, and extends them to new forms of financial instruments, tangible or intangible property, and redefine and enforce the rights of victims of new technologies and activities while protecting the environments from newly emerging risks.[74] The judicial reform shall therefore make the laws to be adapted to the dynamics of the social and economic system.

[74] Buscaglia, Edgardo Jr., Law and Economics of Development, 1999, in: Encyclopedia of Law and Economics, p. 564. (http://encyclo.findlaw.com/)

Chapter 2

Legal System and Civil Process in China

In the absence of fundamental political reform that would validate abandonment of the reigning ideology, Chinese law is likely to ... remain an assortment of disparate institutions lacking some of the elements that Western ideals take a s essential in a meaningful formal legal system such as hierarchy of sources of law, differentiation from other organs of state power, procedural regularity and control of discretion in decision-making, and adherence to professional values among the officials in the system. (LUBMAN)[75]

I. Introduction

A country's legal system plays an important role in adjusting social order and economic development. A capable legal system will enlarge the range of anonymous market transactions[76] and reduce the market transaction costs with the rules.[77] In China, high costs in defining property rights and the difficulties in building up a well-functioning market mechanism to large extent relate to the functioning of civil law. As China has more than 2000 years of Confucianism tradition, informal law still has a strong influence in Chinese society today. For example, in urban areas, the resolution of disputes still relies heavily on customs, morals, trust and reputation. 'It has admittedly been observed that the tradition of Confucianism... leads to a dim view of law and a characteristic tendency to resolve disputes otherwise than by recourse through the courts'.[78] Due to the long tradition of Confucianism and its influence on dispute resolution, the legal system does not work efficiently. The influence of Confucianism sometimes even hinders the development of legal development.

From history, informal means of dispute resolution have a long tradition in China and are

---

[75] Lubman, 'Studying Contemporary Chinese Law: Limits, Possibilities and Strategy', in: 39 American Journal of Law, 293 (1991).

[76] North, D. Institutional Change and Economic Performance, Cambridge Univ. Press, 1996. Also see Schaefer, H.-B., The Significance of a Well-Functioning Civil Law in the Process of Development, Paper presented at the Conference of the Latin Americans Law and Economics Association in Quito (Ecuador(June 15th to June 17th 1998, Manuscript, 1998, pp. 1, 2.

[77] Coase, R., The Problem of Social Cost, Journal of Law and Economics, 1960, p. 1.

[78] Zweigert & Koetz, An Introduction to Comparative Law, Cambridge, 1999, p. 287.

enormously more important. The legal system in China has roots in its culture and social background with distinctive features. The law in China "differs fundamentally from legal families of Western laws which are used for purpose of dispute resolution by issuing a conclusive and binding judgment and taken as a means of ordering social life".[79] From historical viewpoint, social relations are regarded as part of the natural order in China. Such a view is found in the doctrines of Confucianism[80], which has long tradition and strong influence on Chinese social life and the development of legal system in China. Confucianism was adopted as the ruling tool in Han Dynasty when Tun Chung-Shu (174 to 104 BC) incorporated elements of his philosophical thoughts into Confucianism and produced a doctrine of cosmic harmony.[81] The suggestion of "abolishing other thoughts, only respect Confucianism" was accepted by the emperor Han Wu (156 to 87 BC). Since then the thoughts of Confucianism have ever since dominated the legal development and social life of the Chinese for more than 2000 years. It is this form of Confucianism, which constituted the ideology of the Chinese empire until the revolution of 1911. The long influence of Confucianism has lead to a dim view of law and is also the main reason nowadays that formal law is not fully respected. Although state law, or formal law, was also admitted by Confucians to regulate human conduct, the ancient Chinese codes,[82] which appertained to criminal and administrative law, were invoked only where the state must impose a criminal sanction because cosmic order has been very seriously disturbed, or where the organization of the state administration is in issue according to Confucian doctrine.[83] Comparatively, Western legal systems are fundamentally different, social life should be regulated by the rules of objective

[79] Zweigert & Koetz, An Introduction to Comparative Law, Cambridge, 1999, pp. 286, 287.

[80] Confucius lived from 551 to 479 BC. In the "Chun Qiu" time (770 to 476 BC) and "Zhan Guo" time (476 to 222 BC), the law developed from custom law to coded law. The representatives of this time are Confucius and Meng, Ke (ca. 372 to 289 BC), who stressed on the importance of god, Wiseman, especially the importance of the rulers and its advisers, they also stressed the importance of ethical education and argued that "ethics first, penalty comes to the second". On the contrary, the representatives of the same time, Shang, Yang (390 -338 BC) and Han, Fei (280 to 233 BC) emphasized the importance of law; they did not agree the importance of the wise and the God, but stressed on the force and constraining effect of the law.

[81] The doctrine of cosmic harmony is a form of Confucianism which constituted the ideology of the Chinese empire until the revolution of 1911. It starts from the proposition that man and God, Heaven and earth, all things living and inert are organic parts of a harmoniously ordered and intergraded universe. The most important goal of man must therefore be to keep high thoughts, feelings, and actions in perfect accordance with cosmic harmony; in particular men must so conduct themselves as not to disturb the natural balance of their existing relations. The rules of 'proper' behavior were called 'li' and their content characteristically depended on the social status of the person to whom they applied, his status in his family, in his clan, in the neighborhood, in the official hierarchy, and in the state. Compare Zweigert & Koetz, An Introduction to Comparative Law, Cambridge, 1999, p. 288.

[82] Even before the imperial unification of China there were codes. In 221 BC the Ts'in (Qin) dynasty emerged and centralized administration was set up; the regime also passed draconian laws. After Ts'in regime, legislation in each dynasty was focused on criminal and administrative law.

[83] Zweigert & Koetz, An Introduction to Comparative Law, Cambridge, 1999, p. 290.

law rather than simply by conventions, habits, or mores. Admittedly some say, the tradition of Confucianism leads to a dim view of law and a characteristic tendency to resolve disputes by other techniques and informal means other than lawsuits,[84] whereas in a modern market economy, it is much more important to apply the formalistic law in disputes resolution since a sound civil law system with disputes resolution by recourse of court services will provide remedies to the parties in time and at the same time extend sanctions to unfaithful behavior. Conversely, the failure of legal sanctions against would incur a high cost to the society. This problem seems to be much more serious in China. "Trust Crisis", or "Trust Failure", has been a bitter topic in 2002, as many firms were under investigation in China due to improper accounting and fraudulent behavior. The loss due to a disorder in the economy and a lack of trust in market transactions caused a reduction in the quota of 10 – 20 % of the GDP, with indirect and direct economic losses of 585.5 billion Yuan[85] each year since then, which is equal to 37% of the fiscal income of the state, and cause at least 2 % reduction in the GNP.[86] Furthermore, law enforcement has become another obstacle of economic development, as the investigation showed, in civil cases against firms arising from disputes of lending and borrowing, banks won 95% of the cases, but only 15% of the court decisions were enforced. "Triangle Debt"[87] in China is about 1500 billion Yuan; the direct loss to banks in China caused by bad debts, is about 180 Billion Yuan. Due to these facts, many firms require their trade partners to pay cash against delivery in transactions and as a consequence additional financial cost of ca. 200 billion Yuan incurred each year. These problems reveal the failure of legal sanctions and the high cost of unfaithful behavior.[88]

The question is therefore raised here: what factors impede the functioning of the courts in

---

[84] Zweigert & Koetz, An Introduction to Comparative Law, Cambridge, 1999, pp. 287, 288, 290.

[85] One US Dollar is equivalent to 8.26 Chinese Yuan.

[86] In an investigation initiated by the State Audit Bureau based on the analysis of balance of sheet, 68% of the 1290 firms did not have proper accounting and violated the financial regulation; the concerned amount was in excess of 100 Billion Yuan. It is an urgent agenda to solve the problems of fake accounting, repudiation of debt, conceiving in transaction, cheating and abuse of market power etc. The illegal production of fake products is a typical case of "Trust Failure" in China, the various loss caused by low quality products and fake products result in a loss of app. 200 Billion Yuan in China each year. The foundation of social and economic trust is endangered by conceiving and cheating in contracts, tax-escaping and cheating, smuggling, inside trade, price trap, cheating in the stock market and the local protection, etc.. See the report from the Conference on 4th of Jan. 2003 on the topic of "Economic Reform and Social Trust" held in the 5th New Year Forum in Beijing University, in Internet Homepage: www.sohu.com (7th of Jan. 2003).

[87] "Triangle Debt" refers to the debts among three parties, normally involving banks, and firms. For example, Bank A had a right over Firm B, Firm B had a right over Firm C, and the court ruled that Firm C should pay back to Bank A. Such relationship existed in many stated-owned firms and the banks. It has been an obstacle of economic reform, especially the reform of state-owned firms when the property rights are not clear in many cases.

[88] Although the revised Criminal Law in August 2002 has strengthened legal sanction against repudiation of debt, but it does not have enough deterring effect. In the case of spreading fraudulent information, there is no legal sanction available yet. Supra note 86.

China? And why does the legal system fail to function well? To answer these questions, first, a historical review of China's legal development will be addressed for the analysis. Since law is closely related to the society, culture and religion through different phases of history, from Confucianism to legal transplantation and the modernization of Chinese law. Further, there will be an examination of the anatomy of the current civil process with an introduction to Civil Procedure Law in China. The problems facing the judiciary will serve as a basis for the empirical study on the civil process in China with respect to court delay and its costs in Chapter 3.

II. The Development of Chinese Legal System in Brief

To anthropologists, law is an active cultural phenomenon. To sociologists, law is a 'Sein', namely, it is concrete social facts and social norms. But according to judicial dogmatists (Rechtsdogmatiker), law is considered a strictly logical 'Sollen', in another words, the culture and the whole society are the background of the law. The judicial system is intertwined with politics, economy, religion, and morality etc.

As mentioned by Chinese scholar Liang Su Min, 'China is a family based society', for more than 2000 years, the society hasn't changed too much. Confucianism and law are paralleled; in fact law is considered assistance to Confucianism and social norms.

Agricultural societies are seen as "anti-litigation-societies", harmony is considered to be the most important element of society, and even such harmony appears only on the surface. It is better that conflicts are settled privately, so that society seems to be in a harmonious state. Individual conflict is 'contained' in the family, village or business. Such conflicts are solved mainly outside the courts. Disputes should first be solved by the head of the family who acts as conciliator, or else a more remote relative or even outsider who is so respected because of their age or high standing in the region or on other grounds that there is no 'loss of face' to either side in accepting the compromise proposed by the conciliator.[89] Though the imperial courts were open to the parties, the parties had to consider his behavior would be castigated by the tight community of which he/she was a part and thus they would sue only in cases of

[89] Zweigert & Koetz, An Introduction to Comparative Law, Cambridge, 1999, p. 291.

desperation.[90] Compromises were more easily made under the conciliators whose prestige enabled them to provide considerable social and moral pressure on the parties. Furthermore, conflict-resolution outside of the courts would also be a benefit to the parties since the court procedure had a reputation of being extremely time-consuming and expensive. In traditional Chinese society, private settlement outside the courts was an important feature of dispute resolution. Individuals stayed rooted in their narrow social context; they disregarded the law and try to stay far away from the law. Such tradition, as already mentioned, is rooted in the Chinese culture, political system and its religion, and such tradition rooted in the social norm and culture shall not be ignored when discussing the rule of law in China.

1. From 2100 BC until 1911: Historical Review

To get a general idea of the legal system in China, a brief review of the legal development follows, from the ancient times to the time before the P.R. China and the period after the P.R. China is established.[91]

a) Legal Development from 2100 BC to 221 BC

The Chinese legal system can be traced back to 21 BC when the empire of Xia , Shang and Xi Zhou were established. During this time, the law was mainly used to impose criminal sanction in order to deter the power of political enemies. During the empire of Xi Zhou (1100 BC to 771 BC), regulations and ethics (moral principles) were established and administered throughout the country. Such regulations covered from important affairs of the empire even to unimportant private matters. Ethics were used as a tool for educating the people to obey and follow the rules.[92] In the time of Chun Qiu (770 – 476 BC, shortly after Xi Zhou), custom law was transformed initially into coded law,[93] which is similar to the codification of Roman Law. These old codes did not survive fully and most of them were lost, but there succession was unbroken in the following dynasties. The most influential person in legal development during this time was Confucius, who argued that "ethics" should be the main principle for the

[90] van der Sprenkel, S., Legal Institutions in Manchu China, A Sociological Analysis, London, 1962.
[91] For a detailed review of the legal development in China, see Zeng, Xian Yi (eds.), The History of Chinese Legal Thoughts, China People's University Publication, 2000.
[92] See Sheng, Zhong Ling, Research on Comparative Law, Beijing University Press, 1998, p. 433.
[93] Ditto.

society[94] and should be supported by criminal sanction (Penalty law). Though many contemporary legal scholars are of the opinion that competition between Confucius and the law is similar to the confrontation between natural law and positive law in Western countries; however, it is wrong to make such a judgment, since Confucius advocated 'rule by man' rather than 'rule by law', whereas both naturalism and the positivism hold 'rule by law' and democracy to be most important. In the Confucian context, it was believed that man was intrinsically good and could be brought by education of the example of the rulers to see the need for virtuous conduct. The ethical man in the eye of Confucianism should resolve dispute equitably by peaceful discussion rather than by insisting on his rights or by calling in a judge. "Anyone who disturbed social tranquility by calling in a state court and trying to put a fellow-citizen in the wrong was regarded as a disruptive, boorish and uncultivated person who lacked the cardinal virtues of modesty and readiness to compromise."[95] This is a so-called "anti-litigation-society". In the past 2000 years, law has served only as a tool to consolidate the feudal autocratic monarchy.

b) Legal Development in Feudal Society from the Ts'in (Qin), Han Dynasty until End of Qing Dynasty (221 BC until end of 19 century)

In 221 BC, the dynasty of Ts'in (Qin) unified China from wars with rival territorial princes and a centralized feudal autocratic monarchy was established in this imperial state. It was the first time in history that the state was under a unified rule. This feudal autocratic monarchic system continued for more than 2000 years until it was ended in 1911, when the capitalism revolution broke up in China.

In the following dynasties after Ts'in dynasty, one of the most famous coded laws, *Tang Law*, was written during the Tang dynasty (618 – 907 AC). It was the first most complete judicial work in Chinese history. The law was based on the main principle of Confucian using "ethics as a main tool, supported by penalty sanctions". *Tang Law* and its explanation have reached top legal development since the beginning of the era of Chun Qiu and has become a law

---

[94] The so-called "San Gang Wu Chang" means the three cardinal guides (ruler guides subject, father guides son, and husband guides wife) and the five constant virtues (benevolence, righteousness, propriety, wisdom and fidelity) as specified in the feudal ethical code. See Zeng, Xian Yi (eds.), The History of Chinese Legal Thoughts, China People's University Publication, 2000.

[95] Zweigert & Koetz, An Introduction to Comparative Law, Cambridge, 1999, p. 289.

model for the dynasties that followed such as Song, Yuan, Min, Qing. Besides, *Tang Law* has had strong influences on neighboring countries like Japan, Korea and Vietnam etc.; therefore, in many research works, the Chinese feudal legal system represented by *Tang Law* and those laws enacted by other countries based on this model are called 'Chinese Law Family".[96]

From review of judicial development, one can find that the law developed in the Chinese feudal autocratic monarchy has had a big difference on laws in other countries, especially the laws during the Middle Ages in Western countries. First, the autocratic monarchy in China dominated the society for more than 2000 years. "The old China leaves us more of feudal autocratic tradition, but less of a democratic legal system".[97] Second, in its long history, China has been more or less united since the Ts'in (Qin) Dynasty of 2000 years ago. The advantage was obvious, the unification promoted the unity of China and its culture, but unfortunately it resulted in the monopoly of law in the long feudal autocratic monarchy. In contrast, in the legal development in Europe, different laws existed simultaneously in the Middle Ages, laws competed with each other in a process of learning and evolving, whereas the Chinese feudal society closed itself to the outside world and rejected influences from other cultures, consequently it was not possible to have a law similar to Roman Law which had great vitality originating from the process of competition and evolution.[98] Third, since the Han Dynasty, which ruled the country for more than four centuries, the Confucian doctrine became the ideology of the state and the guiding directive in the judicial field. The spiritual and philosophical basis of the Chinese state was challenged only in the 19th century by the influence of capitalist culture.[99] The long tradition of the doctrine of cosmic harmony has resulted in a dim view of law in respect to litigation, protection of legal right by law, jurisprudence, etc. Unlike in many Western societies, the domination of Christian theology was challenged by judicial theory during the capitalist revolution in the 18th century. Fourth, in the Chinese feudal society, penalty law was the dominating law and all other forms of laws like civil, administrative and procedural law were all annexed to penalty law.[100] To the contrary, in the history of Continental Law, private law has had a dominating position in the

[96] Sheng, Zhong Ling, Research on Comparative Law, Beijing University Press, 1998, p. 436.
[97] Abstracted from: Selections from Deng Xiao Ping, Book 2, p. 332.
[98] Sheng, Zhong Ling, Research on Comparative Law, Beijing University Press, 1998, pp. 443 – 446.
[99] Zweigert & Koetz, An Introduction to Comparative Law, Cambridge, 1999, pp. 288, 292
[100] Sheng, Zhong Ling, Research on Comparative Law, Beijing University Press, 1998, pp. 443 – 446.

long term development. Even in the English Common Law system, which is independent of continental law, private law has also played a very important role in England's legal system. The development of commercial law in Western countries to a large extent has promoted the development of capitalism and fostered trade, whereas the law in Ming (1368 – 1644) and Qing Dynasties (1616 -1911) even became obstacles for the development of capitalism due to its restrictions on business development.[101]

2. Legal Transplantation (1911-1949)

Legal transplantation in China occurred in the 1911 when the feudal system was overturned and abolished by the revolutionary capitalism movement.[102]

After the Opium war,[103] China went from a country with a feudal society to a half colonial and half feudal society. Under social pressure, the government established the first law school in China and invited law professors to teach students for the purpose of translating and introducing foreign laws into China. The main goal was to unite the Chinese traditional legal system with the Western civil law system by revision of its existing laws and enacting new laws. Unfortunately, these laws were unable to be enacted due to the downfall of Qing dynasty and the establishment of the Republic of China (1911 –1949) led by Guomintang or the Nationalist Party. Again in the 1920s, the government of the Republic of China enacted laws by invoking Western laws, namely continental law and to some extent accepted the judiciary principle and system of civil law, for example judicial independence, public hearings, lawyer system, judicial review etc.. The whole of private law was codified following Japan's example taking advantage of the Japanese experience. The Codes were principally based on German and Swiss Law.[104]

---

[101] The emergence of capitalism began in Ming dynasty. In Qing dynasty, from abut 1860 China had to enter many 'unequal treaties' with Western powers and opened up ports and trading centers. The national capital emerged under the influence of Western capitalism.

[102] It is argued that legal transplantation and the adoption of civil code would assure as quickly as possible a minimal security of social relationship. See Faundez, Julio (ed.), Good Government & Law: Law and Institutional Reform in Developing Countries, Macmillan Press Ltd., 1997, p. 3.

[103] The opium war broke out in 1839 and ended in 1842 between the Qing Dynasty and the Britain.

[104] Buenger, Zivil- und Handelsgesetzbuch sowie Wechsel- und Scheckgesetz von China (1934), in: Zweigert & Koetz, An Introduction to Comparative Law, Cambridge, 1999, p. 292. Compare: Zeng, Xian Yi (eds.), The History of Chinese Legal Thoughts, China People's University Publication, 2000, & Sheng, Zhong Ling, Research on Comparative Law, Beijing University Press, 1998, pp. 435, 436.

3. The Current Legal System in P. R. China (from 1949)

a) Socialist Law (since 1949 until 1978)

After the P.R. of China was established in 1949, China took most of it's laws from the Soviet Union. All the legislation of the National Party period was abrogated due to being 'reactionary' and 'Western in spirit'. In 1950, apart from the marriage law nothing was put in its place. In the 1950s, criminal code and procedure codes were promulgated but it ground to a halt when the 'Culture Revolution' began in 1960s. In the beginning of 1950s, most of the filed cases were criminal cases. Civil cases were mainly solved through the People's Arbitral Committees, which were set up throughout the whole country in 1953. The courts were under the administration of higher courts and the local governments with a pattern defined as "double leadership".[105] The development of the legal system was interrupted during the 'Cultural Revolution' from 1969 to 1978 and the apparatus of justice, which had been created in the Soviet image, broke down completely during this period.

b) The Second Phase of Legal Construction and Transplantation (Since 1978)

A gradual but profound reform of China's legal system has been undertaken since the "Culture Revolution" ended in 1978. After more than 20 years of legal reconstruction, the country is in the midst of a slow and gradual process of establishing a solid legal infrastructure to facilitate economic and social development. Many laws have been enacted or revised according to the new social and economic situation. In recent years, the speedy enactments of laws aiming at a sound legal system has been based on Western models and in many respects the law has made room for entrepreneurial initiative.

The current Chinese Constitution has experienced several revisions after being enacted in 1954. It was revised in 1975, 1978, 1982; and further amendments were made in 1988 to accommodate the change in the social and economic system. The latest revision has been made in March 2004 and it is the first time in the history that the constitution clearly guarantees that the lawful private wealth shall be protected by the state. Administration law

[105] It was stated in the Regulation of Court Organization (1951) that the Courts at each level should be under the administration of the governments at the same level, although the Constitution promulgated in 1954 addressed the principle of independent jurisdiction of the courts, in reality the courts were constrained by the local governments with respect to personnel and budget. The reliance of judiciary on the administration leads to difficulty in the jurisdiction, especially relating to administrative cases.

was almost blank in the past until the Administration Procedure Code was enacted in 1990 and Administration Review Act was enacted in 1999. Administrative cases must now be disposed in the administrative tribunals, which are annexed to the civil courts.

In the early 1980's, a criminal code and a code of criminal procedure were introduced.[106] An amendment to the Criminal Code in 1991 has abolished some articles and adopted some of the general principles and the spirit of Western penalty law. The Criminal Procedure Code was enacted in 1979 and was amended in 1996.

Finally, a court structure based on the Civil Procedure Code (draft) came into force in 1982 and much was amended in 1991. The Civil Code was drafted in 1986 and is divided into 9 Chapters with only 156 Articles.[107] However, Civil Procedure Code faces many critics because of its rough legislation in many aspects, especially in respect to evidence, filing and disposition, duration, litigation cost, etc..

Amendments and new enactments in legislation since the 1980's are partly based on the experience of others countries. The new enactments and amendments in economic law are mainly a result of a learning process by adopting and integrating most of the internationally recognized trade laws into its legal system.[108]

III. Civil Procedure Code (1991) and Civil Process

The procedure law involves the structure of the courts and is considered to be the most important branch of law, and is regarded as the heart of the legal system.[109] It is therefore no surprise to see that many countries are reforming and improving their procedure laws to enhance the efficiency of their legal systems.

---

[106] The criminal code was under draft in 1950 but was interrupted. In1979 the code was promulgated. In 1991 amendment was made.

[107] The Civil Code in translation is: "General Rules on Civil Code". It consists of the traditional and general rules like the BGB, together with some specific regulations on civil matters. Unlike many codifications in Western civil law countries, the Chinese civil code is not systematically enacted, for example, family law and contract law are separately enacted and are not incorporated in the civil code. However, the discussion of codification of civil law ,similar as the model of German BGB, is under way.

[108] This is much obvious after China joined WTO in 2001 and then revised most of its economic laws to conform with international standards.

[109] Gilles, Peter, Prozessrechtsvergleichung, Prozessrechtliche Abhandlungen, Prueting, Koeln-Berlin-Bonn-Muenchen, 1995, p. 50.

1. Objectives and Functions

The main objectives and functions[110] of Civil Procedure Code are mainly summarized as follows:

a) Protecting the Litigation Right of the Parties

   It is a basic constitutional right for people to be able to protect their own legal rights through litigation and by recourse through court services. The civil procedure law, therefore, provides a fair mechanism for fact-finding and protection of legal rights.

b) Procedural Guarantee for Jurisdiction

   Civil Procedure Code is a procedure law, which provides procedural rules and procedural guarantees for the jurisdiction of civil cases, fact-finding and appropriate application of the law. The procedure applies general rules to public hearings, collegial panels, two-tier jurisdiction in civil litigation and procedural rights in trials, appeals, retrial procedures etc.

c) Court Remedy

   The Court is to define the rights and liabilities among the parties and the disputes are seen to be resolved only when the rights and obligation of the parties are defined through civil procedure; further, through application of law, legal sanction is imposed against unfaithful behavior and breach of law, and thus the legal rights of the parties are protected after the trial.

d) Legal Education

   Civil Procedure Code further serves the purpose of legal education to the general public, since the civil process is a process of realization of justice,[111] and through public hearings and trials the general public will able to get more procedural and substantive legal knowledge, and in the meantime avoid civil disputes.

2. Structure of Civil Procedure Code

The current Chinese Civil Procedure Code was drafted in 1982, but was not enacted until

[110] Art. 2 of Civil Procedure Code.
[111] Cai, Hong and Li, Han Chang, Civil Procedure Code (Text Book), China Judiciary Publication, 1999, p. 32.

09.04.1991 after 9 years of practice.

The Structure of the Civil Procedure Code 1991 can be briefly described as follows:

Civil Procedure Code (1991) is divided into 4 Sections, with 29 chapters and 270 articles. Table 2.1 gives a brief description of the Civil Procedure Code (1991).

Table 2. 1 Activities of the Courts under Civil Procedure Code

		the District Courts	the Intermediate Courts	the High Courts	the Supreme Court
Jurisdiction:	(a) Pecuniary:	up to 3 million RMB	up to 30 million RMB	up to 50 million RMB	no restriction
	(b)Non-pecuniary				
Member of Collegial Panel:		3 to 5 judges	3 to 5 judges	3 to 5 judges	3 judges
Trial:		All the four hierarchies have the jurisdiction on trial cases			
Appeal:		within 15 days after the date of court order; 2-tier system, the jurisdiction of appellate court is final			
Retrial:		The parties can raise a petition to have a retrial under judicial supervision procedure if the judgment is not persuasive			
Limitation of Period:		within 2 years after the dispute arises (otherwise the litigant loses the procedural right)			
Time Limit for Disposition:		6 months for trial cases and 3 months for appeal cases			
Decision of the Courts and the Burden of Cost:					
a	In favor of the litigant:	The losing parties shall compensate the loss and the court fees to the litigant in accordance with the court decision. Lawyers' fee is normally borne by each party.			
b	The litigant withdrawn:	The litigant can withdraw the case from the court, he can also proceed an out of court settlement. The litigation cost will be on the account of the litigant.			
c	Against the litigant:	the litigant has to bear all the costs in connection with the lawsuit			
d	Dismissed:	The case can be dismissed by the court in case of non-conformity of procedure			
Enforcement of the Judgments:		The party shall follow the court orders/decisions. In case of rejecting to comply with the judgment, the winning party may apply for compulsory enforcement. The judges or executors shall notify the party to perform his duty within the appointed time limit. In case of failure to perform within the deadline, compulsory enforcement will follow.			
Penalties:		In case of despise of court orders by illegal actions against the enforcement or by violent means, additional penalties or legal sanctions can be imposed against the debtor			

3. Court System

According to the regulation of Civil Procedure Code, the jurisdiction of the courts in China has some distinctive features in contrast with other civil law countries, especially in respect to judicial hierarchy, two-tier jurisdiction, collegial panel, trial committee, retrial procedure etc.

a) Judicial Hierarchy

The establishment of court system is based on the Constitution Law and the People's Court Organization Act.[112] According to the People's Court Organization Act, the courts are divided into four hierarchical levels, which consist of the Supreme People's Court, the High People's Court (provincial level), the Intermediate People's Court (city level) and District Court/County Court.[113] The so-called "local courts" in each province are divided into 3 hierarchical levels, namely the High People's Court, Intermediate People's Court and District People's Court (including the court in each county in China). The Supreme People's Court supervises the jurisdiction work of all local courts; the jurisdiction work of lower courts is subject to the supervision of higher courts in each province and autonomous region.

The jurisdiction follows the principle of "4 hierarchies, 2-tier jurisdiction", which means that the appeal judgment is deemed to be final. As an exception, the judgment made by the Supreme People's Court shall be final in any case.[114]

Unlike Western civil law countries, the courts in China have no distinction between review of the facts and the application of law in appeal cases; in the appellate phase, judges can review both fact-finding and the application of law. In Germany, for example, the courts distinguish 3 types of appeal, namely: 'Berufung' - review of the facts and application of law; 'Revision' - review of application of law; 'Beschwerden' - complaint of unfair judgments to the Supreme Court.[115] Furthermore, in German Civil Procedure Law (ZPO), under a "leap-frogging" procedure, Art. 556 allows the parties who file in the County Court or District Court to appeal directly in the Federal Supreme Court and by pass the Court of Appeal if the parties only disagree on the law.

---

[112] It was enacted in 1979 and amended in 1983.

[113] Besides civil courts, special courts like maritime courts and railway courts are established in some big harbor cities or railway transportation centers for the jurisdiction of relevant cases.

[114] Art. 21 of the Civil Procedure Code stipulates that the Supreme People's Court has jurisdiction over complicated trial cases, or when it is necessary for the court to conduct the trial. But until now there are no trial cases filed or accepted by the Supreme People's Court.

[115] The German ZPO distinguishes the appeal between Berufung (appeal petition against fact and application of law), Revision (appeal petition against application of law) and Beschwerden (complaint against the court decision). See Art. 511, 543, 567 German ZPO, Baumbach/Lauterbach/Albers/Hartmann, Zivilprozessordnung, Verlag C.H. Beck, 61. Auflage, S. 1549 – 1656.

b) Collegial Panel

In the organization of trial, either a Collegial Panel will be formed to proceed with the trial, or a single judge will be appointed by applying a simple procedure.

In the first instance, except in simple cases which are able to be under the jurisdiction of a single judge, a collegial panel must be formed to make a judgment on the case. A collegial panel consists of judges or judges together with jury.[116] If an appeal case is returned by the appellate court to the court of original jurisdiction, the collegial panel must be newly formed to re-open the procedure.

In the appeal stage, a collegial panel shall also be formed to review the case[117] to decide whether the decision made by the court of the first instance contains any mistake in the application of law. Besides, each court has a Trial Committee responsible for summarizing experience and discussing complicated cases or other judicial work.

In the retrial procedure,[118] a new collegial panel shall be formed to review the court judgments or decisions made by the courts of the first instance or the appellate courts; or a collegial panel shall be formed in the higher courts under supervision procedure for retrial cases.

Further, it is regulated by the law that the judges or the relevant personnel of the courts[119] shall not take part in the litigation in special circumstances, for example, when the parties or the lawyers are their relatives or if personal interest might be involved in the cases, or their presence may affect the fairness of the judgment;[120] besides, in the retrial procedure, judges involved in the jurisdiction of the case shall not be present in the newly formed collegial panel for retrial.[121]

---

[116] Generally speaking, for those complicated cases, the collegial panel shall be formed with judges and some jurors who have relevant knowledge or expertise. The law does not stipulate the proportion of the jurors and judges in the collegial panel, and the number of jurors is subject to the necessity of the court, normally 2 to 5. In reality, jury system does not play an important role in the jurisdiction due to the problems of organization, budget constraint and possibility of causing court delay.

[117] Art. 41 of Civil Procedure Code stipulates: "Collegial Panel shall be formed when the people's court makes judgment on the appeal cases".

[118] Retrial procedure, according to the explanation of Civil Procedure Code, is a procedure under which the cases shall be reviewed if the court finds any mistakes in its judgments or mediation agreements, which are legally effective. Retrial procedure can be held either by the court of first instance, or by the appellate court, or by the higher court. But in practice, the parties file for retrial normally after appeal, therefore the retrial cases are normally under the jurisdiction of higher court.

[119] They are jurors, clerks, translators, appraisers, and inspectors.

[120] Art. 45 I of Civil Procedure Code.

[121] Art. 41 II, III and Art 184 II of Civil Procedure Code.

c) The Trial Committee

The Trial Committee is established in each court for the purpose of a collective decision on complicated cases, which encounter difficulties in the application of law by the judges. Normally it consists of the president of the court and members from collegial panels. The Trial Committee is to discuss cases (but is not to make any decision) and provide advice to the judges who are responsible for the trial of the cases. In practice, the court decisions are very often made by the Trial Committee rather than by the judges or the collegial panels. The involvement of Trial Committee has been viewed as a contradiction to the spirit of judicial independence and causes a lengthy procedure in trial.

d) Retrial Procedure

The preconditions for retrial of a case are regulated in the Supervision Procedure in the Civil Procedure Code.[122] The purpose of retrial is to correct mistakes found in the original court orders/decisions, which are already effective and binding on the parties and the retrial procedure is to provide substantive and procedural justice to the parties. In practice, the parties may make use of the retrial procedure and apply for retrial again and again, and challenge the finality of law. It is criticized that such overstress of substantive justice leads to a long duration in court and a waste of judicial resources.

4. Litigation Cost

Litigation cost is mainly regulated in the Civil Procedure Code 1991[123] and the Regulation on Litigation Cost (1989). The rationale of the litigation cost is to relegate part of the cost burden as "taxation" on the court users. It would be unfair if society were burdened with all of the costs since most people do not go to court during their life. Litigation costs borne by the parties are mainly categorized as follows:

a) Litigation Fee

The fee charged against the litigants can be divided into two types: the first is a litigation fee for non-pecuniary cases such as divorce,[124] infringement of personal rights,[125] patent,

[122] Art. 177-188 of Civil Procedure Code.
[123] Art. 107 of Civil Procedure Code: " The parties shall pay litigation fee according to the regulation in the civil litigation...". Thus, the Regulation on Litigation Cost (1989) is the base for the calculation of litigation cost.
[124] 10 to 50 Yuan will be charged for each divorce case. However, 1% will be charged for the part over 10,000 Yuan if the

copyright, trademark,[126] labor disputes[127] and other categories of non-pecuniary cases.[128] The second type relates to pecuniary cases. The litigation fee of pecuniary cases is calculated according to the 'Dispute Value' as stipulated in the Regulation of Litigation Cost (1989). In case of security of title, the applicant must prepay a fee based on the value of the title.

There is fee shifting according to the outcome of the judgment. Normally, the losing party must bear the litigation fee if the litigant wins the case. However, judges in China have the discretion to allocate the litigation fee among the parties according to the degree of liability in causing the dispute.

b) Other Fees

Besides the litigation fee, there are still other fees relating to litigation. According to the *Regulation on Litigation Cost* (1989) and *Some Opinions on the Application of Civil Procedure Code*,[129] and the relevant regulations of the Supreme People's Court, some actual costs incurred in the litigation shall be borne by the parties. These court fees mainly incur in the following litigation procedures:

(1) Application for Execution

According to Regulation on Litigation Cost, extra fees must be paid in case of application for execution of court orders/decisions. For cases with a dispute value under 10,000 Yuan, each case will be charged 50 Yuan; for cases with dispute values exceeding 10,000 Yuan, an additional 0.5% will be charged to the part exceeding 10,000 up to 500,000 Yuan and 0.1% will be charged for the part exceeding 500,000 Yuan.[130]

In case of compulsory execution of arbitration awards made by arbitration authorities, or debts in notarized form, or penalties ordered by the courts, the fees are regulated by the judicial administration separately and differ from court to court and region to region.

(2) Application for Security of Title

The parties must prepay a part of the fee in case of application for security of title. When the

divorce case further relates to division of family wealth.

125 Personal rights are related to the right of name, copyright, personal pictures, fame and honors etc. Each case will be charged 50 to 100 Yuan.

126 For cases concerning infringement of patent, copyright and trademark, each case will be charged 50 to 100 Yuan

127 Each case will be charged 130 to 50 Yuan.

128 Each case will be charged 10 to 50 Yuan.

129 It was issued by the Supreme People's Court on 14.07.1992. The regulation is regarded as official judicial interpretation of the Civil Procedure Code which is aiming to solve the problems arising from civil process.

130 Art. 8 of Regulation on Litigation Cost (1989).

property value for security of title is under 1000 Yuan, 30 Yuan will be charged; additionally, 1% will be charged for the part above 1000 up to 100,000 Yuan, and 0.5% will be charged for the part over 100,000 Yuan.

(3) Seizure of objects in Maritime Issues

For seizure of vessel, 1000 – 5000 Yuan will be charged for each case; 500 Yuan will be charged in case of claim against the ship owner; for detaining the cargo or fuel, 500 Yuan will be charged for each case; and it should be not less than 500 Yuan in case of application for limiting the owner's liability.

(4) Other Actual Costs

Besides the above mentioned fees, in property cases, the actual expenses incurred in the litigation are on the account of the parties, whereas in non-property cases, part of the expenses will be borne by the state. According to the *Regulation on Litigation Cost (1989)*, the expenses to be borne by the parties are:

- Inspection fee, appraisal fee, announcement fee, translation fee and other fees according to the administrations.
- The actual expenses incurred in the civil procedure related to the cases,
- The actual expenses incurred for security of title, advance execution.
- Expenses from copy of materials and legal documents
- Expenses (transportation, accommodation, living allowances, and allowances for absence from work etc.) for witness, appraiser, translator.

c) Prepayment of Litigation Fee

(1) Prepayment of Litigation Fee

The party who files at the court shall prepay the litigation fee within 7 days after having received the notification of requesting payment.[131] Otherwise the case is considered to be withdrawn, if the litigation fee is not paid within those 7 days. The party who appeals to the higher court shall also prepay the litigation fee within 7 days to the appellate court after the petition. Otherwise the case is considered to be withdrawn if the litigation fee is not duly paid.

[131] The exceptions not to pay litigation fee in advance include: i) cases concerning class action when the number of persons are not clear, ii) cases concerning claim for living expenses and remuneration; iii) cases concerning corporate bankruptcy, in which the litigation fee will be charged from liquidation.

The prepaid litigation fee shall be transferred to the appointed court in case of assignment of the cases.[132] The litigation fee will not be reimbursed by the court in case of withdrawal or dismissal of case. Further, if the case is remanded by the appellate court to the court of first instance for reopening of the procedure, the litigation fee prepaid to the appellate court will not be returned; but the party does not have to pay the litigation fee again in the case of appeal after the retrial procedure. The litigation fee will be shifted to the losing party if the litigant wins the case.[133]

For the application fee in case of security of title, seizure of the vessel, registration of debt, lien on goods and fuel etc., the applicant shall prepay to the court.

(2) Prepayment of Other Fees in Litigation

In case of possible costs arising from inspection, appraisal, announcement, translation, transportation, accommodation and allowances etc., the courts will ask the parties to prepay these costs according to the standards regulated by the state; with respect to the expenses for copy of materials and legal documents, the court will also inform the parties to prepay the fees according to its cost calculation.

(3) The Administration of Litigation Fee

The actual litigation fee will be calculated after the completion of the legal procedure and the parties shall cover the difference if the prepaid sum is not enough. However, the parties have the right to ask the courts to review the calculation in case of disagreement.

According to the Regulation of Litigation Cost (1989), all payment to the court shall be transferred into specially appointed accounts in a bank under the uniform administration. The local government and its audit authorities have the right to supervise the use of litigation fees.

5. Duration of the Civil Process

Under the current judicial system in which a 2-tier hierarchical system is applied in the civil process, the duration of a case is strongly influenced by the time consumed in the court of first instance and the appellate court.

---

132 Art. 36, 37, 38 of Civil Procedure Code.

133 As mentioned previously, judges may allocate the fee among the parties according to the degree of liability causing the dispute.

According to the Civil Procedure Code and the normal practice, the duration is divided into 5 phases.

a) Filing and Acceptance of the Cases

After receiving the claim of the litigant, the court shall check whether the claim is in accordance with the conditions stipulated in the Civil Procedure Code and shall reply to the litigant within 7 days whether the court accepts or rejects going further to the next step in the procedure of civil litigation.[134]

b) Pre-trial Procedure

Before hearing the case, judges shall prepare for the trial in due time by forming a collegial panel, investigation of the facts and collecting evidence and informing the parties to take part in the litigation. After the court accepts hearing the case, it should send the content of the claim to the respondent. The respondent is asked to provide arguments against the claim within 15 days.[135]

At the same time, the court shall also inform all of the relevant parties to participate in the hearing and inform them of their rights and obligations the parties might have; further, the court shall also inform the parties of the composition of the collegial panel[136] so as to avoid unnecessary appearance(s) of court personnel at the request of the parties.

The Court shall check the relevant litigation materials and find out the central point of dispute and applicable laws and regulations for the case. Further, apart from the evidence, which shall be collected by the parties, the court shall collect evidence within its discretion.[137]

It is also a common practice that the parties shall exchange their certificates and evidence in advance if the case is complicated.[138] Those evidences and certificates, which are not

---

[134] Art. 108, 110, 111 of Civil Procedure Code (1991).

[135] Art. 113 of Civil Procedure Code (1991).

[136] The court shall inform the parties within 3 days of the composition of collegial panel, according to Art. 115 of Civil Procedure Code.

[137] Art. 64, II of Civil Procedure Code: "Evidence shall be collected by the courts if it is beyond the ability of the parties and their representatives.or the evidence can be collected by the court if the court regards as necessary". It is criticized that the courts have too big discretion under such regulation and could induce corruption.

[138] In the current judicial reform in Chinese courts, "One Step to Court" is commonly adopted by the courts. It means that before trial begins, the court shall not contact the parties and read any evidence. All claims together with evidence shall be shown only during the trial. The judges shall examine the evidence only until the trial begins. Such reform enhances the obligation of the parties in evidence collection and avoids the prejudice of the judges. It is argued that such pattern of trial helps to curb corruption since the judges cannot have pre-trial contacts with the parties. However, it should be pointed out that "One Step to Court" procedure is applicable for simple and easy cases, but it is not efficient to apply such procedure in complicated civil cases like class action, complicated contract disputes, product liability and severe accidents, since these complicated cases need more time for the parties to narrow the arguments so as to save time and avoid delay. On the other hand, the parties may also reach an agreement (reconciliation) even if the cases are complicated, it is not necessary to open

exchanged before trial are not allowed to be presented in the hearing. Such a system is used in order to identify the central point of disputes and avoid the hiding of important evidence for the purpose of winning cases by sudden tactical procedural assault on the other party.

The experience in the Western countries shows that the two main legal systems (Civil Law system and Anglo-American Legal System) do not adopt a direct trial procedure in the court; on the contrary, the courts have adopted pre-trial procedure before the trial in the court. Article 16 of American Federal Rules of Civil Procedure confirms the pre-trial procedure. In an assessment made in 1983,[139] it was concluded that the pre-trial procedure has been very effective since its application. Pre-trial procedure helps to avoid sudden procedural assault by showing unknown evidence. It further reduces the times of disposition and also saves time of trial by focusing on the central point of dispute, as well as avoiding re-opening of the procedure and court delay etc. Specifically, pre-trial procedure may even help the parties to reach reconciliation before appearing in the court.[140] Of course, pre-trial procedure is much more suitable for complicated cases, whereas for simple cases, such procedure seems to be excessive. The Continental legal system also adopts the practice of pre-trial procedure in litigation. For example, the German Civil Procedure Code (ZPO) used to have a continuous trial before the American experience was adopted, but after the amendment of its Civil Procedure Code, pre-trial procedure is adopted so as to reduce the times of trial and enhance judicial efficiency.

c) Public Hearing

The court shall hold public hearings for the cases filed in the court and shall investigate the facts and the authenticity of the evidence provided by the parties.[141] Further, judges shall organize and coordinate the debates.

d) Decision Making by the Collegial Panel

After a hearing, the collegial panel can make court decision right away or in many cases they

---

the trial procedure under this circumstances. It must be stressed that the pre-trial procedure helps to reduce times of opening of procedure and save time in disposition.

[139] The assessment of pre-trial was made by the Federal Rules Consultant Committee during the amendment meeting in 1983.

[140] Wright, J. Skelly, The Pre-trial Conference in American Court Systems, Readings in Judicial Process and Behavior, Sheldon Goldman and Austin Sarat, 1978, p. 120.

[141] Art. 124 & 125 of Civil Procedure Code (1991).

will hold an internal a deliberation and make a decision on the case after the hearing. In case of difficulties in fact-finding and application of law due to the complication of the cases, the cases will be submitted to the Trial Committee for further discussion.

e) Settlement

A case is seen as settled when a decision is made by the court and the writ is delivered to the parties. In practice, due to geographical location, it takes time to post the writ to the parties where as modes of transportation is not convenient in China. Time taken to deliver a writ is also considered as one of the main factors of court delay.

IV. The Current Structure of the Court System

1. Two-tier Jurisdiction

Most of the civil law countries adopt a three-tier jurisdiction; however, in the Chinese jurisdiction it is based on a two-tier system under its 4 judicial hierarchies. It is considered that a two-tier system is much suitable to China in consideration of its social and economic background, and its territory with a vast rural area where population is large and communication facilities are backward. More hierarchies involved in the jurisdiction may therefore cause longer a duration of the court process and instability of the legal relationship. Two-tier jurisdiction has its advantage in respect to reducing litigation cost and court delay.[142] In the two-tier jurisdiction system, if the parties does not agree with the court decision made by the trial court (the court of first instance), he can appeal and file the case further to a higher court (appellate court) for final jurisdiction, the judgment made by the appellate court will be final.[143] There is no separation of common courts and administration courts, nor criminal courts and civil courts in China.[144] In general, there are 4 tribunals in each court, namely the civil tribunal,[145] criminal tribunal, economic tribunal[146] and administration tribunal, and normally two panels are established under the civil, economic and criminal

---

[142] Cai, Hong and Li, Han Chang, Civil Procedure Code (Text Book), China Judiciary Publication, 1999, p. 68.

[143] The two-tier jurisdiction is the basic jurisdiction system in China. Exceptions are those cases with special procedure, supervision procedure, public notification procedure and bankruptcy procedure, as well as the trial cases filed in the Supreme People's Court.

[144] In contrast, administrative courts are set up in the court system in Germany and other EU countries.

[145] The civil tribunal mainly deals with cases related to personal injury, tort, accidents etc.

[146] The economic tribunal deals with cases related to property, contract disputes, economic claims etc.

tribunals respectively.[147] Chart 2.1 illustrates the structure of the court system in China.

Chart 2. 1 Civil Court System in China

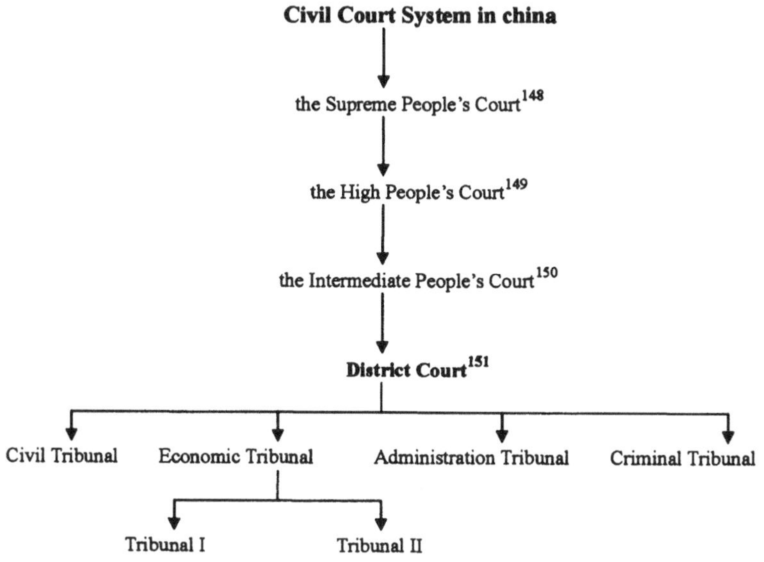

[147] In a reform plan approved by the state on 08.08.2000, the economic tribunal will be integrated into the civil tribunal and there will be 4 divisions under the civil tribunal in the Supreme People's Court: the first will be for family disputes, personal rights, and real estate dispute etc.; the second will be for contractual disputes, and tort cases; the third will be for copyright, trademark, patent, technical contracts which are related to property right; the forth will deal with maritime issues. Under such a reform scheme, the division of work in judgment is seen as clearer and more scientific. see: Reform Plan for Organization in the Supreme People's Court, 2000.

[148] The Supreme People's Court of China was established under the People's Court Organization Act, 1954. It is responsible for judicial interpretation and enjoys wide appellate jurisdiction in constitutional, civil, administration, and criminal cases. Since the beginning of economic reform, the Supreme People's Court is also responsible for the interpretation of laws. Further, the rulings of the Supreme People's Court and its legal interpretation of laws are binding on all the courts in the country.

[149] The High People's Court of China is the highest hierarchy of jurisdiction in each province, or the municipality city which is under direct administration by the Central Government (Beijing, Shanghai, Tianjin and Chongqing). There are 32 High People's Courts in total, among which 28 are set up in provinces and 4 in the cities of Beijing, Shanghai, Tianjin and Chongqing. The High People's Court deals with complicated cases within its territorial jurisdiction. The judgments of the High Courts can be reviewed only when the conditions for retrial or appeal prescribed in the regulations are satisfied.

[150] The Intermediate People's Court is set up in every city in China for the trial of original cases and appeal cases within its jurisdiction. The Intermediate People's Courts and the District Courts in China solve most of the cases, accounting for more than 80% of the total filings.

[151] The District Court is in charge of all disputes within its territory of jurisdiction; normally it is responsible for the cases in the each district of the city.

As to the cases or disputes in the counties or rural area, in practice, the local village governments will first deal with the disputes among the local people, normally by mediation or arbitration by the local officers. In case of bigger cases or cases which cannot be resolved by the village governments, then the parties may go to the County Court for court remedy. In China, the county is the basic unit of administration; the County Courts have the same functions as the District Court in the city.

The Chinese Civil Procedure Code also stresses on the importance of mediation by the courts, as stipulated in Art. 9 of the Civil Procedure Code, the court shall first mediate the parties to reach agreement; only when mediation does not work, the court then shall make judgment duly. This rule is strongly influenced by the Chinese traditional culture in which lawsuits are not encouraged and disputes shall be resolved through a peaceful manner.

Currently there are about 3406 courts in China with approximately 14,000 tribunals in total. Table 2.2 gives a brief illustration of the jurisdiction of the four levels of courts and the total number of courts.

Table 2. 2 Jurisdiction of the Courts and the Number of Courts

The Supreme People's Court (jurisdiction of whole country)	1
High People's Court (corresponding provincial jurisdiction)	33
Intermediate People's Court (corresponding city jurisdiction)	365
Court in the District/County level (corresponding County/District level)	3007
In total:	3406

Source: Compiled from China Law Year Books and relevant reports. The number of courts is more or less fixed but may slightly increase due to the increase of administrative regions.

2. Division of Work

In civil cases, the principle of jurisdiction is based on the nature of the case, complexity of the case, social influence, convenience for litigation and convenience for jurisdiction of the courts. Most of the civil cases are under the jurisdiction of the District Courts and County Courts. As the courts of first instance, District Courts and County Courts dispose of more than 80% of the total civil cases filed in the courts in China.[152] The rest of the cases filed and disposed by the Intermediate People's Courts and High People's Courts mainly are complicated in nature or involve a high 'dispute value'.

With respect to pecuniary cases, they are accepted by the courts according to the "dispute value". Normally, the higher the dispute value of the case, the higher hierarchy of court that will be assigned for jurisdiction of the case.

[152] Estimation according to the statistics of filings and dispositions as per China Law Year Book, 1988 – 2000.

a) The Supreme People's Court

The Supreme People's Court is mainly responsible for review and jurisdiction of complicated cases and appeal cases; it is also responsible for the supervision of the lower courts, interpretation of laws and rules, as well as for judicial administration and reform etc.

Although the Supreme People's Court can also dispose of original cases, so far there have been no original filings in the Supreme People's Court. The Supreme People's Court mainly deals with appeal cases and complaints regarding judgment made by the courts of lower hierarchy.

b) The High People's Court

The High People's Court is mainly responsible for appellate jurisdiction and supervision of the lower courts within its province.

The cases in civil and economic issues filed in the High People's Courts of first instance shall meet the requirement of the "dispute value" in accordance with the regulations of the Supreme People's Court, as indicated in Table 2.3 and Table 2.4.[153] The number of filings is also limited in consideration of its burden.

For civil cases concerning property disputes and foreign countries (incl. the regions of Hong Kong, Macao & Taiwan), the High People's Courts will accept the filing for trial according to the dispute value of the cases, however, the level of "dispute value" varies in different provinces and cities.

[153] See the Notification of the Supreme People's Court with respect to the original trial cases, 1999.

Table 2. 3 "Dispute Value" of the Trial Cases with respect to Property Disputes[154] filed in High People's Court

	Beijing, Shanghai, Guangdong	Fujian, Zhejiang, Hainan, Hubei	Jiangsu, Shangdong, Anhui, Hunan, Guangxi, Henan, Sichuan, Chongqing, Tianjin, Hebei, LiaoNin, Heilongjiang	Other Provinces
1. Value of Property Dispute	>100 Million	>50 Million	>30 Million	>10 Million
2. Value of cases concerning with foreign countries (incl. HK, Macao & Taiwan)	>80 Million	>30 Million	>20 Million	>8 Million
Number of total cases accepted by each High People's Court	Max. 10 cases	Max. 8 cases	Max. 5 cases	Max. 5 cases

Source: the Supreme People's Court's regulation on trial case filed in High Court and minimum of the dispute value. This regulation is effective since 1999.

For cases in economic issues,[155] the regulation is slightly different from the property issues in respect to the provinces listed, and there is no restriction of the number of filings.

Table 2. 4 "Dispute Value" of the Trial Cases with respect to Economic Disputes filed in High People's Court

	Beijing, Shanghai, Guandong Hainan	Shangdong, Jiangsu, Liaonin, Zhejiang	Fujian, Tianjin, Hubei, Hunan, henna, Jilin, Heilongjiang, Guangxi, Chongqing, Anhui, Jiangxi, Sichuan, Shanxi, Hebei, Shangxi	Other Provinces
1. Value of Property Dispute	>100 Million	>50 Million	>30 Million	>10 Million
2. Value of cases concerning with foreign countries (incl. HK, Macao & Taiwan,)	>80 Million	>30 Million	>20 Million	>8 Million

Source: the Supreme People's Court's regulation on trial case filed in High Court and minimum of the dispute value. This regulation is valid since 1999.

[154] Cases with respect to property issues refer to those cases heritage, family property and insurance etc.
[155] Case with respect to economic issues refer to those cases mainly relating to contractual disputes.

c) The Intermediate People's Court

The Intermediate People's Court has either jurisdiction on trial cases and appellate jurisdiction. With respect to the original trial cases filed directly with the Intermediate People's Court, the level of "dispute value" is different in each province, the respective High People's Court has the right to regulate the dispute value of the original cases filing in the Intermediate People's Court in different cities according to the economic development in the province. For example, Table 2.5 shows the "dispute value" of cases filed in the Intermediate People's Court in Xiamen City shall normally be bigger than 2 million Yuan for civil disputes and 3 million Yuan for economic disputes.

Table 2. 5 "Dispute Value" of Trial Cases filed in the Intermediate People's Court in Xiamen City

	Civil Cases	Economic Cases
"Dispute value"	> 2 million Yuan	> 3 million Yuan

d) The District People's Court/County Court

Most of the cases concerning family issues like marriage, divorce and cases with small value are filed directly in the district courts or county courts, the "dispute value" varies in different cities; take the district court in Xiamen City as an example, the dispute value for civil cases is up to 2 million Yuan, and the dispute value for economic cases is up to 3 million Yuan.

Table 2. 6 "Dispute Value" of Trial Cases filed in the District People's Court in Xiamen City

	Civil Case	Economic Case
"Dispute value"	Up to 2 million Yuan	Up to 3 million Yuan

In accordance with the *Some Opinions on the Application of the Civil Procedure Code,*[156] the jurisdiction of cases concerning foreign country, patent, maritime affairs and others are

[156] '*Some Opinions on the Application of Civil Procedure Code*' is a judicial interpretation issued in 1992 for the purpose of better application of Civil Procedure Code.

explained in Articles 1-3 of the Opinion on Application of the Civil Procedure and these cases shall be subject to the jurisdiction of the Intermediate Courts.

3. The Trial and Appeal Procedure

a) The Collegial Panel and the Trial Committee

According to the People's Court Organization Act, a collegial panel or a single judge shall be formed or appointed for the judgment.[157] In practice a single judge is appointed for judgment of simple cases during the first instance in District/County courts and the collegial panel is applicable for complicated cases in District/County courts. For courts of a higher level, normally a collegial panel shall be appointed for the judgment in consideration of the higher dispute value and complexity of the cases. The collegial panel normally consists of 3 judges for judgment.[158]

In accordance with People's Court Organization Act, the Trial Committee is established in the court as collective leadership in supervising judgment work; the Trial Committee shall discuss complicated cases or cases with a large dispute value.[159] The Trial Committee shall review the cases, in cases where the president of the court finds mistakes contained in fact-finding and application of law and submits the case to the Trial Committee for discussion of whether retrial is necessary.[160] The role of Trial Committee is the most controversial issue among the law professionals, since it enjoys a great deal of discretion over case decisions and often interferes with the court decisions made by the judges.

b) The Procedure: Filing and Disposition

With respect to filing, the court shall inform the litigant within 7 days whether the case submitted fulfills the conditions of the filing or is not according to the regulation on filing. After filing and acceptance, the court will decide whether a single judge or a collective tribunal shall be assigned for jurisdiction according to the complexity of the case. In case the

[157] Art. 10 of Court Organization Act.
[158] Art. 11 of Court Organization Act, Art. 147 of Criminal Procedure Act.
[159] Art. 11 of Court Organization Act.
[160] Art. 14 of Court Organization Act; Art. 177 of Civil Procedure Code; Art. 63 of Administration Procedure Code. In accordance with these articles, the judgment made by the collegial panel or single judge is effective unless it contains mistake or it is requested by the president of the court to review the judgment, otherwise the Trial Committee has no right to interfere into the case. In reality this is not the case, according to the empirical study made by Prof. Su Li, in his "Investigation of the Trial Committee in the Local Courts", the Trial Committee very often intervenes the cases even without the request of the president of the court if it regards that the cases contain mistakes in fact-finding or application of law.

litigant or defendant disagrees with the judgment made by the court of the first instance, they can appeal to a higher court. In case of appeal, the lower court must transfer the documents to the higher court within 7 days from the day the appeal is made. In the second trial at the appellate court, the trial is final. However, each party still has the constitutional right to apply for retrial under the supervision procedure. In case of application for retrial, the Trial Committee of the court will review the case and decide whether the case is necessary for retrial.

In brief, the filing and disposition can be put in a simple manner with 7 phases described as follows:

1. Filing and pre-payment of litigation fee by the litigant
2. Time for meeting appointed by the judges
3. Pretrial preparation: evidence-collection, witness, expert view and inspection etc.
4. Hearing
5. Internal discussion made by the Collegial Panel
6. If no consent, further hearing and discussion would be repeated.
7. Judgment made after consent of the judges

Phase 3, 4 and 5 are variable since pretrial normally consumes a lot of time, especially in respect of collection of evidences; a hearing may be repeated in case new evidence becomes available; the proceedings will be lengthy when the Trial Committee takes part in discussion of cases. In case of retrial procedure in the same court, phase 3, 4 and 5 have to be repeated.

4. Retrial Procedure under Judicial Supervision

According to Civil Procedure Code, the courts, the procuratorates and the parties can start the supervision procedure or retrial procedure; the parties can apply for retrial if the court orders/decrees are found to contain material mistakes in fact-finding and application of the law. In general, the supervision procedure under the current Chinese legal system includes:

- self supervision by the courts (proposal by the president of the court to have a retrial);[161]
- retrial procedure initiated by the parties;[162]
- retrial procedure in case of challenges of court orders/decisions by the procuratorates..[163]

161 Art. 177 of Civil Procedure Code.
162 Art. 179 of Civil Procedure Code.
163 Art. 185 of Civil Procedure Code.

From legal point of view, the effective court orders/decisions are compulsory to the parties and shall not be changed for the sake of the stability of the law. The court orders/decisions made by the courts are final and binding on all parties. As soon as the court orders/decisions are made by the appellate courts, the finality of law shall be assured and court orders/decisions shall be enforced with no delay.

However, the finality of law does not mean that the court orders/decrees cannot be challenged. In the judiciary, judges may make mistakes in fact-finding and apply the law improperly due to negligence or lack of professional knowledge and practice experience or due to an imperfect supervision mechanism and the influence of local protections, and corruptions etc. Mistakes and miscarriage of justice in jurisdiction thus deviate from the spirit of rule by the law. Therefore, the supervision procedure is to correct the mistakes or avoid miscarriage of justice contained in the court orders/decrees so as to provide further substantive and procedural remedy to the parties by an ex-post supervision.[164]

a) Retrial Procedure

Retrial procedure can be started by the parties according to Art. 179 of Civil Procedure Code, or by the courts according to Art. 177, 184 of Civil Procedure Code; further, retrial procedure can be started when the procuratorates challenge the court orders/decisions according to Art. 185 or Civil Procedure Code. The retrial can be either undertaken by the court, which generates the original court order/decision or by a higher court.

Judicial supervision is seen as a continuation of trial, but it differs from the regular order of the first instance and appeal procedure: first, according to the civil procedure in China, judicial supervision is considered as a remedy to 2-tier jurisdiction in which the court decision made by the appellate courts will be final. The application of retrial procedure can only be allowed when new evidences are found and it is sufficient to overturn the original court decisions, or when mistakes are found in fact-finding and application of law, or when

[164] In China, judicial supervision is a broad term, which further includes the supervision of the ruling party in the courts, and supervision from the state organs, social organizations, other existing parties in China, press, as well as the public who are eligible to supervise the judicial activities of the courts based on the constitutional right. This concept of supervision in judiciary is however different from the judicial supervision mechanism in legal procedure. Such broad term of supervision of judiciary by the state organs, social groups and individuals is not defined in procedural law and is regarded as an external supervision. For example, the People's Congress may require the courts to reopen the legal procedure if mistakes are found in the court orders/decrees. Whereas the judicial supervision in the form of retrial procedure is mainly initiated by the parties or by the courts and the procuratorates. Whether the supervision procedure (retrial procedure) can be realized depends on the examination of the courts. From this point of view, judicial supervision mechanism is an internal supervision by the courts.

the procedure is violated and miscarriage of justice might happen. Second, the filing procedure in the first instance and during the appeal phase is initiated by the parties who have the substantive right in the case, whereas retrial procedure can not only be initiated by the parties, but also by the court itself and the procuratorate under judicial supervision procedure. Third, retrial procedure is a remedy of 2-tier jurisdiction under the current legal framework in China to ensure substantive justice. Retrial procedure can only be approved after the court affirms that the original court decision contains mistakes and therefore it is necessary to correct such mistakes so as to realize substantive justice. In retrial procedure, a new collegial panel with new members must be formed.[165]

No doubt, in retrial, procedural rights of the parties shall be treated as the same as the procedure in trial and appeal. In practice, such rights are not fully respected, especially with regard to public hearing. Judges often discuss the cases by reading the filing documents rather than spending time to have hearings. According to Art. 125 of Civil Procedure Code: "Cases under the jurisdiction of the People's Court shall have a public hearing, except those special cases defined by the law". Justice can only be guaranteed and corruption can be effectively deterred and prevented only with a public hearing, it is no exception with a retrial. There are almost no public hearings in retrial and it normally proceeds with inquiries in writing and some investigations. Such practice causes many problems[166] since most of the retrial cases are based on new findings in evidence, which could overturn the original court decisions. Only with public hearing and the inquiry by the judges with the presence of all parties, the objectivity, legitimacy and relevancy of the evidence can be justified; otherwise, it is difficult to guarantee justice in a retrial.

b) The Problem concerning Finality of Law and Duration

As per Art. 179 of Civil Procedure Code, the court shall retry cases if the parties have new evidences, which are sufficient to overturn the original judgment, or the main evidences are insufficient to support the original court decision. Normally it is very difficult to collect all the evidences relating to the fact, and judgment is always made when the evidence from the

---

165 In the first instance, one judge can be selected to make the trial.

166 Reference as per Guan, Pi Liang, "Getting out of Wrong Direction of Judicial Supervision", in: Bejing Judiciary Press, on 09.02.1996.

parties is able to prove the fact reasonably. The stability of the court order and finality of the law would be very difficult to be maintained if retrial procedure is allowed whenever there is new evidence available.[167]

It would contradict the finality and speediness of the law if the original court orders/decrees were frequently subject to change due to new evidence presented. Unlike the civil law, it is much more reasonable for penalty law to apply retrial procedure when new evidences are available, since the evidences are collected by the court itself, but in civil cases, the evidences are mainly collected and provided by the parties and therefore the parties should present the evidences to the court as quickly as possible. The parties shall be liable for any delay in providing the evidences. If retrial procedure is allowed whenever there are new evidences available, then it will be difficult to regulate the time limit for evidences; furthermore, the parties may make use of such procedure to delay litigation. In practice, the parties may keep some of the important evidences in the first instance and present it in the appeal, in a consequence, the appellate court may change the original court order/decree made by the court of the first instance or send the case back to the court of the first instance for re-opening of the procedure. Such strategic behavior impedes the impartial jurisdiction by the trial court and damages the interest of the other party. In some cases, the parties even keep some of the evidences waiting for retrial procedure. It must be pointed out that it is waste of the time and the energy of the judges and it is contrary to judicial efficiency without restriction of evidence. The current reform on evidence strengthens the obligation of the parties to collect and provide evidence to the court within the time limit.[168]

5. The Functioning of 2-tier Jurisdiction versus 3-tier Jurisdiction

The purpose of setting up a 2-tier jurisdiction system instead of 3-tier jurisdiction system in China is to facilitate the jurisdiction of the appellate court within its territorial limit and the convenience of filing for the parties; furthermore, a 2-tier jurisdiction is suitable for the

---

[167] It is argued that the instability of law is not very much related to the state of law, but the evidence which is related to the fact. See Adams, Michael, Ökonimische Analyse des Zivilprozesses, Königstein/Ts., 1981, p. 80.

[168] The Supreme People's Court: Some Regulations on Civil Litigation Evidence, effective on 01.04.2002. Art. 33 stipulates that the parties may agree upon the time to provide evidence to the court, otherwise the court shall appoint the time, which shall be more than 30 days.

geographical situation of China which is vast in terrain and population.[169] Due to the high ratio of retrial cases, the 2-tier jurisdiction does not reach the goal of providing speedy and inexpensive redress; besides, 2-tier jurisdiction has some obvious defects: first, since cases must be judged within a certain territory of jurisdiction, local protection is always involved in the jurisdiction; further, due to the social connections and personal relationship, it is difficult for the judges to ignore the social networks around them and they are likely to be influenced.[170] Out of this consideration, many scholars proposed that the Supreme People's Court shall act as an appellate court when the cases involve parties from different regions so as to avoid local influence. Second, 2-tier jurisdiction leads to low quality in judgment as most of the civil cases are filed in the local courts (trial court and appellate court) and in these lower courts judges are more likely to have a different version of understanding in the application of law, consequently the uniform rules of law would be affected. Third, since there is no uniform regulation on time limit of the supervision procedure, it often gives an excuse for court delay; moreover, private autonomy in civil law is affected since retrial can be initiated by the courts and the procuratorates. In consideration of these factors, it is argued that a 3-tier jurisdiction would be more reasonable to replace the supervision procedure.[171] But in a 3-tier jurisdiction, millions of civil cases may be brought to the High Courts or the Supreme Court, the civil procedure would be lengthy and the duration of litigation would be too long. Besides, the parties will have to pay more litigation costs, time and energy and the courts have to invest in more human capital and facilities to finalize the procedure of a 3-tier jurisdiction. From the current limited judicial resources in China, this proposal is still considered as unrealistic and is not suitable to the situation in China.[172]

V. The Problems Facing the Chinese Judicial System and its Restructuring

Judiciary, together with the branch of executive and legislative, forms the corner stone of state power. Judiciary shall be independent from other branches. Due to the influences of political, economic system and judicial culture, tradition, etc., judiciary plays different rolls in

[169] Chen, Gui Ming, Litigation Justice and Procedural Guarantee, China Judiciary Publication, 1996, p.113.
[170] Chen, Gui Ming, Litigation Justice and Procedural Guarantee, China Judiciary Publication, 1996, p.123.
[171] Fu, Yu Lin, The Principle of Structuring the Judicial Hierarchy: a comparative analysis, in: China Social Science, (4) 2002, pp.87, 88, 89.
[172] Liu, Tong Hai and Zhu, Xiao Long, Is the Court Fee Reasonable? in: China Lawyer (12) 2002, p. 22.

different state power structures. Consequently, the understanding and the goal of the judiciary are also different. As a socialist state, the Chinese judiciary is strongly affected by the highly centralized planned political and economic system. In the 1960's, the judiciary was simply considered by the state as the tool for the ruling and even was viewed as an obstacle to the spontaneity of social processes. The apparatus of justice broke down completely and law professions were forbidden at that time. The legal system is under a new era of development since the renewal of belief in the value of legal order in the 1980's. In the past 20 years, the reform and the open policy is mainly undertaken in the area of economics, whereas little in the political system and judicial system. It is still difficult for the Judiciary to be independent from the state administration, and localism in the judiciary becomes an obstacle of judicial and economic development. The lack of human capital affects the pace of judicial reform and in the mean time often has to do with a low quality of judgment. The difficulty in law enforcement has been a bottleneck of the judiciary in China. The general public is dissatisfied with the judiciary with respect to the long duration of court cases, high cost in litigation and miscarriage of justice. It is therefore no surprise to see that the reform in the judiciary in the recent years has attracted quick social attention and reaction. Further, it must be addressed that the problem of court delay is not an independent phenomenon; it is rather a complex outcome due to the problems existing in the judiciary.

1. Judicial Independence: A Dilemma

Judicial independence is regarded as the heart of the judiciary. However, under the current social and economic system, the local courts have little budget autonomy and little discretion in personnel management. In the judiciary, the civil procedure is often violated by local interference; judges are unable to make decision before they are instructed to do so[173] or they may have a bias to judge in favor of local firms.

In an empirical study on "Judicial Reform" through questionnaires assigned to 288 judges, most of the judges admit that in China there is no judicial independence and none of them

[173] The administration pattern of the court system in China requires judges to report the cases to the president or the Trial Committee of the court. Final decisions are normally made with the consents from judges of higher positions, for example, the president of the court or the Trial Committee, but not presiding judge himself.

agreed that independent jurisdiction in accordance with the constitutional law has been completely realized. 164 judges (56.9%) viewed that it has been 'to some degree' realized; 98 judges held the view that 'basically' it hasn't been realized, and 26 judges held the view that it was 'not' realized, these two parts accounted for 43.1%.[174] This indicates that judicial independence is only written on paper, and the principle of judicial independence is not respected due to constraints from the political system, judicial administration, social and economic influences and other factors.

a) Budget

It is a basic feature in the modern judicial system that jurisdiction is exercised by the judicial organs independently. In China, judicial independence as a basic principle is written in the Constitution and in relevant laws. According to Article 126 of the Constitution, which was approved by the National People's Congress in December of 1982, "The courts excise its jurisdiction independently in accordance with the laws the regulations, and it shall not be interfered by the administration and any individual".[175] But in reality, the principle is very difficult to respect. According to a financial arrangement, the budget for the salary of the personnel and the budget for the operation of the courts is arranged by the local governments (for more details see the survey in Chapter 4) and subject to the examination and approval of the local National People's Congress. The material foundation of judicial independence does not exist when the "economic lifeline" of the judiciary is under the control of local governments and the administrations. As a result, it is difficult to realize the independence of jurisdiction when the courts and procuralorates in all levels and cities have to rely on the budget granted by the local governments and administrations. Individually, as a judge or a procurator, it is a dilemma for him/her in jurisdiction since on the one hand it is an honor to be a judge who brings justice to the society, but on the other hand it is difficult for him to keep the balance in the procedure when the career and income resource are under strong influence of the local governments and administrations. Further, as a cultural tradition, the

---

[174] Jiang, Hui Ling, "The conditions and ways to realize judicial independence in China", in People's Judiciary (3) 1998, p. 16.
Whereas in Latin America, more than 55% of judges interviewed in Argentina, Chile, Ecuador, and Venezuela said that lack of independence was one of the main barriers to justice. Compare: Edgardo Buscaglia Jr., Maria Dakolias, and William Ratliff, Judicial Reform in Latin America: A Framework for National Development, Stanford University 1995, p. 12.

[175] Art. 126 of the Constitution Law of China.

parties usually make an effort to make use of their "relationships" in the government and administration so as to influence the outcomes of lawsuits rather than emphasize proper application of law. Such a tradition has resulted in adverse effect on judicial independence.[176]

b) Localism in the Judiciary

The judiciary as a branch of state power shall be highly centralized rather than decentralized. In this consideration, jurisdiction in all level of courts shall be part of the state power and shall not be divided in different regions. In reality, one of the most severe problems facing the judiciary in China is the local protectionism in the jurisdiction and it is considered as one of the main causes of the miscarriage of justice. Localism can be in various forms in the civil process, e.g. the courts may have pre-selection of filings and territory of jurisdiction, or may settle disputes simply in the interest of the local parties, or may have bias in the enforcement of court orders/decisions. In practice, it is very often the situation that many local courts do not accept the filings[177] or simply delay the filings if the claims are lodged by parties from other regions. The judgment made is always prejudiced against the parties from other regions. Court orders/decisions would be very difficult to enforce when the parties from other places win the cases.[178] In some cases, judges in local courts even distort or hide facts for the benefit of the local parties.[179] As a consequence, parties are always frustrated about going to a court, which is not situated in the same region of jurisdiction due to the difficulties in winning or the enforcement of the law in case of winning. The risk of having a bigger loss is likely to incur in case of filing outside of local courts since at least the litigation costs and traveling cost will be saved without filing. Localism has severely affected the public's confidence in resolving disputes by recourse through the courts and damages the credibility of the judicial system when jurisdiction becomes a tradable object.

Localism in the judiciary is causing harm to the sound development of a market economy in which a stable legal system (Rechtssicherheit) and a relatively predictable outcome in civil

---

[176] As known, it is very common and frequent that the parties involved will first try to find "relation" in the courts through their friends, acquaints or relatives. In many cases local government officials can influence the outcome of the case by a phone call , writing note or instruction.

[177] This happens in the case when several courts have the right of jurisdiction over the case.

[178] So far there is no data available in this respect. However, it is a general view among the parties and the general public that the risk of losing the case will be high in case of filing at a court which is out of one's own territory of jurisdiction.

[179] Zhan, Shun Chu, President of High People's Court of Hunan Province, "Correcting local protectionism to guarantee the uniform judiciary and the respect of jurisdiction", in: Jurisprudence Comments, 1st ed., 1991.

litigation shall be guaranteed so as to encourage domestic and international investment. To deter or eliminate the localism in jurisdiction, reform shall be undertaken to the current judicial administration. For example, it is proposed that the cases shall be under jurisdiction of a higher judicial hierarchy and appeal cases shall be submitted to the Supreme People's Court for jurisdiction when the parties come from different regions as a way to avoid local protectionism.[180] But it might cause adverse effects since the Supreme People's Court will not be able to burden such workload within its limited capability in respect of availability of judges and budget; further the parties will have to bear additional travel costs across regions. Such a suggestion is not appropriate since the Supreme People's mainly focuses on interpretation of law and supervision of the judiciary, but not on jurisdiction of cases.[181] Despite formal structural independence "guaranteed" by the national constitution, the organization of the courts, personnel, and budget are administered by the local governments, it is inevitable that the interest of the local courts is intertwined with the local interest, thus, it is difficult to realize justice and eliminate localism in the judiciary unless reform is made to the current judicial administration with respect to organization of the courts, personnel and budget. To reach the goal, the state shall subsidize the judiciary and reform the current budget scheme. A minimum budget for the courts in all levels shall be guaranteed. Personnel and budget autonomy are essential elements in the reform since they are basic principles and preconditions for judicial independence.[182]

2. Lack of Human Capital

In most of the countries, judges and procurators are well trained by legal education and shall have rich practical experiences; they are normally selected from law school or from experienced lawyers who have professional education and practical experience. On the contrary, the standard for judges in China is still far from that of other countries. The admission of judges is not strict.[183] In the 1980's and 1990's, large number[184] of demobilized

[180] Wang, Li Ming, Research on Judicial Reform, China Law Press, 2000, p. 422.
[181] Ditto.
[182] There are many reform discussions in Chinese literature, which cannot be presented in details in this thesis. The main point is about how the state shall assure budget autonomy and personnel autonomy. In respect of budget autonomy, the main suggestion is that the state shall guarantee a minimum budget, whereas the gap shall be then covered by the local fiscal budget.
[183] According to Judge Act and Procurator Act, to become a judge or procurator, one shall have a law degree and one year's

army officials entered into the courts. Legal training was simple, normally they received a 'certificate', which was deemed as university degree after 3 or 4 months of training and were put into positions.[185] Unlike the 2 years' of training for law students in Germany or other Western countries, law students in China stay about 3 months in the courts before graduation from universities. Most of the judges have little practical experiences before admission or were admitted as judges shortly after their 4 year university education. It is simply not enough training/education for them to make judgments when they have little on-the-job training or are just beginning their occupation with little practical experiences.

First, one can admittedly say that that the average quality of Chinese judges is very low. According to a report, among the 270,000 calibres[186] in the court system in 1997, 5.6% of the judges were graduates (bachelor degree), and 0.25% of the judges are post-graduates (master degree); among the 180,000 calibres in the procuratorate system, 4% were graduates, and 0.15% the judges were post graduates.[187] With unqualified calibres and judges in judiciary, the law cannot be correctly interpreted and the right of the parties cannot be effectively protected. Consequently, the quality of the judgment will not be high, especially when the judges in the lower courts, which deal more than 80% of the civil cases, do not have enough professional knowledge to cope with complicated legal problems; it is no surprise that the rate of appeal is very high in China.[188]

Secondly, as a result of low level of human capital, the average disposition is also very low. As shown in Table 2.7, in 1989, the number of judges amounted to about 120,000[189] and 3,182,192 cases were settled in this year, with an average of 26.5 cases settled by each; in

work experience or a high school degree with knowledge in law and 2 years' work experience. Judges are mainly divided into 4 types according to the positions, namely the president and vice president of the court, the presiding and vice presiding judge of the tribunal, judges, and assistant judges.

[184] According to interviews and personal observation, the demobilized (retired) army official may have a share of 20 - 30% of the personnel in the courts in the 1980s. The rate decreases in the 1990s when more and more university graduates enter into the courts.

[185] It must be admitted that in the 1980s and at the beginning of 1990s, law education was just renewed and there were few graduates. The officials from the army were considered to have higher moral standard and more disciplined. Furthermore, the admission to the courts serves as a job assignment.

[186] According to the Chinese Court Organization Act and Judge Act enacted in February 1995, the qualification of judge is very simple and those who do not have legal education and training can be also admitted as judges.

[187] Zhang, Wei Li, China Needs Human Capital for Judiciary", in: Judiciary Daily, on 03.10.1997.

As an endeavor to reform the judicial system and improve human capital, Judicial Examination was initiated in 2002 to improve the quality of judges. Passing the exam is a precondition for law professions. Also in: Gan,Wen, Some basic questions with respect to justice, in: China Jurisprudence, 5th edition 1999.

[188] Source: compiled from China Law Year Book, 1988 –2000.

[189] Source: compiled from China Law Year Book, 1988 – 2000.

1998, there were more than 170,000 judges in all courts in China,[190] and 5,864,274 cases were settled in the same year, with an average of 34.5 cases settled by each judge in the year; in 2002 the number had increased to approximately 210,000,[191] and approximately 6,850,000 cases were settled in this year, with an average disposition of 32.6 cases disposed by each judges. Table 2.7 illustrates the increase of judges in different time and the average dispositions

Table 2. 7. Number of Judges in different Time and the Average Dispositions

Year	Number of judges	Total Dispositions (per year)	Average Disposition (per year)
1989	120,000 (app.)	3,182,192 cases	26.5 cases / per judge
1998	170,000 (app.)	5,864,274 cases	34.5 cases / per judge
2002	210,000 (app.)	6,850,000 cases	32.6 cases / per judge

Sources: Compiled from China Law Year Book, 1988, 1998 and Legal Daily 09.03.2002.

Compared with the average cases settled by judges in other countries/regions, the average disposition by Chinese judges is very low. It may attribute to the procedure and court system and has much to do with the improper proportion of the judges and assistant personnel. For example, in 1998, the number of judges is 170,000, but the number of personnel in the courts amounted to 280,000, namely, judges share 61% of the personnel of the courts. In contrast, the number of judges in the United States in 1984 accounts for 5.9% of the court employees in total; in Taiwan, the proportion of judges in the total court personnel is 15.6%.[192] Though the proportion of judges is big, the quality is not satisfied. The aim of the current reform shall consider a proper proportion of the number of judges to assistants and replace those unqualified personnel with well-trained law students and law professionals so as to improve the human capital of the courts.

[190] See China Law Year Book 1998, pp. 1238, 1241-1243; the figure of judges does not include the clerks, court police and other personnel who are not engaged in the judgment.
[191] See report made by the President of the Supreme People's Court, in: Legal Daily 09.03.2002.
[192] Su, Yong Qin, Reform of Judicial Reform, Yue Dan Publication/Taiwan, 1998, p. 333.

3. Administrative Pattern[193] in Judiciary

It is commonly regarded that the judiciary is heavily influenced by the bureaucratic administration of the government.

First, in China courts are much more localized and decentralized instead of in a centralized and vertical structure. Regarding the relationship between the courts and the local government, despite formal constitutional guarantee, the courts are seen as a department of the local government and are under the administration of local governments in terms of personnel and budget.[194] The nomination of a president of a court is based on his position in the government (bureaucratic position) rather than his professional background. The admission of judges is just as the admission of civil servants in the local governments.[195] Such a pattern of administration has a long tradition since the planned economy in which separation of judiciary and administration of the state did not exist.

Besides the hierarchical positions in the courts, the judicial personnel are ranked according to the bureaucratic standards of the governments and their corresponding honors and salaries are in accordance with the positions. The legal knowledge of the judges was simply weighed according to the bureaucratic rankings.[196] The nomination and selection of judges are subject to the local administration and local congress.

The dependence of the courts on the local administration in respect of budget autonomy, personnel management and even housing etc. leads to weak control of executive power. Courts are even unwilling to accept the filings of administrative cases by using excuses or delaying the disposition, or even ask the litigant to withdraw the cases.[197] In adjudication of administrative cases, the judiciary lacks power and strength. According to the statistics, filing of administrative cases is comparatively small, for example, administrative cases filed in the trial courts in 1997 amounted only to 79,527, which is only 5.29% of the economic case or 2.57% of the civil cases.[198] The judiciary does not function well in guaranteeing the rule of

[193] The 'administration' here refers to the administration of local government rather than judicial administration.
[194] Zhang, Wei Ping, Review on Judicial Reform, Vol. 3, China Judiciary Publication, 2001, p. 3. So far there is no statistics available to see how many percentage of cases are judged in favor of the administration. The parties often ask for administration review instead of suing in the courts; even lawsuit is brought against the administration, the influence of the local administration is obvious under the current relationship.
[195] Wang, Li Ming, Research on Judicial Reform, China Law Press, 2000, pp. 33, 181.
[196] Infra Footnote 200.
[197] Wang, Li Ming, Research on Judicial Reform, China Law Press, 2000, pp. 120, 121.
[198] Compiled from China Law Year Book 1998.

law and controlling the executive power. According to an empirical study, the public lack confidence in the judicial control over the executive power of the administration and are doubt the competence of the judiciary in disposing of administrative cases. 26.08% of the interviewed believed in the judiciary's competence 'completely', 26.68% 'to a certain degree', 32.82% 'lack of confidence', and 14.12% 'does not believe'.[199] This indicates that around half of the people do not trust in the competence of the judiciary in respect of administrative cases. Furthermore, the judgment of administrative cases is difficult to be enforced.

Secondly, there are too many administrative departments within the courts and the bureaucratic characteristics are very obvious. According to an investigation made in one province, there are around 14 departments within the District Courts, 19 in the Intermediate Courts, and 23 in the High Court. Among 84 court personnel in a District Court, 39 of them (46.4%) are high rankings officials for administrative matters.[200]

Thirdly, regarding the jurisdiction and judicial administration within the courts, judges have to report the decisions to higher-ranking administrative officials (from president of the collegial panel, vice president and president of the court, and the Trial Committee). Complicated cases must be submitted to the Trial Committee for further discussion and approval, the views and decisions of the president and the Trial Committee often dominate the outcome. Thus the trial and decision are separately executed. The administrative power dominates the judgment.[201] In this long process of reporting and decision-making, court delay is more likely to occur.

One can distinguish that judicial administration is different from jurisdiction. Judicial administration shall be mainly enforced by the president of the court in terms of management of personnel, budget and facilities of the courts; whereas the current judicial administration extends too much discretion to the president and the Trial Committee of the court in jurisdiction and often leads to interference. Though the experience, ability of individual judge may vary from one another, the judgment made by each judge should be equally respected.

Generally speaking, the judicial functions and the composition of personnel in the court

---

[199] Xia, Yong, Towards An Age of Rights,China University of Politics and Law Publication, 1999, p. 62.

[200] See Wu, Dong Yu and Hua, Shi, An Investigation and Comment on the Internal Setup and Categorized Personnel Management of the People's Courts, in: Zhang, Wei Ping, Review on Judicial Reform, Vol. 4, China Judiciary Publication, pp. 438, 336, 447.

[201] Ditto.

system are not established in accordance with the principle of the jurisdiction, but based on the pattern of governmental administration. The system is the same as a bureaucratic and centralized governmental department, which results in centralization of power, backward management, overstaffed organizations, inefficiency, etc. and these become system-illnesses which cannot be self overcome.[202]

4. Dim View of Procedural Justice

Unlike the philosophy of "priority of procedure" in Western society, the viewpoint of procedural justice does not exist in the history of judicial development in China. Dim views to procedural justice and violation of procedure are very common practice.

In judiciary, the rule of law comes together with the procedural justice. The implementation of law can only be secured and the legal value of justice can only be realized under a justified procedure. From such a point of view, some procedural elements like judicial independence, public hearing, have become the basic principles of the rule of law.[203] Since 1979 China has promulgated three procedural laws, namely Criminal Procedure Code, Civil Procedure Code and Administration Procedure Code, but due to the tradition of a dim view of procedure justice and the selfish departmentalism[204] in the judiciary, many procedures serve only as soft constraints to the courts,[205] for example, the courts can find many excuses not to dispose of cases within the time limits, in the worst cases, even deprive the right of the parties to lodge a claim. Court delay is a common phenomenon not only in disposition but also in enforcement of law.

5. Severe Problem of Corruption

Corruption has penetrated into the judicial field after the opening policy of China. Take the statistics from 1993 to 1997 as an example: in all cases concerning corruption, bribery, and abuse of power investigated by the procuralorates, there are 16,117 persons from the

[202] Sheng, De Yong, Reform of Judicial System, in: Judicial Research 1996, 8th edition.
[203] Wang, Li Ming, Research on Judicial Reform, China Law Press, 2000, p. 49.
[204] It refers to the self interest and rent-seeking behavior by the administration in judiciary.
[205] Ma, Jun Ju & Lie, De Zhong, The existing problem in current Chinese legal system and the way for improving, in: Legal Comments, 6th edition, 1998

government administrations, and 17,214 persons from judicial organs.[206] In 1998, there are 1,641 persons in procuralorates were accused of violating the law and 2,512 persons in the courts were accused of violating the law or regulations.[207] In one city court in Anhui Province, 8 judges, including the vice president of the court and the chief judge of one tribunal, were found to have committed corruption; in some provinces, even presidents of the high courts were charged with abuse of power or committed corruption.[208] The corruption has not only damaged the image of the courts and the authority of law, but also social justice.

6. *The Problem of Delay in Court*

Reducing court delay has been a main task nowadays in the judiciary. In China, caseloads have increased rapidly since the reconstruction of the civil law system in China in 1978 when the "Culture Revolution"[209] was over and a new era of social and economic reform started in the country. As statistics show, during the 10 years from 1990 until 1999, the total cases disposed of by the courts amounted to ca. 42,490,000, with an average of ca. 4,249,000 cases being disposed of by the courts per year,[210] the average number is 3.4 times the total cases disposed of in the previous 13 years from 1978 to 1989. The main features can be summarized as: a continuous increase in cases as a result of more and more social and economic interaction and an improving legal education among the people; the growth rate of appeal cases is higher than the growth rate of cases filed at the courts of the first instance, which may indicate that the quality of judgment in the first instance is low, as a result, cases are brought frequently to the appellate courts.

The problem of court delay has been a serious problem for the past years, especially in appeal and retrial cases; delay and backlog result in no justice to the people and distrust to the judicial system. To the litigant, a long duration may result in waste of using civil process; to creditors, it may lead to loss in profit or interest, or increase of cost during the wait. A long

[206] The figures are from the annual report made by the Supreme People's Procuralorate on 19.03.1998

[207] The figures are from the annual report made by the Supreme People's Procuralorate on 10.03.1999.

[208] In Yun Nan Province, the president of the High People's Court of the Province was accused of violating the law and its vice president of the High People's Court was charged for corrupting 250,000 Yuan; In Hainan Province, the prosecutor (a high ranking official) was charged for corruption of 300,000 Yuan.

[209] A political movement from 1968 until 1978 almost ruined the country's economy and severely damaged the Chinese culture. Civil law system was absent and the legal system was based on centralized public rules.

[210] Source: compiled from China Law Year Book regarding statistical data for all cases disposed from 1990 to 2000.

duration may also lead to bankruptcy of firms due to the increasing burden.[211]

Delays and backlogs coupled with corruption incur a high cost to the private sector and the public in general. While court congestion and problems of law enforcement are acute in most courts in China, it is important for the country to initiate a nationwide judicial reform to enhance efficiency. As addressed by the President of the Supreme People's Court:

"All judicial activities of the courts shall follow the principle of public hearing, legitimacy in procedure, justice in outcomes and strict enforcement of the court orders; Meanwhile, it must also follow the regulation on time limit and enhance efficiency. But in practice, there exists the problem of violation the regulation of time limit and result in court delay in many cases, the parties are dissatisfied (with the courts). The criticism of 'unable to pay for the time' is the reflection of the problem of judicial efficiency. Only when judges dispose the cases within the time limit, the legal rights of the parties can be effectively protected, and the meaning of justice can then be realized... '[212]

"Justice and Efficiency" have become the main topic and a task of the Chinese courts in the new century. As the country has realized, a well-functioning judicial system and the rule of law belong to the most important mechanisms for constructing a modern market economy. The following chapters are an attempt to analyze the problem of court delay and its cost in China through empirical studies of the primary and secondary data based on the samples collected from the courts, as well as the statistics of cases from the Supreme People's Court.

[211] Gerking, Wiebke, Die Wirtschaftlichen Folgen langer Verfahrensdauer, in: Schmitdtchen/Weth (Hrsg.), Der Effizienz auf der Spur, Nomos Verlagsgesellschaft, Baden-Baden, pp. 38 – 42.

[212] See the interview to the President Xiao, Yang of the Supreme People's Court during the People's Congress of China in 2002, in *Legal Daily*, 09.03.2002.

Chapter 3

A Survey of the Functioning of Court System: Duration of the Courts

The assessment of the civil justice is based on: litigation cost, time necessary to solve the disputes, and the exactitude of fact-finding and application of law. Court delay, high litigation cost and miscarriage of justice are all symptoms which impedes access to justice.

This chapter is devoted to an empirical study of court delay in China and the functioning of the judiciary. Further, a critical evaluation on the functioning of the court system will be made and suggestions for restructuring the court system will be presented. Because of the exhaustive nature of the issues covered, this chapter is divided into two parts. The first part deals with the empirical study of court delay in China. The second part presents a critical evaluation of the court system and gives proposals on restructuring the court based on the study of first part.

Part I : Survey of the Duration of the Court

I. Introduction

A nation needs an efficiently functioning judiciary coupled with available ADR mechanisms provided by the private sector to foster the necessary balance between equity and efficiency in the provision of justice.[213] Backlogs, delays and payoffs increase the cost, implicit or explicit, of accessing the judicial system. Growing times of disposition and high litigation costs impede the use of court services by the general public for redressal of their grievances within the court system.

In a transition economy and society like China, the desire and expectation of the general public is growing for an efficient and equitable court system to solve disputes. However, the

[213] Buscaglia, Edgardo, Law and Economics of Development, in: Encyclopedia of Law and Economics, Vol. II, de Geest and B. Boukkaert (eds.), 1999, p.584; also see homepage (http://encyclo.findlaw.com/).

situation is not optimistic, there are many serious problems currently facing the judiciary in China. First, courts are in shortage of finances; and due to the short history of legal education, the lack of specially trained human capital cannot meet the challenges of the increasing workload and complexity of cases; many judges cannot apply and interpret the law properly; some collude with the parties and engage in other rent-seeking activities; corruption increases the cost of using the courts implicitly; court congestion and law enforcement have become a big concern in China; the 2-tier jurisdiction system cannot function well when dealing with appeal and retrial cases. Secondly, the problems and irrationalities originating from the plan of the economy is obvious in the current judiciary, like the selection and administration of judges, the bureaucratic organization within the court system and remuneration for judges, the reliance of budget on local governments and case flow management etc. Thirdly, despite a speedy legislation and quick establishment of the judicial system since social and economic reform started more than 20 years ago, the laws are still too rough and many gaps are still to be filled. In environment such as this, where the law is rough or still blank, court delay is more likely to happen.

The general public views that the civil courts are unable to provide adequate redress because of court delays, high litigation costs and the complexity of the legal procedure. Moreover, law enforcement has become a tough task for the judiciary since court orders/decrees are unable to be enforced. The legal system is unable to provide speedy, inexpensive and simple redress to the people in general.

In this context, the empirical study in this chapter was done to make a critical evaluation of the functioning of the court system in respect to court delay based on primary and secondary data, as well as interviews. First, an overview of the filing and disposition in all the courts will be made with data collected from China Law Year Books,[214] in which yearly filings and dispositions in the courts[215] are categorized. Secondly, the empirical study of the duration of court process will be further based on the primary data, which were randomly collected from the District Court and Intermediate Court in Xiamen City with the help of a questionnaire.[216]

---

[214] This annual publication is an official yearbook of the Supreme People's Court. Like the German judicial journal NJW, it not only collects new enactments, legal interpretations issued by the Supreme People's Court, but also legal discussions about cases, jurisprudence, law education, introduction of foreign laws and the statistics of total filing and sttlement with category-wise illustration.

[215] See Appendix III (judicial statistics from 1988 to 2000).

[216] Appendix I (Questionnaire 1).

For evaluation the problems of court delays in the High Courts and the Supreme People's Court, samples are selected from secondary data (published cases) with details of the filings and settlements at each stage. In order to cover all procedures in the 2-tier jurisdiction and supervision procedure (retrial), cases with appeals and retrials are chosen to evaluate the total duration of the cases.

Based on interviews conducted, views of the parties, judges and the lawyers in Xiamen City, Chongqing and Beijing with regard to the functioning of the courts are presented. In addition, personal observation about the functioning of the courts has been also taken into consideration. Furthermore, with the help of a questionnaire,[217] judges' views on the functioning of the courts have been collected from courts in Jiangsu and Chongqing region.

II. Filing and Disposal: A Nationwide Overview and Analysis

Civil cases have increased very quickly in China after economic and social reform started in the 1980s. During the 10 years from 1990 until 1999, accumulative trial cases disposed by the courts have reached app. 42,490,000, with an average of app. 4,249,000 cases per year, which is 3.4 times of the average cases disposed in the past 13 years before 1990.[218] At the same time, the number of judges is also increasing from app. 120,000 persons in 1989 to 170,000 persons in 1999. However, increasing workloads leads to excessive burden on the judges and delays seem inevitable. The following presents some basic features of the cases in the 10 years from 1990-1999.

1. Continuous Increase in Filing and Disposition

a) Total Number of Cases Filed and Disposed by the Courts

The total cases filed and disposed by the courts, including trial cases, appellate cases and cases under judicial supervision[219] continue to increase. In 1990, the total disposed cases

[217] Appendix II (Questionnaire 2).
[218] Source: compiled from the statistics in China Law Year Book, 1991-2000, see Appendix III.
[219] Cases under the procedure of judicial supervision especially refer to those cases with large dipute value and complicated cases. These cases shall be reviewed by the Trial Committee of the courts. It is regulated in Chapter 16 of the Civil Procedure Code.

were around 3,211,758, and in 1999 it increased to around 6,229,512.[220] Table 3.1 / Graph3.1 shows the number of all trial cases and appellate cases filed in the courts and Table 3.2 / Graph 3.2 presents the total cases disposed by the courts from the year 1990 to 1999.

Table 3. 1 Total Cases filed in the Courts in China (1990 – 1999)

	1990	1991	1992	1993	1994	1995	1996	1997	1998	1999
Trial Case	2,916,774	2,901,685	3,051,157	3,414,845	3,955,475	4,545,676	5,312,580	5,288,379	5,410,798	5,692,434
Appellate Case	213,000	229,690	231,907	215,408	241,129	272,792	323,995	347,651	380,274	438,313
Judicial Supervision	81,984	83,573	81,926	69,531	64,377	70,885	76,094	86,425	89,687	98,765
Total	3,211,758	3,214,948	3,364,990	3,699,784	4,260,981	4,889,353	5,712,669	5,722,455	5,880,759	6,229,512

Source: compiled from statistics made by the Supreme People's Court, in China Law Year Book, 1991-2000. The total number includes pending cases of previous years.

Graph 3. 1 Total Cases filed in the Courts in China (1990 – 1999)

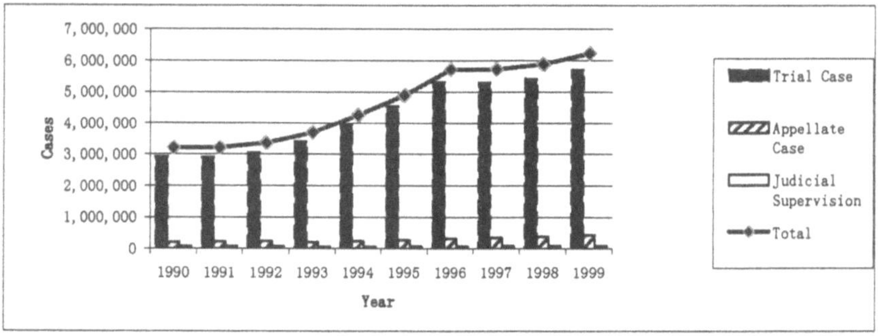

Source: compiled from statistics made by the Supreme People's Court, in China Law Year Book, 1991-2000. The total number includes pending cases of previous years.

Table 3.2 and Graph 3.2 further illustrate the total cases disposed by the courts in China from 1990 until 1999.

[220] Data compiled from China Law Year Book, 1991 and 2000.

Table 3. 2 Total Cases disposed by the Courts in China (1990 – 1999)

	1990	1991	1992	1993	1994	1995	1996	1997	1998	1999
Trial Case	2,921,806	2,950,880	3,049,959	3,406,467	3,943,095	4,533,551	5,285,171	5,249,260	5,395,039	5,698,705
Appellate Case	208,409	230,864	236,800	219,628	239,938	271,741	321,962	340,896	379,206	436,804
Judicial Supervision	86,397	84,538	83,226	73,121	67	70,865	75,230	83,512	90,029	96,793
Total	3,216,612	3,266,282	3,369,985	3,699,216	4,250,321	4,876,157	5,682,363	5,673,668	5,864,274	6,232,302

Source: compiled from statistics made by the Supreme People's Court, in China Law Year Book, 1991-2000. The number includes pending cases of previous years.

Graph 3. 2 Total Cases disposed by the Courts in China (1990 – 1999)

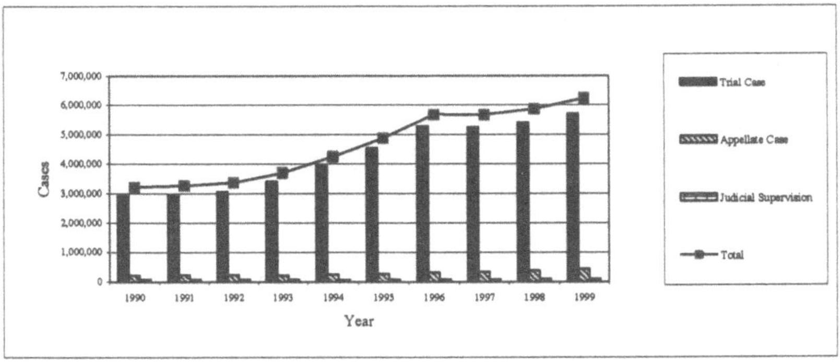

Source: compiled from statistics made by the Supreme People's Court, in China Law Year Book, 1991-2000. The number includes pending cases of previous years.

b) Total Number of Civil / Economic Cases[221] Disposed by the Courts

Among the total cases, civil and economic cases increased very quickly and 85~90% (compared from the figure shown in Table 3.1, Table 3.2 and Table 3.3) of the total filing and disposition are civil/economic cases.

The steady and quick increase of the filing and disposition of civil and economic cases can be explained by the fact that more conflicts and disputes are rising from increasing social and economic activities and change of social norms and moral attitude of the general people since the reform began in China more than 20 years ago. For example, very few divorce cases were brought to the courts before the economic reform (1980's), but this changed when the moral

[221] In China, there is still a distinction between civil cases and economic cases in a narrow concept. In most of the countries, cases for economic issues are categorized as civil cases. Since the year of 2000, the Supreme People's Court begins to integrate its economic tribunals into civil tribunals. Many local courts follow the reform and classify economic cases as civil cases. Therefore, in this research, 'civil cases' and 'economic cases' are included in the category of civil cases in a broad concept.

attitude and income level changed, cases involving divorce and family issues share approx. 50% of the civil cases filed in the first instance (mainly in District and County Courts).[222] In appellate cases, there is an obvious increase in filings related to real estate and contract disputes which reflects the quick development of local economies especially in real estate and trade, which is coupled with many problems and disputes arising from the increasing activities.[223] Table 3.3 and Graph 3.3 illustrate the total filing and disposition of civil /economic cases in the courts from 1990 to 2000.

Table 3. 3 Civil cases / Economic Cases disposed by the Courts in China (1990 – 1999)

	1990	1991	1992	1993	1994	1995	1996	1997	1998	1999
Civil trial cases	1,849,728	1,910,031	1,948,949	2,091,651	2,382,174	2,714,665	3,084,464	3,242,202	3,360,028	3,517,324
Economic trial cases	598,317	583,771	648,018	894,410	1,045,440	1,271,434	1,504,494	1,478,139	1,456,247	1,543,287
Total Trial cases	2,448,045	2,493,802	2,596,967	2,986,061	3,427,614	3,986,099	4,588,958	4,720,341	4,816,275	5,060,211
Civil appellate cases	114,401	128,396	129,079	116,638	123,005	138,585	159,702	177,317	204,958	244,550
Economic appellate cases	33,476	39,761	43,791	45,804	56,682	69,678	83,808	86,347	89,261	95,379
Total Appellate Cases	147,877	168,157	172,870	162,442	179,687	208,263	243,510	263,664	294,219	339,929

Source: compiled from statistics made by the Supreme People's Court, in: China Law Year Book, 1991-2000. The number includes pending cases of previous years.

Graph 3. 3 Civil / Economic Cases disposed by the Courts in China from 1990 – 1999

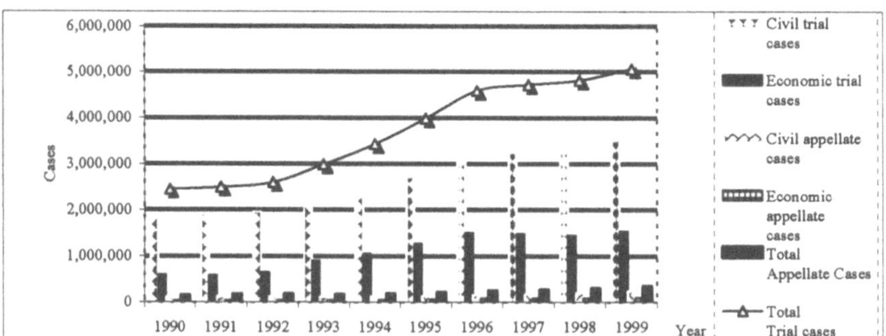

Sources: compiled from statistics made by the Supreme People's Court, in: China Law Year Book, 1991-2000. The number includes pending cases of previous years.

[222] The estimation of percentage is based on the cases filed in the courts.
[223] Real estate has developed very quickly in China. In the earlier stage, there were many speculations in the market with active buy-in and sell-out or unfaithful conducts in the sales. The loose regulation of the state in the sector in the 1990's caused many disputes among the real estate developers, the constructors and the owners with respect to property rights.

Based on the above statistics compiled from China Law Yearbooks, one can see that the settlement ratio for all the cases has been 90 ~ 95% each year. However, it would be too simple to draw a conclusion that the court system is functioning well and court delay has not been a problem in China based on the official statistics showing a high settlement ratio. There are some simple reasons behind this: the settlement ratio does not reveal the real picture in China, and it is confirmed even by judges in both the Supreme People's Court and the lower courts, and by lawyers. First, the high settlement ratio has to do with the time bound program in each court. Under this program, a target settlement ratio is established and the court must follow it.[224] Second, it is a normal practice for the courts to fraudulently report inaccurate statistics and data is changed so that the settlement ratio appears to be high. In some courts, judges treat filings in October of that year as new filings for the coming year so that there will be less backlog in the courts. In many cases, especially at the end of the year, the litigants are asked to postpone filing until the coming year, or withdraw the filing and file it again in the coming year, or to settle the cases quickly by court-arranged mediation.[225] Judges often even sacrifice the interest of the involved parties at the cost of procedural and substantive justice in order to pursue a high settlement ratio.

With regard to this issue, it is not to say that the time bound program is not effective or is bad, in fact, the time bound program increases pressure on the judges for a speedy settlement and helps reduce delay and backlog. However, the time bound program shall take the caseload and the number of judges in each court into account and a more realistic settlement ratio should be established. The time bound program should include some necessary measures like framing more effective criteria in granting adjournments so as to avoid a pure pursuit of high settlement ratios by the judges.[226]

---

[224] The normal target settlement ratio established in each court is around 90%, and the target seldom takes the caseload and the availability of judges into account. Such time bound program is confirmed by the judges and lawyers in the interviews.

[225] In an interview with judges in the Supreme People's Court, judges doubt the authenticity of the statistics provided by the lower courts. In another interview with one judge who is responsible for statistics in the district court and further interviews with lawyers, they all confirmed these usual practice in jurisdiction.

[226] Judges in China have strong incentive to realize the target settlement ratio since the promotion, salary and bonus are bounded to the performance of the judges. It is therefore frequently complained by the parties and the lawyers that many irrationalities exist in the civil process.

c) Increase of Other Cases (Criminal and Administrative)

Apart from civil and economic cases, the number of the criminal cases has also increased (The number of criminal cases accounts for 8-10% of the total disposed cases indicated already in Table 3.1 and Table 3.2). The administrative cases do not compose a large share of the total cases, but it had a tendency to increase between 1990-1998, however, in 1999 the increase ceased due to effectiveness of the Administration Review Act which led to some disputes being resolved through administration review.[227]

Graph 3.4. shows the increase percentage of civil/economic cases and criminal cases from the year of 1990-1995 respectively, as given above, the civil/economic cases not only share 85%-90% of the total cases, but also continue to rise at a high rate.

Graph 3. 4 The Percentage of Increase of Civil/Economic Cases and Criminal Cases from 1990 to 1995

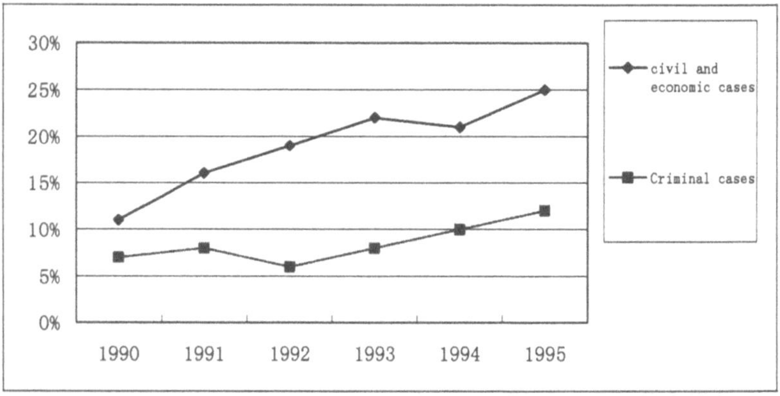

Source: compiled from China Law Year Book, edition 1991-1996

Compared with criminal cases, civil cases have a high percentage of increase each year. The quick increase of civil/economic cases challenges the capability and capacity of the judges. Under the condition of a low quality of human capital in general, and the limited number of

[227] As referred by the an official in State Department, in 1999 when the Administration Review Act came into force, there were more than 32000 cases filing for administration review, among which 40% of the previous administrative decisions/orders were canceled or changed. The enactment of administration laws shows a big change in the judicial development: the executive power and its administration shall be subject to judicial supervision under judicial framework. See He, Bin, Restructuring the Mechanism of Dispute Resolution, in: Peking University Law Journal, Vol. 14, No.1 (2002), p. 6.

judges, caseloads are heavy in some of the courts and delays are likely to occur. This raises the question of the burden of caseloads for each judge and how efficiency can be improved to cope with the continuous increase in cases and reduce delay.

d) Average Cases Disposed by Each Judge in the Year

The workload of the judges has been increasing due to a rapid increase in cases. Take the year of 1997 as an example, there were around 170,000 judges in all of the courts, the cases disposed in 1997 were 5,673,868, with an average of 33 cases disposed by each judge per year, 2.87 per month. In one provincial Intermediate Court, around 2,000 cases were disposed by more than 100 judges, the average number of cases disposed by each judge per year is less than 20 cases.[228]

Although the burden of cases differs greatly from region to region in China, the average disposition of cases is extremely low compared with the average workload of judges in other countries. In America, one judge disposed yearly of 300 – 400 cases on average, approximately 15 times the average number of cases disposed by Chinese judges.[229] Whereas in Germany, one judge in the district courts (Amtgericht) disposes of 700 cases each year on average, approximately 3.26 cases each day; most of the cases were disposed or dismissed very quickly[230] and 33% of them were mediated, around 230 of the 700 cases were mediated. The low efficiency in jurisdiction in China can be attributed to the following reasons: first, the average quality of judges in general is very low due to the lack of legal education, training and experience. Most of the judges are not professional and are not experienced enough in making judgments independently; second, judges in China spend much more time in collection of evidence[231] which consumes time unnecessarily. Compared with American judges who are not obliged to collect evidence and whose main work is to decide the cases in the courts, Chinese judges have to take part in the collection of evidence and spend a lot of time in legal reasoning. Moreover, Chinese judges have to spend their time in political study

[228] China Law Year Book, 1997, pp. 1238, 1241-1243.
[229] Source: from Annual Report of Judicial Administration of American, 1990.
[230] In 1996, in the local courts (Amtgericht), 48.2% of the cases were settled within 3 months, 28.5% within 6 months and 17.5 within 12 months. See Qi, Shu Jie, Research on Reform of Civil Procedure Law, Xiamen University Press 2000, p. 19. Also see Franzen, Hans, Was kostet eine Richterstunde? – Berechnung und Folgerungen, in: NJW 1974 Heft 18, p. 785.
[231] Procedure reform is undergoing in Chinese courts in the recent years and one major reform is to shift the burden of proof (evidence-collection) to the parties. Judges in China have to take more time in evidence-collection partly due to the low engagement of lawyers and the lack of necessary legal knowledge of the parties in civil process.

and some social programs like birth control and legal education program for people living in countryside,[232] consequently reducing the time available for trial.

2. Quick Increase in Appellate Cases

According to the statistics created by the Supreme People's Court from 1997 -1999, appellate civil and administrative cases increased rapidly.

Civil appellate cases increase by 14.34%, 13.36%, 18.85% respectively in the years of 1997, 1998 and 1999;[233] whereas civil trial cases increased 5.93%, 2.97% and 4.27% respectively,[234] as shown by the Graph 3.5.

Graph 3. 5 Percentage of Increase of Civil Appeal Cases and Trial Cases in 1997, 1998 and 1999

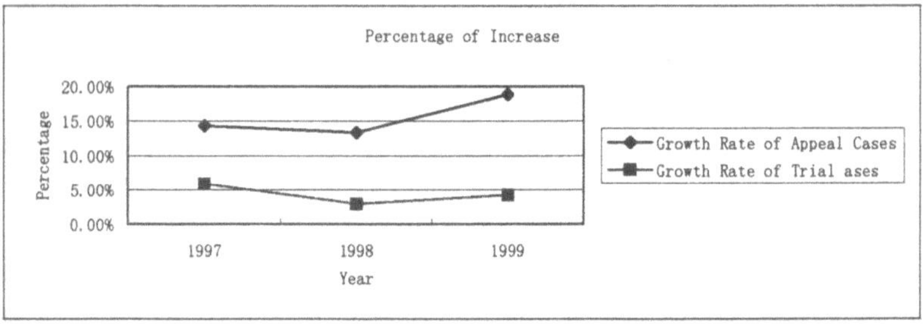

Sources: compiled from the statistical data issued by the Supreme People's Court, in China Law Year Book, 1998-2000

Graph 3.5 shows the percentage of increase in civil cases filed in the courts of the first instance and appellate courts respectively. From the comparison of the growth rate in civil cases filed in the courts of the first instance and the appellate courts, it is revealed that appeal cases increased at a comparatively higher rate.

Similar statistics were reported for the increase in administrative cases. The appellate cases related to administration increased 11.35%, 12.36%, 25.92% in the year of 1997,1998,1999 respectively;[235] whereas

[232] Judges sometimes are sent to poor countryside for education programs, birth control and government food programs etc. See Wang, Li Ming, Research on Judicial Reform, China Law Press, 2000, p. 421.
[233] Source: compiled from China Law Year Book, 1998, 1999, 2000.
[234] Source: compiled from China Law Year Book, 1998, 1999, 2000.
[235] Source: compiled from China Law Year Book, 1998, 1999, 2000.

the growth rate of trial cases were 13.24%, 8.61% and 8.12% for the year of 1997, 1998 and 1999 respectively,[236] as illustrated in Graph 3.6.

Graph 3. 6 Percentage of Increase of Administrative Appeal Cases and Trial Cases in 1997, 1998 and 1999

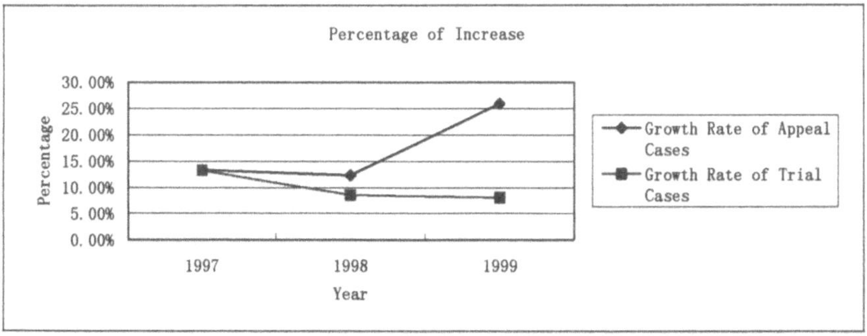

Sources: compiled from statistical data issued by the Supreme People's Court, in China Law Year Book, 1998-2000.

The above comparison between civil and administrative cases filed in the courts of the first instance and the appellate courts indicate an increase in original filings of trial cases and an increase in appeal cases. Furthermore, it is obvious that the growth rate of appeal cases is bigger than that of the trial cases.

It must be also mentioned briefly that appeal in respect of criminal cases also increases, while the growth rate of appeal cases is almost the same as that of trial cases.[237]

---

236 Source: compiled from China Law Year Book, 1998, 1999, 2000.

237 The rate for appeal in criminal cases (1987-1996) is reduced since the sanction is normally not so heavy in judicial practice, as a result, the defendant will not go for appeal. On the other side, the prosecutor cares much more about the nature of the case but comparatively less about the extent of the penalty. With regard to economic cases (1989-1997), the filing for appeal is reduced since the economic cases are dealt with more care, as a result, the quality of the judgment is higher. With respect to administration cases, more judgments deviate from the law since the decisions of the courts are affected by the administration organs (especially the local governments), as a result, the appeal ratio of administration cases is high. Therefore, the judgment quality of the civil cases and economic cases is the crucial criteria for assessing the quality of the judgments, since the quantity of the civil/economic cases share more than 80% of all cases. Compared He, Bin, Restructuring the Mechanism of Dispute Resolution, in Peking University Law Journal, Vol. 14, No. 1 (2002), p. 4, Footnote 7.

3. Improved Efficiency in the Past 10 Years (1989 – 1999)

In 1989 there were 120,000 judges in the Chinese courts and 3,182,194 cases were settled, thus the average number of cases settled by each judge annually was 26.5. In 1998 there were more than 170,000 judges in all Chinese courts and 5,864,274 cases were settled, with an average of 34.5 cases settled by each judge annually.

Table 3.4 presents the average number of cases settled annually by each judge in 1989 and 1998 respectively.

Table 3. 4 Average Number of Cases Settled Annually by each Judge in 1989 and 1998

	1989		1998	
	Cases Settled	Number of judges[238]	Cases Settled	Number of judges
Pieces / Persons	3,182,194	120,000	5,864,274	170,000
Average	26.5 cases per judge		34.5 cases per judge	

Sources: compiled from statistics made by the Supreme People's Court, in: China Law Year Books.

The number of judges in 1998 increased approximately by 41.67%[239], more than that of 1989; whereas the cases settled increase 84.28%.[240] The average number of cases settled by each judge increased 30.19%.[241] The above statistical figures indicate that the courts have sped up the settlement of cases and improved efficiency over the past 10 years..

4. Imbalance in Filing and Disposition

a) Imbalance in Filing and Settlement

Filing and settlement are not balanced. As shown in Graph 3.4, the average settlement ratio is higher than the average filing ratio in each month. From 1989 till 1998 the lowest point of accumulated filing is in February, with approximately 2,000,000 cases and the highest point of accumulated filing is in December, with approximately 4,400,000 cases. This shows a big

[238] In China judges may not have legal education from law school. Especially in the 1980's, many judges were assigned by the local government and they were given app. 3 months of training before they took the positions.
[239] (170000 – 120000) / 120000 = 41.7%.
[240] (5,864,274 – 3,182,194) / 3,182,194 = 84.28%.
[241] (34.5 – 26.5) / 26.5 = 30.19%.

gap in filing between the lowest level (in February) and the highest level (in December), with a difference of 2,400,000 cases from the lowest point (February) and the highest (December). With respect to settlement of cases, the lowest point of accumulated settlement of cases is in January, with approximate 1,250,000 cases; and the highest point of accumulated settlement of cases is in December, with app. 6,700,000 cases. The gap between the lowest point (January) and the highest point (December) is app. 5,450,000 cases. This indicates the fluctuation of settlement in each month is higher compared with the filings. Graph 3.7 presents some features of the accumulated cases filed and settled in all courts:

Graph 3. 7 Number of Filing Cases and Settlement in each Month from 1989 to 1998

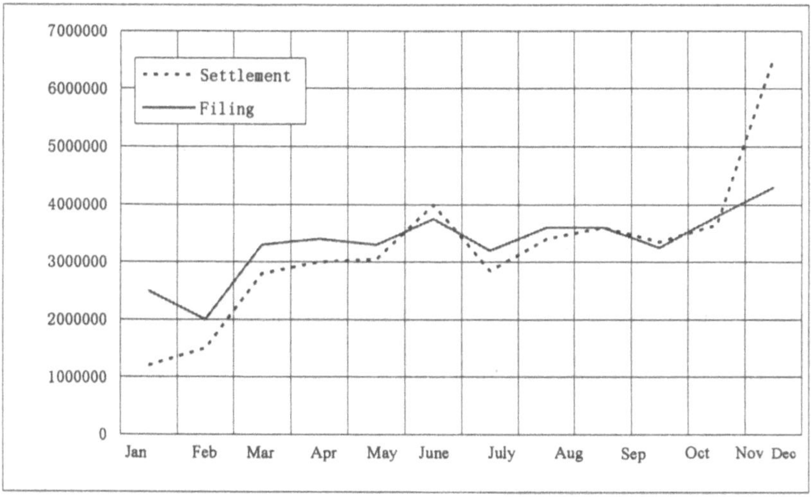

Source: compiled from China Law Year Book, 1990-1999

With respect to settlement of cases, it reveals a feature of "3 high, 2 low", that is, the accumulated cases settled in February, July, October were comparatively lower than the neighboring months; the accumulated cases settled in June, Sept., December are comparatively higher than the neighboring months; in December, the accumulated number of settlement reached the highest point. However, from 1989 till 1998, the number of cases (accumulated) settled in January is only 1,250,000 and the number of settlements (accumulated) in December (6,700,000) is app. 5.36 times the number settled in January. Furthermore, a comparison of accumulated cases settled in each month during the 10 years indicates that the figure in August is close to the average, from January till May it is lower than the average, and the figure from September till December is higher than the average. As revealed in Graph 3.7, the accumulated number of settlements in each month is not even, but has a high fluctuation as shown in the curve. In January and February the number reaches its bottom point and in December it is at the top.[242]

Graph 3.8 shows more obviously a big fluctuation of settlements in each month from 08.1997 to 05.1998, especially in January, February, and December.

Graph 3. 8 Cases Settled from 08.97 to 05.98

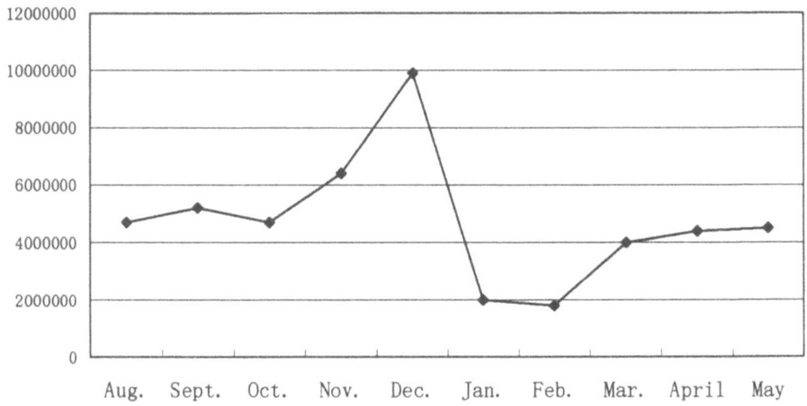

Sources: compiled from statistical data issued by the Supreme People's Court in China Law Year Book 1998 & 1999

b) Imbalance of Settlement by Each Judge in Different Month

The settlement of cases in January 1998 by all courts in China has an average of 7,162 cases per day (excluding official holidays - 9 days, the remaining 22 days are working days), and it

242 The high ratio of settlement in December can be attributed to the time bound program and the pressure of annual work report to be submitted to the People' Congress Assembly, in which the Government, the Supreme People's Court & the Supreme People's Procuralorate shall present annual reports to the National People's Congress. In order to show better work efficiency, the courts in all level try to settle the cases by the end of the year by speedy trials, and even refuse to accept new filings at the end of the year. The low rate of settlement in January and February has much to do with the holidays in January and Chinese Spring Festival (normally at the end of January or in February).

means that only 0.9 cases are settled per judge in a month, or an average of 24 days is needed for each judge to settle one case. In December of 1998, the average number of cases settled per day was 43,599 cases (excluding official holidays - 8 days, the remaining 23 days are working days). The average cases settled per judge was 5.9 cases and the average time for each judge to reach a settlement for one case was 3.9 days, as indicated in Graph 3.9.

This can be explained by considering that in January, during the Chinese Spring Festival (Chinese New Year), people are busy preparing for the celebration with family members, shopping, traveling and with other social activities; consequently time spent for the judgment is reduced, whereas in December judges are trying their best to settle the cases in order to realize the target established in the time bound program of the court and in order to show good figures in the annual report. Consequently a lot of piled up cases and cases filed in the same year have a greater possibility to be settled in December.

Graph 3. 9 Average Cases Settled by each Judge in Jan., Aug., and December respectively (1998)

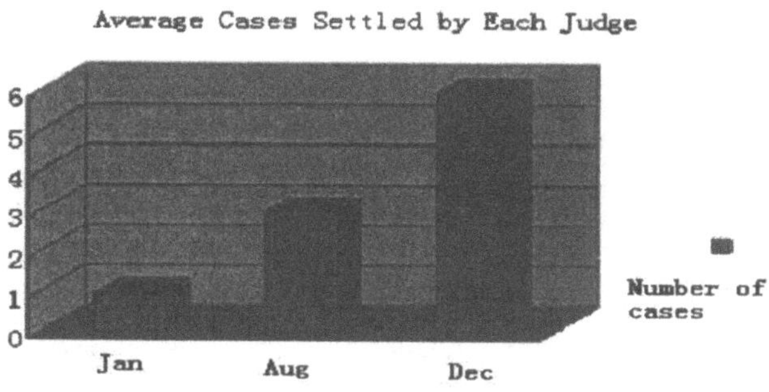

Source: compiled from statistical data issued by the Supreme People's Court, in China Law Year Book, 1999

c) 'Loose" in the Beginning and "Tight" in the End

Graph 3.10 shows the proportion of cases settled in the courts during 4 seasons of the year of 1998, which illustrates the disproportional settlement of cases in different periods of the year. The graph shows that the first season has a low settlement, sharing 13% of the total cases of 1998 and the fourth season shares 36% of the total cases of 1998. In first half of the year it is

22% lower than that of the second half year. The reason may be the same as mentioned in point b), as in the second half of the year judges work harder to settle the cases in the year so as to realize the target settlement ratio.[243]

Graph 3. 10 Proportion of Settlement in each Season of 1998

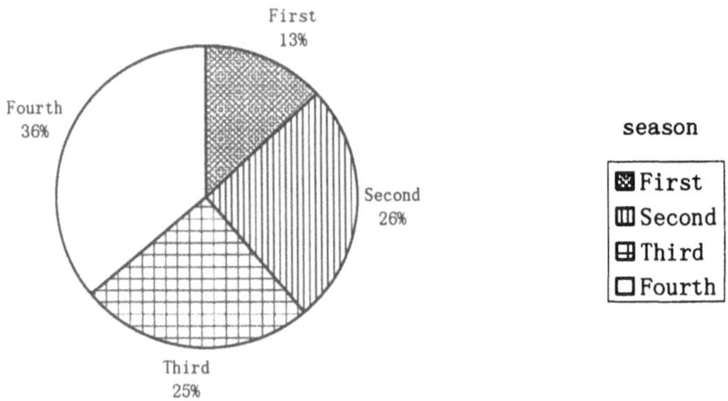

Source: compiled from statistical data issued by the People's Supreme Court, in China Law Year Book 1999

5. The Problems Caused by the Imbalanced Progress in Disposition

Though efficiency of the courts has been improving over the past 10 years, there are still many problems facing the judgment due to the disproportional number of settlements. First, backlogs incurred in the first half of the year increased pressure to resolve cases in the second half of the year. Take the year of 1998 as an example: at the end of June 1998 all the congested cases for the whole country reach 858,631, namely 5.05 cases for each judge on average; at the end of December 1998, the backlogs reach 378,911, namely 2.2 cases for each judge on average. Secondly, the rush for settlement at the end of the year resulted in a low quality of judgment. For example, if a civil case concerning an economic issue settled in the trial court in December of 1997 were appealed in the appellate court, then it should be judged

[243] Each court establishes a settlement ratio according to the previous caseload and the number of judges in the court. In the interviews, it was told that the court normally set the ratio at around 90%.

and settled in April 1998 according to the time limit of disposition stipulated in the Civil Procedure Code, whereas in the second season of 1998 the ratio of re-judgment[244] ordered by the appellate courts reached 33.28%, which is higher than other seasons, this means that the cases appealed to the appellate courts contained mistakes and a high percentage (33.28%) of these appellate cases were returned to the trial courts for re-judgment,[245] consequently the concentration of settlement at the end of the year does not solve the problem of backlogs since the appeal rate is high in the coming year due to the low quality of judgment made in the past year, and this again increases the workload of the courts and wastes judicial resources, as well as the litigation costs of the parties. Third, as a consequence, the workload is increased sharply in the second half of the year and affects time available for legal study, training and other judicial programs. The imbalance in disposition of cases affects the goal of judicial efficiency.

6. Reasons of the Imbalance in Disposition

The reasons for imbalance in disposition of cases can be summarized as follows:

(1) Holiday Effect
During the New Year and Chinese Spring Festival, which is normally in January or February, judges spend their holidays with their families and leave the disposition of cases aside tentatively. The holiday effect reduces the time availability of judges and the work efficiency of the courts.

(2) Bureaucratic Burden
Reports at the end of the year take too much time in the Chinese courts; judges have to spend time summarizing the work of the past year and dispose cases within the time limit, consequently it increases the workload of the judges.
Judges have to face the internal and external examination[246] of judicial work; further, judges have to spend time to write plans for the coming year. As a result, the availability of time for

---

[244] The cases are returned to the court of first instance for reopening the procedure.
[245] China Law Year Book, 1999.
[246] The internal examination is an assessment of performance of each judge and the external examination refers to the check of work in the lower courts by the higher courts.

disposition is reduced.

(3) Inefficient Case Flow Management

The current judicial administration of the Chinese courts is still backward. The courts, especially District Courts and County Courts, lack a computer system for support and management of cases. In addition, case flow management is still new to many courts. Thus, improving the management of cash flow shall also be included in the reform agenda.

(4) The Time Bound Program

The courts in China are strictly required to settle the cases within the time limit according to the Civil Procedure Code and the *Regulation on Strict Implementation of Time Limit (2000).*[247] Each court has to establish a time bound program in which a target settlement ratio is to be established. The performance of the judges according to the time bound program will affect the remuneration, bonus and promotion opportunities of the judges. Judges have pressure (and incentive) to settle the cases at the end of the year.

7. Findings

In the study based on primary data, which was compiled from the China Law Year Book and other relevant publications, some findings can be presented as follows:

(1) There is a steady increase in filings and disposition of cases, as per Table 3.1 and Table 3.2. Meanwhile the average disposition of each judge has improved from 26.5 cases in 1989 to 34.5 cases in 1998, as per Table 3.4. This average is lower than the developed countries like the US and Germany.

(2) Civil case and economic cases share 80 – 90% of the total filings and disposition, criminal cases have a stake of 8 – 10% and the rest is administrative cases.

(3) There is an imbalance in filing and disposition in the courts, with a feature of "3 high, 2 low", namely, the accumulated cases settled in February, July and October are comparatively lower than the neighboring months. The accumulated cases settled in June, Sept., December are comparatively higher than the neighboring months, in December, the number of settlements reaches the highest level, as per Graph 3.7 and Graph 3.8.

[247] The regulation was promulgated by the Supreme People's Court in 2000.

(4) The study based on secondary data reveals that the settlement ratio is very high in China. The settlement ratio is higher than 90% (refer to Table 3.1 and Table 3.2) each year based on the yearly filing and disposition as per the China Law Year Books.[248] The question is, court delay has been a frequent topic and a tough task in judiciary in China, such a high rate could be explained that the statistics might not be authentic enough due to some improper practices in statistics.[249] Additionally, it might justify many assertions that the high cost behind the high settlement ratio: the sacrifice of procedural rights of the parties and miscarriage of justice.[250] Nevertheless, it must be admitted that the high settlement ratio has heavily to do with time bound programs in there jurisdiction. Under the time bound program, judges are under strong pressure to realize the target settlement ratio as established by the court. However, the time bound program should take the caseload and the number of judges in each court into account and a more realistic settlement ratio should be established. The bound program should include some necessary measures like framing more effective criteria in granting adjournments so as to avoid a pure pursuant of a high settlement ratio by the judges while sacrificing the procedural and substantive justice of a speedy trial.

8. Suggestions

Despite a high settlement ratio, the above investigation also indicated that the efficiency of the courts should be improved. The time availability for disposition of cases should be readjusted so that cases will not be concentrated and congested at the end of the year whereas only a small proportion of cases are settled in the beginning of the year. The time bound program for settlement should also consider its workability in each court according to the caseload and availability of judges and time for judgment. Furthermore, under a better

[248] Judge Huang, Song You of the Supreme People's Court, argued that the problem of court delay has been deterred after the promulgation of *the Regulation on Strict Implementation of Time Limit* in 2000 by the Supreme People's Court. In his view, the duration of the courts in China is short due to the application of simple procedure in the lower courts and most of the cases can be settled within 6 months. The efficiency of the Chinese courts is not low compared with jurisdiction in the Western countries. See Huang, Song You, An Analysis of Judicial Efficiency, in: People's Judiciary (11) 2001, p. 21.

[249] In an interview with one judge in the Research Department of the Supreme People's Court on this issue, it was admitted that the local courts very often change the figures in their statistical reports so as to undermine the problem of court delay. According to some lawyers, local courts may ask the litigants not to file in the courts at the end of the year or ask the litigants to withdraw the cases at the end of the year or file in the beginning of the year. The settlement ratio shown in the China Law Yearbooks is overestimated in this sense.

[250] Compare Wang, Li Ming, Research on Judicial Reform, China Law Press, 2000, pp. 358-361.

designed and workable time bound program in which some necessary measures like framing more effective criteria in granting adjournments should be included, judges should settle cases within the time limit as stipulated in the Civil Procedure Code and relevant regulation[251] so as to avoid delay and backlog.

The reform is a complicated work, which requires not only a reform of judicial administration concerning case flow management, but also a reasonable allocation of time availability for disposition of cases. First, judges should bear in mind that court delay is justice denied. Delays not only waste time but also increase litigation costs, judicial costs and judicial resources. Second, the work of writing annual reports, examination within the court system, and planning for the coming year should be allocated optimally within a certain time limit so that more time can be available for judgments. Third, from filing through judgment to settlement of the cases, all the information should be processed more efficiently and improved by a computer system. The Supreme People's Court has now set up a computer system to record filings, settlements and documentation; such a system could be spread out to cover all of the courts in China so that the judges can check records and supervise the cases in a scientific and easy manner. Fourth, the rush for settlement at the end of the year, which merely seeks for a settlement ratio just to satisfy the congress in the annual judicial work report, must be changed. Fifth, the court shall arrange an optimal holiday plan for judges so as to avoid cases being congested during certain periods of time.

III. Empirical Study of Functioning of the Courts

Due to the rapid increase of filing and low efficiency in the judiciary, court delay has been a disputed issue and is seen as a major obstacle of the judiciary nowadays in China. There are a large number of cases piling up in the courts. For example, from January to July of 2000, the settlement ratio is 69.43%; there are 1,850.000 cases still pending at the end of July 2000.[252] Backlog and court delay severely affected the functioning of the courts. Justice delayed is justice denied, court delay has not only damaged the authority of the courts and the principle

[251] The Supreme People's Court: *Regulation on Strict Implementation of Time Limit (2000)*.
[252] Source: report on 28.09.2000 from the China News Net. These pending cases would be settled by speedy trial in the second half year under the time bound program as indicated in the previous study.

rule of law, but also impedes the rights of the parties and leads to distrust by the general public to the judicial system.

In this context, the empirical study attempts to investigate the duration of the court through a sample survey. In the meantime, this study also tries to find out the causes of delay and provides solutions to remove those delays. While reducing delay in the courts requires sufficient manpower, the increase in judges raises complex political issues. Furthermore, the increase in manpower does not mean that it can solve the problem of supply and demand.[253] Despite the large number of judges in China, the efficiency with respect to the average disposition is extremely low. It seems that improving efficiency by additional judges in disposition is not resolving the problem, but more important is the time consumed for trial and judges' competence to deal with complex cases.

In the simplest terms, delay is a problem of supply and demand; the demand for judges' time has outrun the supply. Furthermore, the size of the backlog will affect the effort to remove delay, since the preferment of removing the cases in the backlog will definitely affect the filed cases. Thus it also raises the question of which cases shall be given priority for trial and the arrangement of such will increase the cost of the other parties whose cases are postponed.

Furthermore, the discussion of court delays and remedies should recognize the basic facts of the pattern of disposition in lawsuits. According to the statistics in the China Law Year Book 1999, 79.7% of civil trial cases were settled by mediation or disposed by trial procedure with court decisions or orders;[254] the remaining were withdrawn or reassigned. To state this quantitatively, approximately 79.7% of the civil trial cases yearly are settled by trial,[255] and the disposition of these cases requires most of the total court time. The problem of court delay therefore is the problem of the time consumed to dispose these cases since these cases take up the overwhelming majority of judge's time. The following sample survey is therefore directed

[253] According to an empirical study, there is no correlation between the efficiency of disposition and number of judges. See Edgardo Buscaglia Jr., Maria Dakolias, and William Ratliff, Judicial Reform in Latin America: A Framework for National Development, Stanford University 1995, p. 9.

[254] In 1998, the total civil trial cases amounted to 3,360,028, among which 1,540,368 were settled by mediation, 1,1515,649 were in favor of the litigants and 22,382 were reversed. The remaining 681,429 cases were withdrawn or settled by other means. According to the law, hearing (trial) must be held in respect of mediation, court decisions/orders, or dismissal of the cases, therefore the cases settled by trial accounted 79.7% of the total cases (1,540,368 + 1,115,849 + 22,382) / 3,360,028 = 79.7%), see China Law Year Book, 1999.

[255] In contrast, most of the cases were settled before trial in America. According to an investigation made in the New York Court, some 71% of all suits were settled without trial and the disposition of these cases requires only 16.2% of the total court time. See Hans Zeisel, Harry Kalven, Jr., Bernard Buchholz, Court in Delay, Little, Brown and Company, 1959, p. 5. Court efficiency can be improved if increasing percentage of cases are settled before trial. Compare He, Bin, Restructuring the Mechanism of Dispute Resolution, in: Peking University Law Journal, Vol. 14, No. 1 (2002), p. 10.

toward the trial cases in the courts. The data was randomly collected from the trial courts and appellate courts respectively. The magnitude of delay is based on cases tried in regular order, as it reflects the best time index of delay.[256]

1. Sources of Data

In order to make an critical evaluation of the courts' efficiency in China in terms of delay and costs, it is necessary to use the data with regards to filing of cases, disposal of cases and decisions of the courts on the cases and opinions on law's delay, thus, the analysis will be based on the primary data and secondary data in the following study. The requisite data is compiled on the basis of:

- Primary data collected from the local courts (City of Xiamen);
- Statistical data from the publications of the Supreme People's Court and case books (secondary data);
- The views of the judges in respect to the problem of court delay;
- The views of lawyers;
- The views of the parties in the litigation; and
- Personal observations.

The District Court and the Intermediate Court

The study of court delay in the lower courts (District Court and Intermediate Court) is based on primary data which was mainly collected by a sample survey in the District Court of HuLi, Xiamen, and the Intermediate Court of Xiamen City,[257] among which some cases were provided by law firms[258] so as to balance the possible difference contained in the data processing between the courts and the law firms. These cases collected from law firms are combined in the sampling.

[256] In the study of District Court of Huli, Xiamen, duration of the cases disposed under simple procedure is also indicated. All the cases filed in the Intermediate Court, the High Court and the Supreme People's Court are disposed under regular order.

[257] It is very difficult to have first-hand data from the courts in China since the courts keep strict regulation on the data administration. The best way to get the information is to get the data through the powerful judges who have discretion to ask the data administrator to do the work for researchers, or through the data administrator who is ready to help. In this study, most of the data are provided by the data administrator in the courts.

[258] The information with respect to the cases from the law firms should be much more accurate since the records are neutral and reflect the reality; whereas the records made in the courts might contain alternation in the records.

These cases concern filing and disposition made by the courts in the year of 2002. From the District Court of Hu Li, Xiamen City, 287 trial cases were collected. Among these 287 cases, there were 63 cases filed for appeal in the Intermediate People's Court of Xiamen. Furthermore 213 cases were collected randomly from the Intermediate People's Court of Xiamen and the law firms (among which 26 cases come from law firms).

The High Court and the Supreme People's Court

Due to the difficulty in getting access to first hand information (primary data) directly from the High People's Courts and the Supreme People's Court, the study of court delay in the High Court and the Supreme People's Court are based on secondary data which is mainly collected randomly from publications and selected case books published by the Supreme People's Court.

The case books include:

Selection of Appeal and Retrial Cases relating to Economic Disputes Disposed by the Supreme People's Court (from 1993 until 1996), Vol. 2, edited by Economic Tribunal of the Supreme People's Court,China University of Politics and Law Publication 1997, and

Selection of Cases Disposed by the People's Court, Civil Cases Collection 1992 - 1999, Vol. 1, 2 and 3, edited by the Research Institute of China Law Application of the Supreme People's Court, China Judiciary Publication, 2000

107 cases were selected from the case books. These 107 cases were tried by the High Courts and were filed for appeal in the Supreme People's Court. As the Supreme People's Court never has direct filing of trial cases, for the sake of convenience, the study of court duration in the Supreme People's Court is further based on these 107 cases filed in the High People's Courts for first trial and the Supreme People' Court for appeal.

In short, the study of court delay is concentrated on the cases filed in the District Court of Huli, Xiamen and the Intermediate People's Court in Xiamen City based on the primary data, since these local courts deal with most of the cases and the study of these courts is very critical to the analysis of court delay in China; further study based on the published data with respect to the High People's Courts and the Supreme People's Court will illustrate a full picture of court duration in China, though the filing and disposition in these higher courts do not have a big stake in the total filings and dispositions in China.

2. Sample Survey

All cases are collected from the filed cases in the courts, especially from the local courts in Xiamen City;[259] some cases are from the filing record in law firms. These cases include 287 cases from the Huli District Court in Xiamen City in which 63 cases were appeal/retrial cases, and 213 cases from the Intermediate People's Court of Xiamen. The collected data are category-wise filed and disposed civil cases. These cases were collected by the method of Stratified Random Sampling from the courts.

Based on a review of filed cases, all of the data were collected by a designed and structured questionnaire 1.[260] The questionnaire also includes some items which interview complainants about their attitude towards court delay and the costs incurred in the cases, these interviews help find out how costs affect the complainants' decision to go to court and how it could affect the speed of the judgment.

Further, a sample survey was also made to discover the duration of disposition in the High Courts and the Supreme People's Court, 107 trial cases filed in the High courts were collected. These cases were further brought to the Supreme People's Court for appeal. The study of these 107 cases not only illustrates the duration of disposition in each tier of jurisdiction, but also the total duration from filing in the High Courts until it's final jurisdiction made by the Supreme People's Court.

a) District Court of Huli, Xiamen

(1) Disposed/Dismissed Civil Cases Categorized

The investigation was made in the District Court of Huli, Xiamen with 287 cases randomly

[259] Xiamen City is located in Fujian Province and is one of the economic centers in south of China; and it is one of the 4 Special Economic Zones which were established by the central government in the beginning of 1980s to attract foreign investment.

[260] Contents of the questionnaire please see Appendix I.

chosen and analyzed. The District Courts and County Courts are responsible for trial cases and have no appeal jurisdiction. Table 3.5 presents the duration of the category-wise cases.

Table 3. 5 The Duration of Cases by the District Court of HULI (N = 287)

Type of Cases	<30 days	30-90 days	90-180 days	180 – 360 days	360 – 540 days	540 – 720 days	>720 days	**Total**	**Percentage**
Family issues, like divorce	18	30	11	3	1	0		**63**	**22%**
Heritage	2	15	2	1	1	0		**21**	**7.3%**
Rental disputes	7	6	8	6	2	0		**29**	**10.1%**
Contract Disputes	18	33	12	8	2	1	1	**75**	**26.1%**
Consumer Products	1	5	5	0	0	0		**11**	**3.8%**
Real Estate	3	13	12	3	3	0		**34**	**11.8%**
Transportation	8	12	5	2	1	0		**28**	**9.8%**
Personal injury	5	17	2	2	0	0		**26**	**9.1%**
Total	**62**	**131**	**57**	**25**	**10**	**1**	**1**	**287**	
Percentage	**21.6%**	**45.6%**	**19.9%**	**8.7%**	**3.5%**	**0.35%**	**0.35%**		**100%**

Source: compiled from the data collected from the District Court of Huli, Xiamen

Table 3.5 presents the category-wise number of 287 cases disposed in the first instance by the Huli District Court in the year of 2002.[261] From the statistics it is evident to see that contract disputes (26.1%) and family issues (22%) dominated the number of cases filed in the court, followed by real estate accounting for 11.8% and rental disputes accounting for 10.1%, the others are transportation (accounting for 9.8%), personal injury (9.1%), heritage (7.3%), consumer products (3.8%) respectively.

Among 287 cases, 125 cases were disposed under simple procedure, 18 of them exceeded the time limit of 90 days according to Civil Procedure Code; 162 cases were disposed by normal

[261] The Huli District Court has disposed / dismissed around 7,000 cases in the year of 2001, 5,800 cases in 2002, as informed by the administrator for the statistics.

procedure, 37 of them exceeded the time limit of 180 days as regulated by the Civil Procedure Code.

Most of the cases disposed within the time limit are concerning divorce, neighborhood conflicts, tort, and small value contract disputes. From the cases collected, 'dispute value' of 70% of the cases is within the range of 1000 – 10,000 Chinese Yuan (app. 121 – 1210 USD). The facts of the cases are clear and evident to all the parties and therefore it is easy for the judges to make decisions on these cases in short time.

(2) Time Taken to Dispose/Dismiss the Cases

In terms of duration, among the 287 cases, 62 cases were disposed within 30 days (accounting for 21.6%), 131 cases were disposed in 30-90 days (accounting for 45.6%), 57 cases were disposed in 90-180 days (accounting for 19.9 %), 25 cases were disposed in 180-360 days (accounting for 8.7%) and 10 cases were disposed in 360-540 days (accounting for 3.5%), 2 cases exceeded 540 days.[262]

(a) Average Duration

Through calculation of the duration of the samples, the average time consumed by these 287 trial cases, which were settled in the District Court of Huli, Xiamen, is 56.5 days for cases with simple procedure and 155 days for cases in regular order.

Graph 3.11 illustrates the 287 cases disposed by the District Court of Huli, Xiamen and the corresponding time.

[262] According to China Law Year Book 1998, the duration of the trial cases in China is short. In 1997, the number of trial cases is 5,349,460, among which 79.61% of the cases were settled by simple procedure within 3 months; 18.43% of the cases were disposed under regular order within 6 months; and 1.96% of the cases exceeded 6 months for disposition. Also see Huang, Song You, An Analysis of Judicial Efficiency, in: People's Judiciary (11) 2001, p. 21.

Graph 3. 11 Cases disposed by the District Court of Huli, Xiamen and the corresponding Time

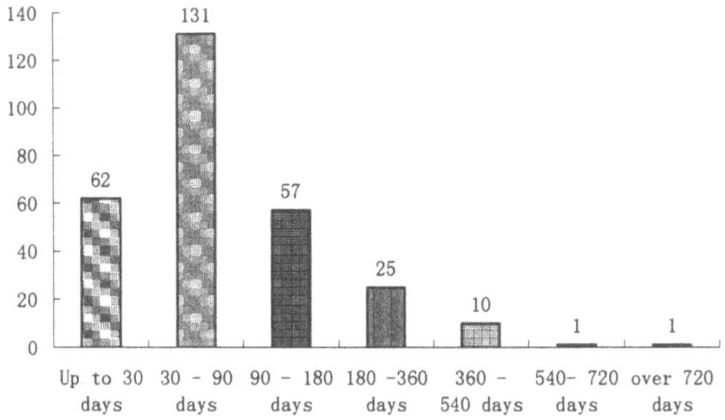

Source: compiled from the data collected from the District Court of Huli, Xiamen

From the statistics one can see, that family issues (especially divorce) and contract disputes dominated filings and disposals; the others are disputes involving transportation, consumer products, personal injury, rental dispute, real estate, heritage etc., which indicates that the District Court mainly deals with cases close to the daily life of normal people; most of these cases are clear and evident in fact-finding and thus can be disposed within the time limit.

(b) Average Consumption of Time in Each Phase of the Trial

Table 3.6 shows the average time in each phase of trial and the total average time of consumption. The advantage of simple procedure[263] (125 cases) in time consumption is very obvious compared to the normal procedure[264] (162 cases) at the court of the first instance (District Court). The application of simple procedure saves a lot of time in the phases of pretrial preparation and hearing.

[263] According to Civil Procedure Code, cases filed in the District Courts shall first apply the simple procedure, and normal procedure shall be applied if the case is found as 'complicated'. Cases under simple procedure shall be settled within 3 months after filing.

[264] Normal Procedure refers to procedure in regular order.

Table 3. 6 Average Time Consumption in each Phase and Average Duration of the Cases in District Court, Huli, Xiamen

	Filing (days)	Pretrial Preparation (days)	Hearing (days)	Discussion/Meeting (days)	Settlement (days)	Average Duration (days)	No. of Cases exceeding Time Limit	Percentage Of Cases exceeding Time Limit
Simple Procedure[265]	3.8	20	15.6	7.9	9.2	56.5 days	18	14.4%
Normal Procedure[266]	5.4	65	52	16.6	16	155 days	37	22.84%

Source: compiled from the data collected from the District Court of Huli, Xiamen.

Remark: among the 287 cases, 125 cases were settled by simple procedure and there were 63 appeal cases filed in the Intermediate Court of Xiamen. The analysis of appeal cases will be further made in b).

Graph 3. 12 reveals the average time consumed in each phase of the cases settled in regular order (Normal Procedure).

Graph 3. 12 Average Time Consumption in each Phase of Disposition

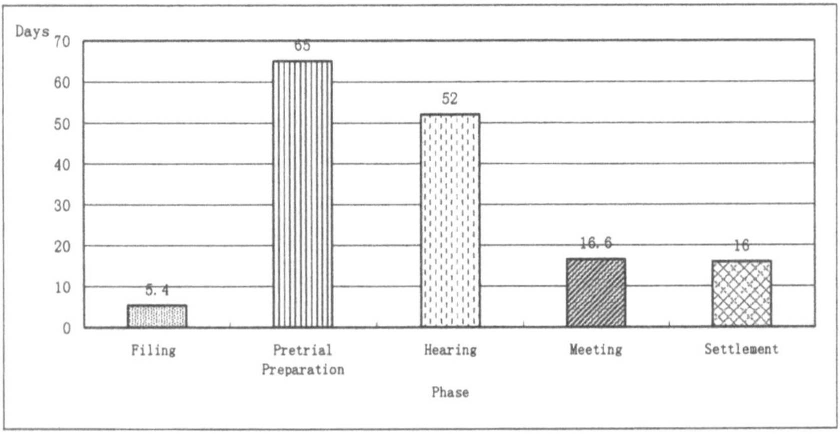

Source: compiled from the data collected from the District Court of Huli, Xiamen

265 According to Art. 142 – 146 of Civil Procedure Code, the Simple Procedure is applicable in the lower courts (District Courts and Intermediate Court, normally for cases filed in the District Court) for cases with clear and evident facts, as well as small dispute values; oral filing is allowed and hearing is much more flexible under simple procedure; one judge can be assigned to make the judgment.

266 In normal procedure, the case shall be settled within 6 months after the date of filing, and it can only be prolonged for another 6 months with the consent of the President of the court. A further prolongation must be permitted by the higher court of the region. See Art. 135, Civil Procedure Code.

It is obvious that pretrial preparation took a large proportion (41.93%) of time consumption in these cases. This also indicates the reform in recent years focusing on pretrial and introduction of an adversarial system in the hearing may have positive effects on the efficiency of judgments.

(3) An Anatomy of Workload in Huli District Court

In Huli District Court there are 28 judges and 5 clerks, the number of cases disposed/dismissed in 2002 is 5,800,[267] with an average of 207 cases in one year for each judge, or 17.25 cases per month for each judge. The high rate of filing and disposition in this court is due to the fact that many residents in the district come from other cities/provinces and work in the industrial zones in the city, consequently, civil disputes and contract disputes happen every day in this area.

The time distribution in daily work is as follows: 5 working days a week, 8 hours each day, the total working days for one year is 239 days.[268] Further, judges have to spend time in other activities, which are not related to disposition of the cases. According to an estimation based on the information available from the courts and personal observation, each year judges will spend:

- 30 days for meetings and study (both political and legal study are organized by the court)
- 10 days for social activities: environment activities, legal consultancy for the public etc. (These activities are also organized by the court or the local government)
- 15 days for traveling (for example, evidence-collecting in other cities)[269]

Thus, the total time available for judgment is 184 days (239 – 55). Based on this assumption, the workload for each judge in District Court of Huli, Xiamen is very heavy. Each judge must

[267] Data provided by court clerk of the court. Caseload varies from court to court in China. For example, in Xiamen city, one District Court has around 90 judges and they dispose around 1,2000 cases in one year; while another one has 22 judges and has filing and disposition of only 230 cases in one year.

[268] 239 working days is calculated by deduction of all holidays in the year: weekends (52 X 2 = 104 days) and 7 days off in May, 7 days off in October, 8 days off in Chinese Spring Festival.

[269] Compared with judges in other countries, the Chinese judges spend more time for traveling to collect evidence.

dispose 1.1 cases each day.[270] This result is however quite different from the findings made previously by the survey on average disposition in all of the courts in China (refer to Graph 3.6): the average disposition in this court is much higher than the average based on the nationwide level. The explanation behind the difference lies in the caseload in different regions. In fact, caseloads are different from court to court and region to region in China. Despite the low average disposition at the nationwide level, in China, most of the courts in the coastal area, especially the district courts, have a high record of filing and disposition due to its high density of population and increasing economic and social interactions among the population. For example, each judge in Huangpu District Court/Shanghai disposed 74.7 cases on average (2.49 cases per day!) in 1999;[271] whereas the filing in the courts located in the western regions are comparatively less. The caseload may be very low in the court, even less than 200 cases per year; in some courts, some judges are assigned for judicial administration and social matters because there are no cases for disposition.

Cases filed in the district courts are normally small claims, tort, family issues etc, they are easy to resolve by simple procedure. The city of Xiamen is a special economic zone in China and has a high level of economic activities and its inhabitants come from all over the country. With more economic activity and dense population, it is no surprise that caseload is high.

In comparison, the working days for a German judge are 215 in a year, after deducting the 30 days of holiday.[272] One judge in the district courts (Amtgericht) disposes 700 cases each year on average, or each day 3.26 cases. 67% of the cases were disposed or dismissed very quickly and 33% of them were mediated, namely, around 230 cases were mediated. In the local courts (Amtsgericht), 48.2% of the cases were settled within 3 months, 28.5% within 6 months, 17.5% within 12 months. The average duration of the local courts from filing until settlement was 4.6 months, but there 4% of the cases were delayed for more than 3 years. It implies that the legal system in Germany is highly efficient.[273]

---

270 5800/(184x28) = 1.1

271 He, Bin, Restructuring the Mechanism of Dispute Resolution, Peking University Law Journal, Vol. 14, No.1 (2002), p. 15.

272 This figure does not take hospital time into consideration, see Franzen, Hans, "Was kostet eine Richterstunde? – Berechnung und Folgerungen", in NJW 1974, p. 785.

273 Qi, Shu Jie, Research on Reform of Civil Procedure Law, Xiamen University Press, 2000, pp. 18, 19.

(4) Findings

Based on the sample study of 287 cases collected from the District Court of Huli, Xiamen, the finding can be summarized as follows:

So far there is no serious court delay concerned with trial cases filed in the District Court of HuLi, Xiamen, and the average duration of disposition is 56.5 days for cases disposed under simple procedure and 155 days in regular order. The average duration is more or less within the time limit[274] as regulated in the Civil Procedure Code. The reason is that most of the cases are small claims and are clear in facts and application of law is easy.

There is no summary court or summary tribunal in lower courts, but all cases filed in the District Court shall first apply simple procedure; only when judges find out that the case is complicated and cannot be solved in a short time, then the procedure will be turned into regular order. The short duration concluded from the sample survey is due to the fact that many of the cases surveyed were settled by simple procedure since the dispute value is small and it is easy for the judge to make decision. In China, around 80% of the cases filed in district courts are settled through simple procedure.[275] But of 287 cases, 125 cases (43.55%) were disposed by simple procedure, which requires the judges to solve the cases within 3 months.

With respect to dispute value, most of the dispute values of the cases (66.86%) ranged from 5,000 to 50,000 Yuan.

The high record of filing and disposition in this court has to do with the density of the population and level of economic and social development found in the region.

Judges in the District Court have heavy workloads due to the increase in cases in recent years. As known, the average qualification of judges is low, especially in the lower courts. Judges in the lower courts spend a lot of time in meetings and social service. The availability of judges and time for trial activity is therefore discounted.

Nevertheless, the efficiency of the court is not low in the District Court of Huli, Xiamen. As indicated, each judge disposes 1.1 cases per working day. This average is comparatively

[274] The time limit for trial cases is 6 months in regular order, a prolongation of 6 months is possible with the permission of the president of the Court if there is special reason. For further prolongation, it must be subject to the permission of the higher court of the region.

[275] Zhang, Wu Sheng, Research on some problems of reform in lower courts, in: Vol. 2 Review of Judicial Reform, China Judiciary Publication, 2001, p. 204. Compare Huang, Song You, An Analysis of Judicial Efficiency, in: People's Judiciary (11) 2001, p. 21.

higher than the average at national level.[276] On the other hand, it may be concluded that the current problem of case overload and personnel shortage in many other courts can be solved through efficiency-enhancement, such as by re-assigning the work of judges from administration to trial, by increasing the working time for trial, and undertaking procedural reform etc.

b) Intermediate Court of Xiamen City

Further investigation has been conducted in the Intermediate Court of Xiamen City, in which 213 trial cases were selected. These cases were chosen randomly from the Intermediate People's Court in Xiamen and some from the city's law firms (26 cases). All the data were collected by a designed and structured questionnaire,[277] based on a review of the filed cases. The questionnaire also included some items to interview complainants about their attitude toward court delay and the costs incurred in the cases, these interviews would help find out how costs affect complainants' decision to go to court and how it could affect the speed of the judgment.

Additionally, 63 cases with appeal or retrial procedure conducted by the Intermediate People's Court of Xiamen were selected from the 287 trial cases filed in the District Court of Huli to see the total duration cases from filing until final jurisdiction; furthermore, the average duration of 16 retrial cases will be illustrated.

(1) Original Filing and Disposition

(a) Disposed/Dismissed Civil Cases Categorized

Table 3.7 presents 213 filed and disposed/dismissed trial categorized cases selected from the Intermediate People's Court.

[276] The burden of cases on the judges differs from region to region. In less developed region, the workload for judges is low as there are few cases; whereas in costal areas where the economy is much more developed, the caseload is very heavy. For example, in Chao Yan District Court of Beijing, one judge disposed more than 400 cases per year; in Huangpu District Court in Shanghai, one judge even disposed more than 700 cases per year; but in some backward regions, each judge may dispose less than 10 cases a year. See He, Bin, Restructuring the Mechanism of Dispute Resolution, Peking University Law Journal, Vol. 14, No. 1 (2002), p. 15.

[277] Contents of the questionnaire please see Appendix I.

Table 3. 7 The Duration of Cases by Intermediate People's Court of Xiamen (N = 213)

Type of case	<30 days	30-60 days	60-90 days	90-120 days	120–150 days	150-180 days	>180 days	**Total**	**Percentage**
Contractual disputes	1	3	3	7	7	29	21	**71**	**33.33%**
Real estate	1	1	3	2	2	12	28	**49**	**23%**
Bankruptcy	0	1	5	7	11	3	15	**42**	**19.72%**
Property right	0	0	3	3	5	3	6	**20**	**9.39%**
Transportation	0	1	2	2	5	8	13	**31**	**14.56%**
Total	**2**	**6**	**16**	**21**	**30**	**55**	**83**	**213**	
Percentage	**0.94%**	**2.8%**	**7.5%**	**9.9%**	**14.1%**	**25.8%**	**38.96%**		**100%**

Source: compiled from the data collected for the Intermediate People's Court of Xiamen.

Most of the cases are related to disputes in contract, real estate and bankruptcy. It reflects that in the process of economic transition, conflicts arising from business interactions are frequent and inevitable. Investment in construction and real estate have become the main economic activity in the country; furthermore, as a result of economic reform, many inefficient state-owned firms cannot survive in the market economy, the role of these state-owned firms fade away in the national economy, whereas the private sector is playing a more and more important role in economic development.

Table 3.7 shows that among the 213 cases, 33.33% of the cases concern contract disputes; 23% of the cases involve real estate; bankruptcy cases share 19.72%; cases concerning property rights share 9.39%; the rest, 14.56%, are cases involving transportation.

(b) Time Taken to Dispose/Dismiss the Cases

Table 3.7 reveals that 2 cases (0.94%) were disposed within 30 days; 5 cases (2.8%) were disposed within 30-60 days; 16 cases (7.5%) were disposed within 60-90 days; 21 cases (9.9%) were disposed within 90-120 days; 30 cases (14.1%) were disposed within 120-150 days; 55 cases (25.8%) were disposed within 150-180 days; 83 cases (38.96%) were disposed more than 180 days.

Some disputes can be solved very quickly, even if the dispute value is large, since the evidences and documents are easy to collect concerning big contracts and it is easier for the judges to make decisions based on clear and evident facts. However, some disputes may take a long time due to the complexity of cases and conflicts of interest. For example, one case disposed by Xiamen Intermediate People's Court has not yet been settled because the court order was rejected by the state-owned trading house; the case has taken more than 10 years to progress through the procedure of trial, appeal, retrial and further appeal for retrial procedure.[278]

(aa) Average Duration

The average time of disposition, based on the 213 trial cases, is 8.7 months (261 days). Compared to the duration of trial cases disposed by the District Court of Huli, Xiamen, the Intermediate Court of Xiamen City, as an example, needs a longer time to dispose trial cases. This may be attributed to a larger dispute value and more complicated cases being filed in the Intermediate Court of Xiamen.

The following Graph 3.13 illustrates the 213 cases disposed by the Intermediate Court, Xiamen and the corresponding time consumed.

Graph 3. 13 Cases disposed by the Intermediate Court, Xiamen and the corresponding Time

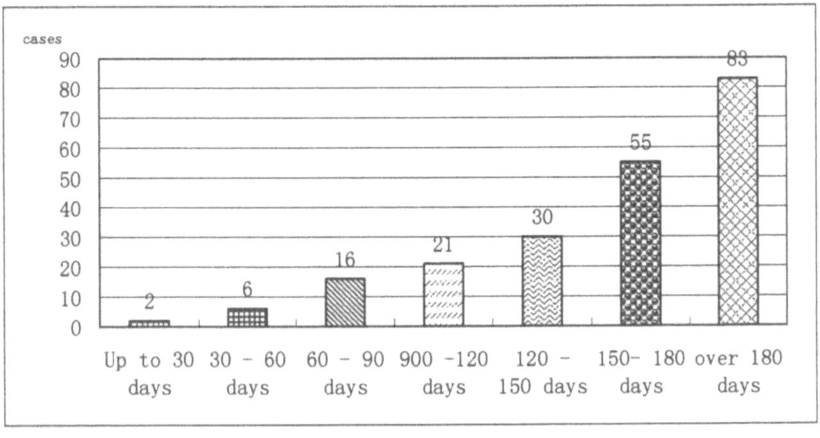

Source: compiled from the data collected for the Intermediate People's Court of Xiamen

[278] Retrial procedure is often used when the parties do not agree with the final decision of the court. As a constitutional right, the parties can complain the unfairness of the judgment to the Supreme People's Court or the People's Congress in local or higher level even after retrial. There is no restriction of times of disposition for retrial procedure.

In contrast, in Germany, most of the lawsuits filed at the regional courts (Landsgericht) can be settled within a reasonable time limit. For instance, in 1996, 38.9% of the cases were disposed within 3 months by the regional courts (Landsgericht), 5% within 6 months, 21.7% within 12 months and 9.6% within 24 months. The average duration of all the regional courts from filing until settlement is 6.5 months.[279]

(bb) Average Time Consumed in Each Phase of Trial

As indicated in Table 3.8 and Graph 3.14, pretrial preparation (93 days) and hearing (82 days) consume most of the time of disposition, since the parties spend time in collecting evidence, fact-finding, and preparing for the hearings. This phase of filing needs 6.5 days on average; discussions by the Collegial Panel consume 43.5 days and this phase of settlement requires 36 days. Compared with the simple cases disposed by the District Court, it consumes more time in each stage of trial, which may affirm the additional complexity of the cases.

Table 3. 8 Average Time Consumption in each Phase and Average Duration of the Cases disposed by the Intermediate Court of Xiamen (as court of first instance. Sample: N = 213)

	Filing (days)	Pretrial Preparation (days)	Hearing (days)	Discussion (days)	Settlement (days)	Average Duration (days)	No. of cases exceeding Time Limit (days)	Percentage of Cases exceeding Time limit (days)
First Instance	6.5	93	82	43.5	36	261	168	78.8%

Source: compiled from the data collected for the Intermediate People's Court of Xiamen

Graph 3.14 reveals the average time consumed in each phase of the cases settled in regular order (normal procedure).

279. Gottwald, Peter, The German Administration of Civil Justice, in: Civil Justice in Crisis – Comparative Perspective of Civil Procedure, Oxford University Publication 1999. Also in: Qi, Shu Jie, Research on Reform of Civil Procedure Law, Xiamen University Press, 2000, pp. 18, 19

Graph 3. 14 Average Time Consumption in each Phase of Disposition

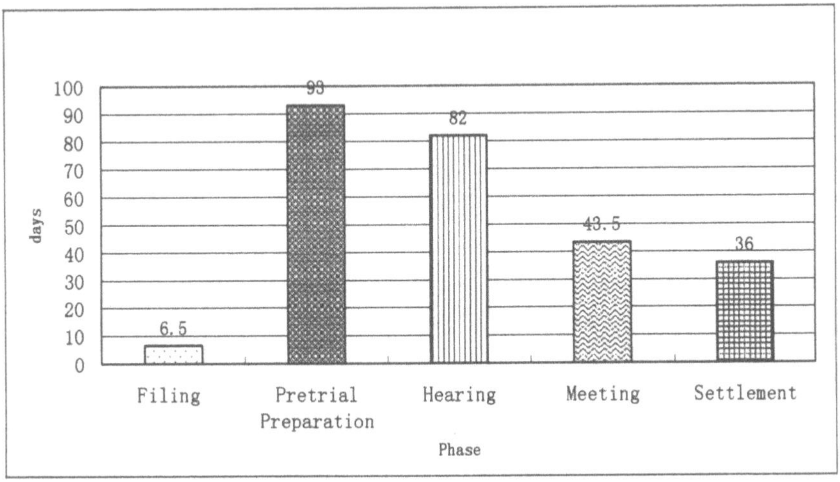

Source: compiled from the data collected for the Intermediate People's Court of Xiamen

(2) Cases under Appeal and Retrial Procedure: from First Instance to Appeal/Retrial

(a) Cases Filed for Appeal in the Intermediate Court

63 cases from the District Court of Huli (among the 287 samples as indicated above) were filed for appeal or retrial procedure[280] in the Intermediate Court of Xiamen for final jurisdiction. The following analysis is to find out the total duration of these appeal cases and retrial cases from it's filing in the original court until final jurisdiction in the appellate court. In 63 appeal cases, 16 were under judicial supervision for retrial.

Table 3.9 reveals the duration from filing in the District Court (as court of first Instance) and the final jurisdiction made by Intermediate Court of Xiamen (as court of appeal respectively.

280 Often, retrial is regarded as a new case filed in the court in statistics. In this study, it is treated as continuation of the trial of original cases.

Table 3. 9 The Total Duration of Appeal Cases made by Intermediate People's Court of Xiamen (N = 63)

Days	<30	30-60	60-90	90-120	120 – 150	150-180	>180	**Total**
First Instance[281]	7	15	6	6	4	12	13	**63**
Delivery of Documents[282]	Very difficult to measure. In reality it is one of the main reasons of delay.*							
Appeal	1	3	12	13	6	11	18	**63**
Retrial[283]	0	0	0	1	2	4	9	**16**

*Time consumed to deliver file from trial court and to appellate court is 'blind' and it is the major reason of delay. After filing for appeal, court clerk needs at least 20 days to pack up the file, 7 days for post and 10 days to notify the litigant to pay. In practice, such period take 1 – 3 months for delivery of file.[284]

These 63 appeal cases concern disputes of property right regarding real estate, contract, tort, heritage, debt and/or loan.

Among these 63 appeal cases, 16 of the cases were further under retrial procedure after the judgments made by the appellate court due to the following reasons: 10 cases were appealed again for retrial by the parties because of discontent with the court orders/decrees; 4 of them were initiated by the president of the court and were presented to the Trial Committee for reconsideration as the president of the court viewed that the judgments made contained mistakes; another 2 cases were complained and challenged by the local procuratorate as they disagreed with the judgments and therefore challenged the court orders made by the court. Thus, 16 cases in total were under supervision procedure for retrial.

(b) Time Taken to Dispose/Dismiss Appeal and Retrial Cases: from First Instance to Appeal/Retrial

Table 3.10 reveals the average duration of cases in each phase of the trial and the total duration from District Court to the Appellate Court. 63 cases disposed originally by the

281 It refers to the trial in the District Court.

282 It is regulated that the file shall be transferred to the higher court within 5 days after filing of appeal. In practice the time limit is very difficult to be respected due to many reasons.

283 There is no regulation on judicial hierarchy in retrial. According to Civil Procedure Code, the court which adjudicates the case can undertake retrial. For example, if the court order/decree is made by the court of first instance, then retrial will be conducted according to the procedure in the court of the first instance; if court order/decree is made by the appellate court, then the retrial will be in accordance with the appeal procedure; in case the higher court and the Supreme Court retrial the case according to the procedure of judicial supervision, the retrial procedure will be then in accordance with appeal procedure.

284 It is confirmed by formal Judge H.J. He, now a lawyer.

District Court of Huli were brought for appeal in the Intermediate Court of Xiamen, among which 16 are under retrial procedure

Table 3. 10 Average Time Consumption in each Phase and Average Duration of the Cases disposed by the Intermediate Court of Xiamen (as appellate court).

Duration	Filing (day)	Pretrial Preparation (day)	Hearing (day)	Discussion (day)	Settlement (day)	Average Duration (day)	No. of Cases exceeding Time Limit	Percentage Of Cases exceeding Time Limit
First Instance	6	45	38.6	28.4	27	**145**	13	20.6 %
Appeal	5.6	56	60	66	30	**217.6**	48	76.2%
Retrial	The parties can apply for retrial within 2 years after the court decision made by the court					**336***		
	5	51	116.5	177	26	**375.5**	No time limit required	

Remarks:

1: *336 days is the time from the date of court order is made by the court until the application for retrial is accepted by the court. It is based on the calculation and estimation from reading of the cases.

2: The parties can apply for retrial within 2 years after the court order is made.

In the appellate stage, as indicated in Table 3.10, pretrial preparation does not consume as much time compared to the time consumed in trial court, the explanation is that the evidence have already been presented to the court, and thus the judges in appellate court can concentrate on hearings and internal discussions with respect to questionable or points of dispute and how to apply the law; Table 3.10 reveals that discussion consumes much more time than the time consumed in the trial court, this may reflect that appeal cases are more complicated with regard to disputes in fact-finding and application of law. In the phase of settlement it makes no big difference in time consumption between the trial court and the appellate court.

(aa) Average Duration from Original Filing to Final Jurisdiction

Duration of most of these civil cases filed in the court of the first instance (District Court) were more or less within the time limit of 6 months, the average duration in the court of the first instance is 145 days. However, appeal consumed much more time compared to trial in the court of the first instance: 16 cases were disposed within the time limit of 90 days as regulated in the Civil Procedure Code; the duration of rest of the cases (47 cases) exceed the time limit of 90 days for appeal cases. The average duration of these 63 cases in the appellate court is 217.6 days. Therefore, the duration concerning appeal cases based on these 63 samples is 362.6 days (145 + 217.6), beginning from filing in the District Court (Trial Court) and commencing when the final court orders/decrees were made by the Intermediate Court of Xiamen (Appellate Court).

(bb) Average Duration of Cases with Retrial Procedure

For the 16 cases under retrial procedure, the duration of the retrial procedure ranges from 1 to 3 years.[285] The average time of disposition for the 16 retrial cases is 375.5 days or 12.5 months from applying for retrial until final judgments was made, and 711.5 days (336 + 375.5) or 23.71 months calculating from court orders made by appellate court until final settlements were made by the retrial court. The average time consumption from original filing until the final settlement exceeds 2 years. Though the retrial cases do not have large proportion in the total filings and dispositions,[286] it has a big stake in appeal cases, and more around 20-25% of the appeal cases were further tried under judicial supervision procedure, namely, by retrial.[287] It is obvious that these cases with retrial procedure consumed not only time and cost, but also judicial resources due to no restriction of time limit and times of disposition in regulation.

(3) An Anatomy of the Workload in the Intermediate Court of Xiamen

There are around 192 personnel in the Intermediate Court of Xiamen, among which 103 have

[285] Some cases consumed even more time under retrial procedure. In the investigation, some cases took more than 9 years until the final judgments were made by the retrial courts. In these 16 samples, such case with more than 9 years duration is not taken into consideration so as to avoid big deviation from the real situation.

[286] According to the calculation based on China Law Year Book, 1990 – 2000, retrial cases or cases under judicial supervision only share 1.5% - .2.5% of the total filings and dispositions in the courts in China.

[287] According to China Law Year Book, 1991-2000.

The proportion of retrial cases is comparatively higher in the High Court. According to a statistics made by the High Court of Hainan province, in 2000, the High Court of Hainan province received 1376 cases, among which 311 cases (22.6% of the total filings) were retrial cases, in the Intermediate Court of Haikou of this province, the court received 1710 filings and 140 cases were retrial cases (8.2%), whereas in the District Court of Xinhua of Haikou city, the court received 3716 cases and retrial cases amounted to 42 (1.1%), this indicated that the higher the judicial hierarchy, the more the filing of retrial cases, since the litigants believe that the quality of the higher court will be higher. See Zhang, Ai Zhen, Some Suggestions on Restructuring the Judicial Supervision in China, in: People's Judiciary (10) 2001, p. 19.

the title of judge; the others are court police, clerks, and administrators.

The total working days for the year are 239 days,[288] 5 working days a week, 8 hours each day.

The workload for the judges in this court is heavy as they have to deal with approximately 4,200 cases each year, including trial cases and appellate cases.[289] The average number of cases adjudicated by each judge in one year is app. 40.78, or 0.17 case each working day.

In reality, the number of judges responsible for jurisdiction is only 53. It means that only around 50% of the judges are assigned for jurisdiction, the remaining judges are mainly engaged in administrative matters.[290] Moreover, judges have to spend their time for other activities such as meetings, social activities and traveling, which are estimated to be the same as the estimation made for the District Court of Huli, Xiamen:

- 30 days for meetings and study (both political and legal study are organized by the court)
- 10 days for social activities: environment activities, legal consultancy for the public etc. (organized by the court or the local government)
- 15 days for traveling (for example, evidence-collecting in other cities)

Thus, the total time available for judgment is 184 days (239 – 55). Based on this assumption, the workload for each judge (53 judges) in Intermediate People's Court Xiamen is very heavy. Each judge must dispose 0.43 case each working day.[291]

(4) Findings:

(a) The duration of cases originally filed in the Intermediate court is longer. The average time for trial cases to be disposed by the Intermediate Court is 8.7 months (261 days). Although the economic cases originally filed in the Intermediate Court of Xiamen has a relatively

---

288 The 239 working days do not excluded the weekends (52 X 2 = 104 days) and 7 days off in May, 7 days off in October, 8 days off in Chinese Spring Festival.

289 Data available through interview with judges in the Intermediate Court of Xiamen.

290 A similar investigation in the setup of courts also reveals that 46.5% of the court personnel engage in administration of the court. Compare Wu, Dong Yu and Hua, Shi, An Investigation and Comment on the Internal Setup and Categorized Personnel Management of the People's Courts, in: Zhang, Wei Ping, Review on Judicial Reform, Vol. 4, China Judiciary Publication, pp. 438, 336, 447.

291 4,200/(184x53) = 0.43

higher dispute value (normally exceeding 2 million Yuan), some can also be resolved quickly and can be settled within the time limit as regulated in Civil Procedure Code, as the parties normally have complete evidence and documents in hand.

(b) There exists serious delay concerning cases under appeal and retrial procedure since most of the appeal cases are more complicated, or have big dispute value. Retrial procedure is not strictly regulated in respect to time limits in evidence collection and times of disposition. The average duration of 16 cases under retrial procedure consume 711.5 days commencing from court orders/decrees made by the appellate court until the final settlement was made by the retrial court.

The workload in the Intermediate Court of Xiamen is heavy. Most of the cities in the coastal areas like Xiamen experienced quick economic development, meanwhile disputes also increased quickly due to the intensification of economic and social interaction between people. The average number of cases disposed by each judge in the court was 40.78 cases per year, or 0.17 cases per working day. Efficiency could be improved if more judge's time could be assigned for jurisdiction of cases rather than administrative matters.

(c) In general, the Intermediate Court in China serves as a court of final jurisdiction. Such a 2-tier jurisdiction system leads to a congestion of appeal cases in the Intermediate Court since 80-90% of the civil cases are filed in the District/County Courts and the Intermediate Courts. The final jurisdiction on civil cases made by the Intermediate Court has severely affected the unification of the application of law and the quality of the judgment, since the local courts are lower in the hierarchy, the understanding and application of law differs from region to region; besides, the application of law is strongly influenced by local interest and interference.[292] Unlike the 2-tier jurisdiction in China, most other countries apply a 3-tier jurisdiction. The High Court or the Supreme Court enjoys final jurisdiction on cases, and very few cases are filed and disposed by the Supreme Court. The final jurisdiction in higher courts and the Supreme Court under a 3-tier system may be better in law application considering the

[292] Zhang, Wu Sheng, Research on Problems of Reform in the Lower Courts, in: Review on Judicial Reform Vol. 2, China Judiciary Publication, 2001, p. 204.

'filtering' function of the lower courts.[293]

c) The High People's Court

The High Courts in China are responsible for important cases within its' territory of jurisdiction[294] and serve as appellate courts for the local courts. The study of the duration of original filing in the High Courts is based on secondary data.[295] 107 original filings in the High Courts were collected to analyze the duration of disposition incurred in the High Courts in China. As the number of cases available in the single provincial High Court is limited, the samples being collected here are not limited to the filings in a specific High People's Court. These 107 cases were brought for appeal. Therefore, further analysis of duration of disposition of cases in the Supreme People's Court is also based on these samples.

(1) Original Filings in the High Courts

With respect to original filings in the High Courts in China, 107 cases filed in the High Courts with appeal in the Supreme Court were collected.

There are some common features in these cases:

- The number of filing in each provincial High Court is limited per year, as already explained above.
- The dispute value of these cases is comparatively big, which is normally over millions of Chinese Yuan.
- Cases filed in the High Courts are normally concerning economic issues, mainly contract and property disputes.

(a) Filed and Disposed/Dismissed Cases Categorized

Table 3.11 reveals both the duration incurred in the High Courts.

---

293 Those cases which are simple, clear and evident in fact-finding can be solved by the lower courts in the first trial, thus, only complicated cases will be brought to the High Courts for appeal.

294 Art. 20 of Civil Procedure Code.

295 These 107 cases are randomly selected from the case books edited and published by the Supreme People's Court. In: Selection of Appeal and Retrial Cases relating to Economic Disputes disposed by the Supreme People's Court (from 1993 until 1996), Vol. 2, edited by Economic Tribunal of the Supreme People's Court, China University of Politics and Law Publication 1997, and

Selection of Cases disposed by the People's Court, Civil Cases Collection 1992 – 1999, Vol. 1, 2 and 3, edited by the Research Institute of China Law Application of the Supreme People's Court, China Judiciary Publication, 2000.

Table 3. 11 Category-wise filed and disposed/dismissed Cases and the Duration in the High People's Courts

Type / Months	<3 m*	3- 6 m	6- 9 m	9-12 m	12-15 m	15-18 m	18-21 m	21-24 m	24-30 m	30-36 m	>36 m	Total No.
Sales	2	20	4	2	2	0	0	0	0	0	0	30
Construction	0	6	3	1	0	0	0	0	0	1	0	11
Credit/Loan Agreement	2	9	4	2	1	0	0	0	0	1	1	20
Guarantee Contract	2	1	7	1	0	0	0	0	0	0	0	11
Agent Agreement	0	0	0	1	3	0	0	0	1	0	0	5
Real Estate	1	2	1	2	2	0	0	0	0	0	0	8
Financial Leasing	0	1	2	0	1		0	1	1	0	2	8
Foreign Exchange & Portfolio	1	0	2	1	3	1	0	0	0	0	0	8
Other Disputes	0	1	1	3	1	0	0	0	0	0	0	6
Total No.	**8**	**40**	**24**	**13**	**13**	**1**	**0**	**1**	**2**	**2**	**3**	***107***

* m represents "months". Source: compiled from Case Books edited by the Supreme People's Court.

Among 107 cases, 30 cases were related to sales contracts with dispute values ranging from 1 million to 10 million Yuan (most of them are around 2 million to 4 million Yuan); 11 cases were related to construction projects with dispute values ranging from 5 million to 10 million Yuan; 20 cases were relevant to disputes from Credit / Loan agreements with dispute values over 2 million Yuan, and most of them exceeded 7 million Yuan; 11 cases are relevant to guarantee contracts between firms and banks and had comparatively higher dispute values; the highest dispute value exceeds 20 billion Yuan; 5 cases were related to agent agreements between parties and another 8 cases were related to real estate disputes; furthermore, 8 cases are relevant to financial leasing, foreign exchange & portfolio; the remaining 6 cases concern other economic issues.

(b) Time Taken to Dispose/Dismiss the Cases

As to the duration of disposition in the High Courts, among 107 cases, 8 cases were disposed within 3 months, 40 were disposed in 3 – 6 months, 24 cases were disposed within 6 – 9 months, 13 cases were disposed within 9 -12 months, 13 cases were disposed within 12 – 15 months and the duration of the disposition of the remaining 9 cases exceeded 15 months. Thus, it is evident that only 48 cases, accounting for 44.86% (of the 107 samples) were disposed within the time limit of 6 months as regulated by the law. 55.14% of the cases did not have disposal within the time limit. This can be explained that due to the complexity of cases and high dispute value, the parties needed more time in pretrial preparation and fact finding; further, judges and involved parties are more carefully engaged in the cases.

(c) Average Time of Disposition

Based on the statistical figures from the 107 filed cases and the sum of the time consumed for each filing, it is easy to calculate the resulting average duration. The average time of disposition of 107 cases was 10.63 months.[296]

(2) An Anatomy of Workload in the High Court

Take one High Court as an example, there are 322 personnel in this High Court but many of the judges are not responsible for judgments. They are involved primarily in administrative activity. In this court, 88 officials are involved in court administration, accounting for 25.1%[297] of the total number of personnel in the court. The High People's Court is responsible for civil trial cases, which have a strong impact within its territory of jurisdiction.[298] Judges travel very often to different regions in the province to supervise judicial work and review some big cases in the province. The court has the highest

[296] The sum of time consumed for these 107 cases is 1137.26 months; 1137.26 months divided by 107 equals to 10.63 months.

[297] In the previous investigation in the lower courts, administrative officials accounts around 50% of the total personnel. In fact, the ratio in the high courts will be higher, since the high courts set up more departments than the lower courts.

[298] Art. 20 of Civil Procedure Code.

jurisdiction on appellate cases within the province. In the year of 2000, civil/economic cases filed in this High Court amounted to 1376.[299]

(3) Findings

According to Table 3.11, 44.86% of the cases under investigation were disposed within the time limit of 6 months as specified by the Civil procedure Code for cases disposed in the first instance; 55.14% of the cases were not disposed within the time limit. This is due to the reason that the trial and appeal cases filed in the court are much more complicated in application of law, or have a high dispute value.

The average duration of disposition is 10.63 months for 107 cases filed in the High Courts. This indicates that many dispositions exceeded the time limit regulated by Civil Procedure Code and delays are inevitable.

Additionally, delays are also due to the current case management system of the court and lack of supervision. As the court for administration and supervision, the High Courts spend much of their time in supervising the judicial work of the lower courts within their territorial jurisdiction and sometimes ignore the regulation on time limit in the jurisdiction of their own cases.[300]

d) The Supreme People's Court

(1) The Function of the Supreme Court

(a) Interpretation of Law

The Supreme Court enjoys the highest discretion in jurisdiction and its judgment on cases is final and binding to all parties. Moreover, the interpretation of the Supreme Court in laws and regulations and its conclusions on cases have a strong influence on the judiciary, the role of the Supreme Court is therefore of great importance to legal development.

The number of judges in the Supreme Court differs in each country.[301] In most countries, the

[299] The high court spends substantial time in judicial supervision, for instance, among 1376 cases, 311 cases are retrial cases.
[300] The impression is concluded from discussions and interviews with some judges and lawyers.
[301] For example, in Germany it consists of 10 judges in the Supreme Court (Bundesgerichtshof); in Netherlands it consists of 26 judges in the Supreme Court; in the US the Supreme Court has 9 judges; in Swiss there are 30 judges in the Supreme Court and in Denmark there are 25 judges in the Supreme Court. The judges in the Supreme Court are not all professionals, the may also come from prosecutors, law professors and senior lawyers.

process of selection and nomination of judges in the Supreme Court is complicated. Judges of the Supreme Court usually enjoy high social status and prestige. For example, in Japan, the Supreme Court consists of 15 judges, among whom 5 are professionals; the others are selected from prosecutors, law professors and senior lawyers. In Japan, the Judicial Conference enjoys the highest discretion in judicial interpretation, judicial review and also serves as the highest jurisdiction on big and complicated cases; furthermore, the Judicial Conference enjoys the highest discretion in judicial administration.

In China the Supreme Court has a total number of about 300 personnel but only slightly more than 50 judges are engaged in judgment activities. One of the main tasks of the Supreme People's Court is to interpret current laws and regulations. As the Chinese legal system is still under progressive construction, there are many gaps to be filled in laws and there exists different understandings of laws in different regions, thus, to unify the legal system and extend guidance to the local courts, every year the Supreme People's Court issues more than 300 interpretations, attempting to improve the uniform understanding and application of the law.[302]

(b) Judicial Supervision

According to Art. 177 of the Civil Procedure Code, the Supreme People's Court has the discretion to review court orders/decrees made by the lower courts and has the jurisdiction to retry the cases or order the lower courts to conduct the retrial procedures and review the cases.

The Supreme Court has jurisdiction both on trial cases as well as in appellate cases,[303] furthermore, it can also review cases filed in the lower courts.[304] Cases filed in the Supreme People's Court[305] normally have national influence, or have a big dispute value. Due to the complexity of cases, it would be no surprise to see that 70% of the cases have disposed more

[302] Fu, Yu Lin, The Principle of Structuring the Judicial Hierarchy, in: China Social Science, Vol. 4, 2002, p. 96. The interpretation of law by the Supreme People's Court is helpful to unify the application of law, but in fact it does not solve the problem of different understanding of law by the lower courts, lawyers and the public in general completely, since most of the interpretations are based on the reports and questions from the lower courts, while the interpreter – the Trial Committee of the Supreme People's Court, does not participate in the trial of the cases and the interpretations made by them with respect to some cases are still abstract, and these interpretations need to be interpreted again.

[303] Art. 21, Civil Procedure Code.

[304] Art. 177, Civil Procedure Code.

[305] So far there is no trial cases (Civil Cases) filed accepted by the Supreme Court. Civil cases filed in the Supreme Court are appeal cases and retrial cases.

than 4 times until they were finally brought to the Supreme Court for final jurisdiction.[306]

(2) The Duration of Disposition in the Supreme People's Court

So far there is no original filing of civil case in the Supreme People's Court, though the Civil Procedure Code allows such. All the civil cases disposed by the Supreme People's Court are appeal cases from the High Courts or retrial cases from the lower courts. The study of duration in the Supreme People's court is based on 107 cases, which were mentioned previously. These 107 cases were original filings in the High Courts and were brought to the Supreme People's Court for appeal or retrial after the first trial. It is therefore very easy to see the total duration of cases filed originally in the High Courts and further appeals in the Supreme People's Court.

(a) Filed and Disposed/Dismissed Civil Cases Categorized

Table 3.12 reveals that most of the 107 civil cases filed for appeal in the Supreme People's Court are economic issues in nature, as already indicated. Most of the civil cases filed in the Supreme People's Court concern disputes arising from sales contracts, construction projects, credit / loan contracts between firms and banks, guarantee contracts, principal-agent contracts, real estate, foreign exchange, portfolio and property, etc.[307]

In these 107 samples, 25 of the judgments made by the High Courts were canceled or reversed; 7 of them are partly revised; 66 of them (accounting for 61.68%) remained unchanged; 1 appeal was withdrawn by the party and 8 of them were settled through mediation by the Supreme People's Court. The higher percentage of unchanged jurisdiction in the higher courts reflects a more accurate application of law in the higher level of jurisdiction. The dispute values of these cases are large compared with those trial cases filed in the lower regional courts. In the survey, the dispute value of most of these cases was above 3 million Chinese Yuan; the highest dispute value was 20 million Chinese Yuan.

With respect to litigation cost, most of the cases cost more than 30,000 Yuan in each filing. Some cases incurred high costs when the case involved various fees like court fees, lawyer's

[306] Sun, Bo Sheng, Analysis of Retrial Cases, People's Court Publication, 1999, p. 23.

[307] See Cases Book edited by the Supreme People's Court. Infra Footnote 308.

fee, and fees for security of title and execution etc.

Table 3. 12 Category-wise filed and disposed/dismissed Cases and the Duration in the Supreme People's Courts

Type / Months	<3 m*	3- 6 m	6- 9 m	9-12 m	12-15 m	15-18 m	18-21 m	21-24 m	24-30 m	30-36 m	>36 m	Total No.
Sales	6	11	3	7	2	0	0	1	0	0	0	**30**
Construction	1	3	1	1	1	0	2	0	1	0	1	**11**
Credit/Loan Agreement	7	3	5	1	1	0	1	1	0	0	1	**20**
Guarantee Contract	2	6	1	1	0	0	0	0	0	1	0	**11**
Agent Agreement	0	1	2	0	0	1	0	0	1	0	0	**5**
Real Estate	0	5	1	1	0	1	0	0	0	0	0	**8**
Financial Leasing	0	1	3	1	0	1	0	0	2	0	0	**8**
Foreign Exchange & Portfolio	1	5	1	0	0	1	0	0	0	0	0	**8**
Other Disputes	0	0	0	1	1	0	0	2	0	2	0	**6**
Total No.	**17**	**35**	**17**	**13**	**5**	**4**	**3**	**4**	**4**	**3**	**2**	***107***

* m represents "months"

Source: compiled from Case Books edited by the Supreme People's Court.[308]

[308] Selection of Appeal and Retrial Cases relating to Economic Disputes disposed by the Supreme People's Court (from 1993 until 1996), Vol. 2, edited by Economic Tribunal of the Supreme People's Court,China University of Politics and Law Publication 1997, and
Selection of Cases disposed by the People's Court, Civil Cases Collection 1992 – 1999, Vol. 1, 2 and 3, edited by the Research Institute of China Law Application of the Supreme People's Court, China Judiciary Publication, 2000.

(b) Time Taken to Dispose/Dismiss the Cases

Among 107 appeal cases settled by the Supreme People's Court, as indicated in Table 3.12, 17 cases were disposed within the time limit of 3 months as regulated by the Civil Procedure Code for appeal cases; 35 cases were disposed within 3 – 6 months; 17 cases consumed 6 – 9 months; 13 cases were disposed within 9 – 12 months; 5 cases were settled within 12 – 15 months; all others were resolved in 15 months or more. From this empirical study, it was found that only 17 cases, accounting for 15.89% of the total 107 sample cases, were settled within the time limit (3 months for appeal cases), the rest (accounting for 74.11%) over ran the time limit. Some cases took a very long time for disposition, for example, several cases were settled after more than 2 years from filing.

(c) Average Time of Disposition Appeal Cases

The average time of disposition of the 107 cases in the phase of appeal, based on the statistics, took **9.**51 months[309].

The average duration from original filing until settlement is the sum of average time consumed in the High Court (10.63 months) and the Supreme Court (9.51 months), which was 20.14 months.

(d) Average Duration of Retrial Cases

Comparatively, the time duration from disposition until final judgment made by the Supreme People's Court under the supervision procedure, was too long.

Among 107 cases, 12 cases were under judicial supervision procedure by the Supreme People's Court and were disposed as retrial cases.[310] Table 3.13 briefly shows the statistics.

[309] The sum of 1017.5 months for all the cases divided by 107 equals to 9.51 months.

[310] Retrial cases has a stake of 20-25% of the caseload of appeal cases, see China Law Year Book, 1991-2000.

Table 3. 13 Time Consumption of Retrial Cases filed in the Supreme People's Court (12 cases from 107 appeal cases filed in the Supreme People's Court).

Month	0-3m*	3 – 6 m	6 – 9 m	9 -12 m	12 – 15 m	15- 18 m	18 – 24 m	> 24 m-
cases	0	1	2	0	0	3	0	6
Average time of disposition: 16.8 months **Total duration****from original filing in the local court until final settlement in the Supreme People's Court: **38.85 months**								

* m is for 'month'

** The total duration includes the waiting time before the acceptance of retrial filing.

As revealed in Table 3.13, 6 cases exceed 24 months, 3 cases needed 15 – 18 months, 2 cases consumed 5 – 8 months and 1 case took 4.5 months. Therefore, it may be concluded that it is these small size cases that consumed the most time for disposition and affected the duration of court.

The average duration of a retrial procedure took 16.8 months and the total duration from original filing in the court of the first instance until final settlement in the Supreme People's Court was 38.85 months.

This indicates that under supervision procedure, there may exist some defects in Civil Procedure Code in which the parties and the courts can present evidence and new arguments for retrial without limit on times of trial and time limit in disposition. The retrial procedure can be repeated in the court and result in a heavy burden on the court. Delay in the Supreme People's Court has much to do with the complexity of the cases and the generosity of the retrial procedure, consequently, the appearances of the parties for hearings is also frequent; according to statistics for retrial cases under jurisdiction in the Supreme People's Court, 70% of the retrial cases were filed and disposed by the lower courts more than 4 times before the cases were finally brought to the Supreme People's Court for final jurisdiction under the supervision procedure.[311]

The law's delay not only proves that justice delayed is justice denied, but also it may imply that improvements should be made on how to regulate retrial in respect of how new evidence

[311] Some of the cases were even disposed more than 7 times before filing for retrial in the Supreme People's Court, see, Fu, Yu Lin, The Principle of Structuring the Judicial Hierarchy: a comparative analysis, in: China Social Science, (4) 2002, p. 98, Footnote 3.

and fact-finding can be accepted as the reason for a retrial. In terms of litigation costs, due to the impossibility of having a speedy redress, the parties not only pay a high amount of litigation fee, but also lose many business opportunities due to the long duration of the court procedure.

(4) An Anatomy of the Supreme People's Court Workload

There are around 300 personnel in the court and only around 50 judges are engaged in judgment activities. The cases filed in the Supreme People's Court have increased quickly over recent years. Currently, the Supreme Court disposes around 3,000 cases each year, the number of filings are about two times the number of dispositions,[312] this indicates that the court is not able to solve all of the cases filed in the court, and delay is inevitable when cases are pending and new filings are increasing. Furthermore, the Supreme Court deals with around 10,000 claims made by post or by visits of individuals.[313] The workload in the Supreme People's Court is high, due to the fact that most of the people hope to utilize the court as their last chance to realize justice, especially when inequality, corruption and interference are frequent in local regions. To reduce the overload of cases, some suggest that the cases filed in the Supreme Court should be 'filtered' by the lower courts based on a 3-tier hierarchy in jurisdiction[314], or by procedural reform, and through increasing the quality of judgment in the lower courts.[315]

(5) Findings

The Supreme Court takes upon itself part of the function of legislature in the form of legal interpretation in China.[316] The Supreme Court serves mainly as an appellate court for complicated cases or cases with large dispute values or those which are of great national influence.

---

312 Ditto.

313 It is very common to see from the newspaper that many people go to the Supreme People's Court or the People's Congress in case they feel justice is miscarried. The large number of claims by personal appearance in the Supreme Court or by post reflects the failure to deliver justice to the public by the local courts and many people see the Supreme Court as the last defense of justice.

314 Fu, Yu Lin, The Principle of Structuring the Judicial Hierarchy, in China Social Science, (4) 2002, pp. 93-96.

315 Tan, Shi Gui, Research on Judicial Reform in China, China Law Press, 2000, pp. 235-238.

316 The Constitution stipulates that the National People's Congress has the right to enact and interpret law. However, in practice, the interpretation of law is made by the Supreme Court.

Among the 107 appeal cases, only 17 cases (accounting for 15.89%) were settled within the time limit of 3 months (for appeal cases).

The average time of disposition for appeal cases in the Supreme People's Court, based on the sample study, was 9.51 months and the average duration of disposition from original filing until settlement by the Supreme People's Court was 20.14 months (10.63 + 9.51).

It must be mentioned that the disposition of retrial cases took longer than necessary at each level of jurisdiction. Likewise, in the Supreme People's Court, sample survey shows that it needed 16.8 months on average to dispose the filing of retrial cases. The average total duration of the cases from original filing in the court of the first instance until the final judgment was made by the Supreme Court was 38.85 months. According to China Law Yearbooks, 20-25% of the appeal cases were brought for retrial.[317] Retrial cases represented a small proportion of the total filings and dispositions. Most of the retrial cases were mainly concentrated in the higher courts and only a small proportion of retrial cases were filed in the lower courts.[318] The empirical study indicated that retrial case consumed a longer time and increased the overwhelming workload of the judges.

IV. Functioning of Court System: Assessment based on Interviews and Questionnaires

1. Views of the Parties: Delay, Cost, and the Factors for Court Success

The parties' views on the functioning of the courts were gathered based on questionnaires, mainly through interviews with 20 litigants and respondents in different cases. The purpose of the questionnaire (questions shown in Part E of Questionnaire 1 – Appendix I) was to find out the views of the parties with respect to the functioning of the court system, especially on the issues of duration of the cases and the cost for litigation.

With respect to the duration of cases, according to the Civil Procedure Code (1991) and *Regulation on Strict Implementation of Time Limit in Jurisdiction (2000)*, the duration of cases under trial in the court of the first instance shall be 6 months and 3 months in the

[317] China Law Year Book, 1991-2000, supra note 287.

[318] Supra note 286. In High People's Court of Hainan, retrial cases had a stake of 22.6% of the total caseload; In Haikou Intermediate Court it had a stake of 8.2% and in District Court of Xinhuan, it was only 1.1%.

appellate court, prolongation must strictly fulfill the relevant regulations.[319] Most of those interviewed were of the opinion that the duration of the court process was too long and there were no objective criteria for granting adjournments. In appeal and retrial, the parties had to wait for more than one month until the documents were delivered by the trial courts and accepted by the appellate courts, despite the time limit of 15 days. The longer the duration of the cases, the lesser the possibility for redress of grievances from the courts, as was the view of the parties.

As to litigation fees, litigants complained that advance payment to the court could not be recovered from the court when the debtor disappeared or went bankrupt. As a result the risk for recovering the prepaid litigation fee is shifted to the litigant even when he/she wins the case.[320] Besides the litigation fee, which is based more or less on objective criteria, many people complained that additional (implicit) costs were charged by the courts, based on arbitrary criteria set by the courts. With respect to bribery, many admitted that they were affected by the lawyers or the opposite parties to bribe the judges so as not to find himself in a weak position in litigation.

The litigants viewed that the success of litigation may be gauged by the extent of compensation settled in favor of litigants and the speed of the trial; further, litigation costs are a great concern to the parties involved, a quicker and less expensive settlement is essential for success.

Furthermore, law enforcement is regarded as an important element of court success, since the court orders/decrees are executed by the courts, the functioning and competence of the courts strongly affect the success of court remedy. Many viewed that the execution procedure is also expensive. Some interviewed were of the opinion that the attitude of the executor is very decisive for success of execution. If the executor acts passively, then it will be very difficult to have the court orders enforced.

---

[319] Before this Regulation was issued by the Supreme People's Court, the research department of the Supreme People's Court conducted an investigation in Henan and Shangdong Province to assess whether the time limit as regulated in the Civil Procedure Code (1991) is appropriate for law practice. In the investigation report conducted in 1999 with subject on: Enhancing Efficiency, Solving the Problem of Exceeding Time Limit, it is found that many cases were delayed, backlog has been a serious problem in many courts under investigation. Thus, the Supreme People's Court issued this Regulation to urge all the courts in China to deal with the problem of court delay.

[320] According to current regulation, litigant must pay litigation fee in advance to the court at the time of filing. In case of winning the case by the litigant, the prepaid litigation fee can only be recovered from the debtor. The risk is shifted to the litigant.

2. Views of the Judges (Interviews)

The views of the judges were gathered through interviews by face-to-face discussions. Most of the interviews were conducted in the District Court of Huli, Xiamen City and Intermediate People's Court of Xiamen, some interviews were done in Beijing with judges in the Supreme People's Court.

Many judges are in favor of more determination in budget supply and judicial independence. They thought that only when the courts do not have to rely on the budget from the local governments, can the influence of the local administration be reduced. Judicial independence requires a reform of the court system with respect to budget autonomy, personnel management, case management etc. As for the Trial Committee,[321] it is still very controversial for many judges: most of them regard the Trial Committee as an obstacle to judicial independence since it has too great power in jurisdiction and judges have to follow the opinions of the Trial committee. Delay is more unlikely when the Trial Committee affects its power for review cases. To some judges, the Trial Committee is a guarantee of quality of judiciary and helps to avoid abuse of power by individual judges, especially when the judges of the lower courts (district courts and intermediate courts) are not competent to deal with complicated cases or are not sure how to apply the law, the Trial Committee is a shield against corruption and miscarriage of justice.[322]

With respect to human capital, most of the judges, especially judges in the higher courts, viewed that the current legal system is not efficient and the quality of the judgment, especially in the court of first instance, is not satisfied since most of the cases are filed and disposed by the district courts and the intermediate courts and that the human capital in these courts is very decisive to the outcome of the judgment. If the courts of the lower level cannot attract talented judges, the functioning of the judiciary and judicial product cannot be guaranteed.

[321] The Trial Committee, according to People's Court Organization Act, is established in each court to discuss the complicated cases filed in the court. In practice, the Trial Committee often interferes into the decision of the collegial panel or the judges in the name of judicial supervision. For more details about the function and problems of the Trial Committee, see Chapter 2, II 3 c) and IV, 3 a) and III. 1 of Part II in Chapter 3.

[322] In an interview with the president of one intermediate court. Compare: Thinking on the Reform of Civil Jurisdiction, in: Contemporary Law, 4th ed. 2000. Judge Huang, Song You of the Supreme People's Court shares this view.

Judges always face a dilemma in judicial activity. When a case is filed, the presiding judge is likely to be influenced by all of the social connections in his surroundings. As the Chinese society is traditionally "a net consisting of numerous private connections", thus "Chinese ethics and law, are elastic in procedure according to relationship between the person and 'himself'."[323] Judges in the Chinese local courts encounter heavy pressure from the "net", consisting of a relationship of family, friends and hierarchies.[324] According to an investigation made of the 5 judicial organs,[325] it was found that "there exists the influence of personal contacts and relationship in 87% of criminal cases and 94% of civil cases, and it is becoming more and more serious".[326]

Meanwhile, many judges admit that the litigation cost is high for the parties involved. Besides the litigation fee, the courts charges additional costs to the parties. The reason for this is widely known to all; the courts have a budget shortage and need more income to cover the expenses of the courts. Some admit that the parties very often bribe the judges so as to influence the outcome. However, it is difficult to know whether the judges interviewed engaged in corruption; although it is a matter of fact that corruption is one of the major obstacles of accessibility of justice. Some high ranking officials in the courts expressed that they normally do not give their phone number to acquaintances so as to avoid approach by these people. It was admitted that many people use their relations and personal contact to approach judges if litigation is brought to the court. Judges say they find it very difficult to balance the interest of the parties, especially when both of the parties have relations and personal contacts in the government administration.

Many judges felt that a lawyer's involvement is not necessary unless it is a complicated case.

---

323 Fei, Xiao Tong, Native Soil of China, 1st ed. In 1947, San Lian Book Publication, 1985, p. 34.

324 Such pressure is very obvious in China. In the traditional ethics, family plays a very important roll among the general people. According to traditional Chinese ethical standards and its corresponding attitudes and norms, family interest is decisive to the people in dealing with various conflicts in daily life. For example, when a person becomes a judge (or other type of official), his relatives and friends may have such expectation: in the litigation, the judge should distinguish the relatives from the others and shall not ignore their close relationship. Such expectation put the judge into a dilemma situation: he may risk himself making unfair judgment and violating the law if he gives up his neutrality – as the judges in China always do. The legal system in China is under modernization but the legal culture is still to a large extent very traditional, therefore, if the judge ignores the relationship, it may cause tension between the judge and his family, relatives, friends and hierarchies. Empirical study shows that a harmonious relationship with the family members is very important to the psychological health of a judge and the law enforcement is very much affected by his psychological health. From this viewpoint, it is suggested that institutional arrangement shall be made to avoid judges to work in the locals where they were borne. See Xia, Yong, Toward An Age of Rights: A Perspective of the Civil Rights Developments in China, revised edition,China University of Politics and Law Publication, 2000, pp. 234, 235.

325 These 5 institutions are: the court, the procuratorate, the police, the judicial administration and the congress.

326 See the People's Court Daily, 07.03.1994.

Lawyers sometimes cheat the innocent party by adding additional charges to the cost of the innocent parties or by just making use of procedural rights and by delaying the cases technically. Lawyers sometimes are also corrupted. In one case the lawyer was aware of what the outcome would be but cheated the party he represented by saying that he needed 50,000 Yuan to bribe the judge to win the case, when in actuality he took the 50,000 Yuan for himself.[327]

Judges interviewed had different opinions on the issue of court delay. First is the concern the calculation of duration. To some judges, court delay is not serious when the duration in the court of the first instance and the appellate court is calculated separately. Due to the time bound program, most of the filings can be disposed by the end of the year; however, some judges opined that delay is severe based on the total duration, calculated from filing until the case is finally settled either in the trial court or the appellate court, and further taking the time of enforcement of court order into consideration. Secondly, on law's delay, judges have different views on delay in notification and delivery of writ. Postal delay, adjournments because of absences of respondents and delay in case of the involvement of the Trial Committee, account for the major reasons. Take the postal delay as an example, one judge in the Supreme People's Court commented that the time to post a file from the trial court to appellate court is 'blind' point, which is a major reason of court delay. But in practice, this 'blind' period is not calculated in statistics.[328] Third, the intervention by government administration, as viewed by the judges, is one of the main obstacles causing court delay, especially in the enforcement of law, court orders are very difficult to enforce when a case has to do with local interests. In the traditional hierarchical structure, the higher rank judges have greater discretion.

As to the high settlement ratio, many judges confirmed that they have to follow the prescribed time limit as regulated by the Civil Procedure Code and the *Regulation on Strict Implementation of Time Limit in Jurisdiction (2000)*. Further, a time bound program[329] of

---

[327] See People's Judiciary, (2) 2001, p. 36.

[328] Interview with judge Wang, Yan Bin of the Supreme People's Court on 27.01.2003.

[329] The time bound program is good in the sense that it establishes a clear task in disposition of cases. But it also causes some problems in disposition, for example, to realize the time bound program in which settlement ratio is given, judges tend to settle the cases by mediation, or asking the litigants to withdraw the cases by the end of the year or even settle the cases by careless trial . This leads to some adverse effects in judiciary, namely, low quality of judgment and miscarriage of justice. The time bound program therefore shall include a workable time limit for the judges.

settlement has been established in each court, both for disposition and law enforcement.

3. Views of Lawyers

In China, law was established and first recognized as a profession after the reform and open policy at the end of 1970s. The engagement of a lawyer in litigation has greatly improved procedural reform.

In interviews with 10 lawyers, most of them opined that current procedural reform is strongly related to the lawyers. From the standpoint of procedural justice, fair judgment can only be guaranteed by a just procedure. The modern procedure law stresses the equality of the parties, respect for legal rights, private autonomy, remedy of legal rights and protection of human rights, etc., these procedural activities need the help of lawyers. Due to the short history of the legal profession and limited engagement of lawyers in civil process in China, civil procedure law contains many irrationalities,[330] thus, lawyers' engagement is viewed to be very important in protecting the procedural rights of the parties.

Lawyers not only play an important role in providing professional legal counsel to the parties, but also assistance to the judges, since many judges in China do not have professional university education, their knowledge and understanding of law is limited; whereas lawyers are professionals who normally have a law degree and are skilled in the application of law. Furthermore, in legal debate, the arguments and suggestions from lawyers may remedy the procedural defects or fill legal gaps. However, some lawyers said many judges were hostile towards lawyers in some cases (The main reason for this is that judges felt the existence of lawyers was a hurdle to their self-interest, especially in specific cases, when conclusion had already been made by the Trial Committee by internal discussions or orders are given by the local administration).

On the issue of procedure justice, all of the interviewed lawyers held the view that the procedure is very often violated. For example, the lower courts very often ask for instruction from the higher courts when they have problems in dealing with cases, the opinions of the higher courts are normally adopted by the lower courts in the judgment. For the litigants, an

[330] Wang, Li Ming, Research on Judicial Reform, China Law Press, 2000, p. 507.

appeal in the higher court would mean the same result because the higher court has already made a prejudgment on the case.

Most of them denied that lawyers acted as middleman for bribery of the judges. They admitted that there may have been some cases in which lawyers bribed the judges in order to win, but they said these few people do not represent the whole. Most of lawyers are self-disciplined and abide by professional ethics.

With respect to delay, all the interviewed lawyers rejected the idea that engagement of lawyers in the court process leads to court delay. The current problem of backlog and court delay, as referred to by them, was attributed to the functioning of legal system in respect of organization of the courts, human capital, legal tradition & culture, intervention, budget, case management, etc. The removal of court delay needs to begin with a reform of the legal system, not only the symptoms.

As for cost, lawyers had different opinions from those of the general public. They viewed that it was a good idea that, under the current reform, the advocate fee was decided by the market and based on mutual agreement. They felt that the Regulation on Advocate Fees and Standards of Advocate Fees of 1990[331] could not adapt to the current market economy and the legal profession.

4. Assessment based on the Questionnaire[332] - The Major Factors Affecting Court Delay and the Effect of Regulation on Time Limit[333]

The reasons affecting the duration and efficiency of the courts are complicated. According to the questionnaire filled out and returned by 70 persons (including judges, assistant judges, clerks and court police) in the courts of Jiangsu Province and Chongqing City, the main results can be summarized as follows:

With respect to the process of litigation, 50% of them opinied that delivery of settlement is the main reason affecting court delay; 36% of them indicated pretrial preparation; 21% of them chose the hearing phase; 10% regard the meeting and discussion of collegial panel

[331] Regulation on Advocate Fee and Standards of Advocate Fee were promulgated in 1990 by the Ministry of Judiciary, Ministry of Finance and State Bureau for Price of Goods and Services.
[332] See attached Questionnaire 2 / Appendix II.
[333] The Supreme People's Court: *Regulation on Strict Implementation of Time Limit, 2000.*

affected the duration of cases; only 7 % of them chose 'filing' as a reason for affecting court delay.

As to the internal and organizational factors, 46% of them opinioned that the human capital of the court affect the duration of cases; 41% regard that budget, case management, court facilities and personnel autonomy etc. affect duration of cases; 31% regarded that waiting for instruction from higher ranking officials or higher courts consume more time in the making of judgment; 24% identified "waiting for the decision of a collegial panel and a Trial Committee"; and only 1% chose "signing of legal documents by the presiding judge or president of the court".

For external reasons, 57% voted for "Complexity of Cases", which indicated a need for time for collecting evidences and authentication; 46% indicated "Intervention of Administrative Bodies"; 44% chose "Difficulty in Delivery of Legal Documents"; 43% identified "Delay in Providing Evidences by the Parties" and only 10% chose "Bad Cooperation from Lawyers".

The problem of court delay is more serious in civil cases compared with criminal and administrative cases. The problem in enforcement of court orders/decrees, as viewed the judges, was that 90% of the court delay are concerning cases of law enforcement. This reveals that the enforcement of judgments is considered to be the toughest task in judiciary in China. The reasons are rooted not only in the courts with respect to human capital, budget, court facilities, case management etc., but also relating to the external social and economic environment, as well as the lagged legislature.

Table 3.14 presents the causes of delay and the percentage based on the survey through the questionnaire.

Table 3. 14 Causes of Court Delay (based on multiple choice)

Items	Percentage
Delay in Exchange of Evidences	27.2%
Excessive Consumption of Time in Audit, Assessment and Appraisal	55%
Difficulty in Delivery of Writ and other Legal Documents	40%
Delay in Hand Over File	4.5%
Waiting for Instruction	20.4%
Cases Concerning Group Action	5.4%
Difficulty in Application of Law	7.3%

a) Arbitrariness and Subjectivity of Judges

Many of judges lack responsibility in judgments and have a dim view towards the time limit. Judges often speed up their court proceedings in order to settle the cases by the end of the year so as to have a better settlement ratio and fewer records of 'exceeding the time limit' because their bonuses, promotion opportunities are closely related to their 'performance'. Some simply apply for prolongation when the time limit is up or revert simple procedure into normal procedure just to avoid exceeding the time limit of 3 months in a simple procedure. Some judges do not prepare and write the writ after the meeting of the collegial panel or do not send the writ in time to the parties.

The low quality of judges also leads to court delay. Judges act very cautiously when they are not confident in the application of law due to their limited legal knowledge and experiences; consequently they cannot make judgments in time and appearances of the parties / hearings will increase. Decisions are not made during the hearing but very often through "close door discussions", which consume much more time. One example in from this investigation shows one case concerning a dispute over a leasing contract of an apartment was finally last settled after 6 hearings and 8 collective discussions by the collegial panel. The total duration of this case took 8 months; in fact, such an easy case could have been concluded within several days.

b) Heavy Workload

Compared with other countries, the average number of cases disposed by the judges in China is low and the number of judges is high, compared to China's population. For example, in 1998, there were 170,000 judges among 280,000 court personnel and the number of cases settled by the courts was 5,864,274.[334] The average number of cases disposed by each judges was 34.5, which is low compared with American or German judges.[335] But, this low average does not mean that the workload of the courts is not heavy. On the one hand, though the number of judges in the courts is great, many judges actually do not engage in judgment of cases. Further, the proportion of judges is too great while the personnel for assistance work is

[334] China Law Year Book, 1999.

[335] The average number of cases disposed by each American judge is between 300 -400 per year and the German judge around 700 cases per year.

not enough;[336] consequently, judges have to spend time in simple work, which normally should be done by court clerks and assistants. From an efficiency point of view, it is waste of judicial resources for judges not to be able to concentrate on disposition of cases. On the other hand, the increase in case load needs more court staff to strengthen the force in judgment. On the contrary, many courts, especially the lower courts, have to reduce the number of personnel under the reform program.[337] Many excellent judges quit the positions in the courts and joined the law firms as the legal profession provides a high income opportunity to them. Take the courts in Chongqing City as an example, in the year of 2000 the case load was about 230,000 cases, but the number of judges and assistant judges and clerks was reduced from 5751 to 5045. To reduce backlog and settle the number of cases assigned[338] to them, some judges concentrated on simple cases first and left the complicated cases for later. Some judges even worked overtime to avoid exceeding time limit.

An overload of cases is one of the main reasons of court delay. The reform should increase the proportion of assistant judges and clerks in the courts by assigning those unqualified judges to these new positions.[339] According to the caseload, it has been suggested that 30,000 judges are needed to dispose the current caseload.[340] The number of judges should be 20-30 (highly qualified judges) in the Supreme People's Court, 10-20 judges in each High Court, 15-20 judges in each Intermediate Court and around 5 judges in each District Court.[341] The aim is to separate the administration from jurisdiction of cases. The remaining highly qualified judges would be competent for disposition of cases when the simple administrative matters are left to the assistants and clerks.[342]

c) The Difficulty and Complexity of Cases

As China is in a transitional economy, new conflicts happen every day and some are beyond the current capability of the law. Thus, court delay is inevitable when it is difficult to apply

[336] More than 50% of the personnel are judges. See the research report of Foshang Intermediate Court: the Research of Assistant Judge and the Number of Judges. In: People's Judiciary (8) 2002, p. 38

[337] Courts at all levels shall reduce 10% of the personnel, according to the reform plan in 2000.

[338] In the court, each judge has a certain amount of cases to complete. Whether he can settle the assigned cases or not, affects his remuneration and future promotion opportunity.

[339] The proportion of judges in the Chinese courts is 61% (170,000/280,000), whereas in the US the proportion in 1984 is 5.9% and in Taiwan the proportion is 15.6%.

[340] He, Bin, Restructuring the Mechanism of Dispute Resolution, in: Peking University Law Journal, Vol. 14, No.1 (2002), p. 7.

[341] Ditto.

[342] Wang, Li Ming, Research on Judicial Reform, China Law Press, 2000, p. 422.

the law to some cases.

The investigation shows that for some cases judges have to spend more time to discuss or wait for instruction from the Trial Committee or higher court; these cases share 20.4% of the total cases, which exceed the time limit. In many civil and commercial disputes, the problem has much to do with financial trust and security; some cases need experts' opinions and advice from special organizations and therefore need longer time.

Moreover, the cases concerning group litigation, which may affect social stability or sharpen the conflict, share 5.4% of the cases which exceed the time limit. For example, in the corporate reform of state-owned firms, disputes arising from bankruptcy catch the attention of the society and government; the development of real estate in China creates new conflicts not only in property rights, but also coupled with tort cases in environmental protection, the right for healthcare, etc. Although the legislature in China is speeding up to tackle these problems, mainly in the form of legal interpretation,[343] judges still find it difficult to apply the law in specific cases. Further, in these cases concerning employment and social stability, local governments frequently intervene in the judgment. Due to these factors, judges find it difficult to apply the law or make proper decision.

d) The Administrative and Functioning Problems of the Courts

The problems with respect to judicial administration and its functioning can be summarized as follows:

(1) Administrative Problem

Judicial efficiency has much to do with the management and organization of the court system in China. The administrative and managerial pattern of the courts is difficult to change in short run. Internally, judges have to report cases to higher officials or higher hierarchies and lack arbitrariness in the judgment of cases; externally, the personnel, budgets and facilities of the courts are dependent on the local governments and the ruling party. As a result, local governments and the ruling party can easily intervene in cases. In some cases, due to the

[343] Legal interpretation is normally made by the Supreme people's Court. Many interpretations are made when there are legal questions from lower courts asking for instructions on how to solve the complicated cases. In China, around 300 legal interpretations are issued by the Supreme People's Court each year. See Fu, Yu Lin, The Principle of Structuring the Judicial Hierarchy: a comparative analysis, in: China Social Science, (4) 2002, p. 96.

existence of localism or the outside interest of certain government sectors, local governments and the ruling party, even the supervisory body frequently interferes with the courts or requests the courts postpone trial or suspend the execution of court orders/decrees. Besides, court delay may occur when the judges have to report to the representatives of the local people's congress who execute the power of supervision in certain cases.[344] As China hasn't enacted supervision laws, there are no systematic or legal procedure regarding the supervision of the People's Congress and the Judiciary. In case of discrepancy in views, the courts have to follow the opinion of the People's Congress; thus, the supervision of representatives in specific cases may affect judicial independence and judicial authority.[345]

According to this investigation, 7.3% of court delay in the samples was related to the above mentioned factors. Taking one particular case as an example, it is difficult to find applicable law in a tort case relating to personal reputation, which has a social impact. A case is filed on 12. June of 2000, as a result of 3 public hearings, 7 meetings and discussions of the collegial panel, 7 reports to the higher court for instructions; it was finally settled on 18.05.2001. The duration of this tort case took almost one year.

(2) Functioning Problem

The regulation on Meetings of the Collegial Panels and Trial Committees is not effective since the contents for discussion in the meeting are too broad and consume a lot of the judges time; besides, delay often occurs when the cases pile up for discussion by the Trial Committee or when the cases are not able to be arranged for discussion in time, due to a conflict in the schedule of the Trial Committee.

(3) Effectiveness of Supervision on Time Limit

Although the *Regulation on Strict Implementation of Time Limit (2000)* was promulgated by the Supreme People's Court in 2000 it still lacks strong sanction in case of violation of the time limit. Many courts have poor case flow management. The regulation has only a

[344] As a socialist country, the Constitution stipulates that the power of the state belongs to the people, and the National People's Congress and its local People's Congress represent the people to enforce power of the state. The National People's Congress is the highest power organ of the state and the local People's Congress represents the power organ of the local; the Constitution stipulates that the National People's Congress has the discretion to select the administration and the judiciary, the procuratorate and has the power to supervise their activities.

[345] Wang, Li Ming, Research on Judicial Reform, China Law Press, 2000, pp. 454, 455.

short-term effect in reducing backlogs and delays. In the long run, reduction of backlogs and delays depends on further judicial reform.

(4) Delay in Transfer of Files

Some court delays are caused by a reassignment of work and training programs of the judges. As a result the files are not transferred to the colleagues in time and it takes more time when new judges are assigned to take over the cases. Such cases share 4.5% of the total court delay. Among its total 18 cases in delay, one court under investigation had 6 delayed cases relating to the problem in transfer of files.

e) The Impact of Economic Development on Judicial Efficiency

One factor must be addressed that the level of local economic development has also great impact on the speed of judgment: first, in west part of China where many provinces are underdeveloped, many counties of these provinces are poor and have a deficit every fiscal year. Although there are some subsidies for local budgets, the sum is still too small for the courts. In some counties, even the salaries and allowances are not able to be guaranteed. Second, backward office facilities cannot meet the functioning of the courts. Due to the lack of sufficient budget to purchase the necessary equipment, the efficiency of the courts is heavily affected. For example, many county courts do not have a computer network to save a vast volume of information. Third, delivery of writ takes too much time and affects the duly settlement of the cases. In some poor regions, transportation is not yet developed; consequently, delivery of writ by courier or by post takes a long time. Moreover, some parties cannot provide accurate addresses of the other parties; some small companies disappeared and nobody was available, in such a situation, the case is regarded as settled only 60 days after the public notification is issued. In the sample survey, 40% of delays were caused by late delivery of writ. Fourth, the legal attitudes of the parties and the participation of lawyers also have an impact on court delay. Normally, in poor regions, due to the educational level and social environment, people do not have the concept of law in their minds. In case of litigation, they do not exactly know the correct procedure for litigation, and delays very often happen when evidence is lost and other legal procedures are not properly done. The engagement of a lawyer involves a high cost to people with a low income. Only 45.2% of cases from the sample survey were engaged by lawyers.

f) Ambiguity of Law and Lag of Legislation

(1) Lack of Definite Criteria in Audit, Assessment, and Appraisal Procedure

One of the main reasons for court delay in civil cases is due to ambiguous criteria with respect to the procedure of audit, assessment, and appraisal of the dispute objects in the cases concerning disputes of quality of construction & architecture, real estate and property rights, etc. According to the Civil Procedure Code, a third party shall be appointed by the courts to proceed with audit, assessment and appraisal, but very often the parties cannot agree on the selection of the audit firm, the materials submitted for auditing, and relevant fees arising thereof. Such disagreement leads to more consumption of time in the civil process; moreover, some items from the disputes are difficult to be appraised. The conclusion from experts differs from each one another. Consequently it is difficult for the court to draw an acceptable conclusion within a reasonable amount of time.

In the sample survey, 55% of the cases were delayed due to excessive time consumption in auditing, assessment and appraisal. For example, among 6 civil cases, which exceeded the time limit, 5 cases were delayed due to the above mentioned reason.

(2) Faultiness of Regulation on Evidence

The survey revealed that 27.2% of the cases were delayed because of excessive consumption of time in collecting evidence by the parties, investigation of evidence by the courts and exchange of evidence by the parties. Although Civil Procedure Code regulates the obligation to provide evidence by the parties in reasonable time,[346] courts are still flexible on this issue. In practice, considering the weak litigation ability of the public in general, most of the courts accept new evidence any time during the litigation; the consequence is that the cases takes more appearances and hearing of the parties and causes court delay.

[346] According to Art. 110 of Civil Procedure Code, the parties shall present evidence to the courts at the time of filing, otherwise the court can specify a deadline for presenting the evidence according to the nature of the evidence and estimated time needed. In case of failure to provide the evidence within the time limit, prolongation can be allowed only subject to reasonable application. Art. 76 of Regulation on Strict Implementation of Time Limit interprets 'reasonable time' as 30 days.

(3) Application of Simple Procedure

According to Art. 142 of Civil Procedure Code, simple procedure shall be applied in District Courts relating to civil cases with clear facts and small dispute values. The aim of simple procedure is to facilitate filing[347] and trial by the courts in quick time[348] and with low cost.

In practice, the application of simple procedure does not reach the goal of legislature, as the cases applicable for simple procedure must be "clear in facts, rights and obligations, and the dispute value shall be not great".[349] The narrow definition excludes most cases even when they are not difficult these cases have to follow the normal procedure. Meanwhile, simple procedure is not applicable in the appellate courts, thus all appeal cases are centralized in collegial panels, which is also be responsible for the trial cases. It has been a bottleneck for judicial efficiency and leads to congestion of cases in the appellate courts.

(4) The Instruction Practice

In some cases, due to the vacancy of law in the transitional economy, judges sometimes cannot find applicable law and have to ask higher courts for instruction on how to apply the law in specific cases, and even on cognizance of the evidence and facts. The procedure for such instruction costs more time for settlement of the cases.

Besides, to avoid responsibility for wrong judgment, many judges depend on the instruction procedure as a shield against possible mistakes in application of law.[350]

(5) No Time Limit on Evidence in Appeal

There is no strict regulation on time limit under the current regulations on evidence. The parties can ask for a hearing when new evidence is found. Parties may make use of new evidence to postpone judgment.

(6) No Regulation on Time Limit for Delivery of Legal Documents

From the date of settlement of the trial court until the date of filing in the appellate court, there is no regulation of time limit, and it is regarded as one major reason for court delay.[351]

[347] Written form is not necessary in some circumstances.
[348] The case shall be settled within 3 month according to Art. 146 of Civil Procedure Code (1991).
[349] Art. 142, Civil Procedure Code (1991).
[350] Due to the fact that many judges do not have formal legal education and training, their understanding of law is limited. Asking for instruction from higher court is often used to avoid mistakes in application of law or shift responsibility.
[351] Wang, Li Wen and Wang, Yan Bin, Understanding and Application of Regulation on Strict Implementation of Time Limit, People's Judiciary, (1) 2000, p. 11.

Civil Procedure Code and its relevant regulations do not have a specified time limit in respect of sending the file between trial court and appellate court and transfer of cases in case of change of place of jurisdiction. In statistics from the courts, the time for delivery of files is not considered. In reality, the total duration is longer than that reflected in the statistics.

(7) Improper Procedural Reform in Pretrial and Hearing

Civil Procedure Code does not specify how much time is allotted for each phase of the trial. In fact, much of the time is consumed before all the evidence and files are ready to be presented for hearing. But in the current reform, the pretrial procedure is lengthy and complicated. Consequently, the low efficiency of the pretrial procedure leads to excessive amounts of time spent in litigation.

V. Findings based on the Empirical Study

1. Sample Study in the District Court and the Intermediate Court

Through an empirical study based on 287 cased disposed by the District Court , Huli, Xiamen and 213 cases disposed by the Intermediate Court of Xiamen, it was found that duration of cases in the District Court is more or less within the time limit of 6 months as regulated by the Civil Procedure Code. The average duration of the 287 cases was 56.5 days for cases disposed under simple procedure and 155 days in regular order. Dispute values of these cases were comparatively small, mostly ranging from 5,000 – 50,000 Yuan; the facts were clear and evident in most of the cases. But many disputes could have been solved in shorter time if simple procedure were more frequently applied in the jurisdiction.

With respect to the problem of court delay in intermediate court, 213 civil trial cases filed in the Intermediate Court of Xiamen were surveyed. It is very common that time limit is violated in this court, no matter if they are trial cases or appellate cases. The average time consumption of 213 cases was 8.7 months (261 days) for trial cases filed in the Intermediate Court of Xiamen (as court of the first instance).

Furthermore, 63 appeal cases filed in the Intermediate Court of Xiamen were selected to survey the total duration of cases from original filing in the court of the first instance until the final settlement. In the court of first instance, the average duration was 145 days, the average duration in the appellate court was 217.6 days, and the total duration from original filing in the court of the first instance until court orders/decrees were made by the appellate court was 416.5 days.

2. Sample Study in the High Court and the Supreme People's Court

The study of the duration of the High people's Court and the Supreme Court is based on 107 civil trial cases collected from the publications of the Supreme People's Court. The average duration of the High Courts was 10.63 months based on the 107 civil trial cases filed in the High Courts, whereas the duration of the Supreme People's Court was 9.51 months.

In brief, from empirical study, it was found that duration in the District Court was more or less within the time limit as stipulated in the Civil Procedure Code. However, the time limit normally cannot be honored in the appellate court. The higher the judicial hierarchy is, the longer the duration will be.

3. Court Delay in respect of Retrial Cases

Court delay is obvious concerning cases under judicial supervision (retrial cases). The caseload of retrial cases is heavier in higher jurisdiction.[352] 20-25% of the appeal cases were further filed for retrial under judicial supervision.[353] Though retrial cases doe not represent a large proportion in total filings and dispositions,[354] it is obvious that it consumes an overwhelming amount of the judge's time and exhausts the parties. It is this small size case that has spread adverse effects to the general public and results in a loss of confidence of the people.

Among 63 appeal cases, 16 cases were under retrial procedure. The duration of these retrial cases were 375.5 days or 12.5 months from the date of applied for retrial until final judgments was made, and 711.5 days or 23.71 months calculating from when court orders

[352] Supra note 287. See Zhang, Ai Zhen, Some Suggestions on Restructuring the Judicial Supervision in China, in: People's Judiciary, p. 19.
[353] China Law Year Book, 1991-2000.
[354] Supra note 286.

were made by the appellate court until final settlements were made by the retrial court. The average time consumption from original filing until the final settlement exceeded 2 years.

Among the 107 samples in which 12 cases were under retrial procedure, it was also found that the duration of the retrial procedure is long. It took 16.8 months on average to dispose the cases by the Supreme Court under retrial procedure. The total duration of these cases also exceeded 2 years on average.

There are some reasons behind the long duration: these cases are complicated and consume a lot of time for evidence-collecting; in retrial procedure, judges focus more on substantive justice[355] and ignore procedural regulations on time limit; furthermore, the parties try to make use of the retrial procedure to revise the court orders/decrees made by trial court or appellate court. The parties can apply retrial procedure within 2 years after the original court orders/decrees and there are no restrictions on times of disposition.

4. The Interviews

There are some implications which can be taken from the assessment based on the interviews and questionnaires. First, court delay seems not to be a big problem considering the high settlement ratio and the duration found in the empirical study. This has to do with the time bound program established in the courts. The time bound program established in the courts is useful in creating incentives and pressure on the judges for a speedy settlement and enhancing judicial efficiency, but the time bound program also causes some problems in disposition, for example, judges are inclined to settle cases through mediation, or to ask the litigants to withdraw the cases at the end of the year or settled by a speedy and even careless trial. In some courts, judges treat the filings in October as the filings for the next year. Judges tend to settle the cases at the end of the year so as to realize the high settlement ratio as established in the time bound program. This leads to some adverse effects in the judiciary, namely, low quality of judgment and miscarriage of justice.[356] A time bound program

---

[355] Similarly, the Italian Civil Procedure Law stresses on the substantive justice. Art. 360 allows the parties involved to apply for substantive review whenever there is a substantive mistake in judgment. Consequently, delay is serious in Italy. The long duration of civil procedure in Italy is very often complained by its member states in EU.

[356] According to the statistics of the Supreme People's Court, cases settled at the end of the year have higher probability to be retried than the cases settled in the previous 3 seasons. This indicates that the speedy trial at the end of the year may result in violating procedural and substantive justice. See People's Judiciary, (4) 2000.

therefore must establish workable time limits for the judges. Second, the parties are of the opinion that the explicit and implicit cost of litigation is too much for them. They viewed that speedy trial is critical for litigation. Third, lawyers' engagement is considered to be important in protecting the procedural right of the parties and the sound development of the judiciary in China, despite the complaint about lawyer's improper conduct in some cases.

5. Some Conclusions

Some conclusions can be drawn from the empirical study based on primary and secondary data, interviews and questionnaire-oriented interviews.

Generally speaking, court delay seemed not to be a big problem in China as far as the results of the empirical work are concerned. There are no serious delays in the district courts and the intermediate court, and this coincided with the results drawn from the study based on the secondary data concerning total filings and dispositions in China. The result is important to the study of duration of the courts since the district courts (including magistrate courts) and intermediate courts dispose 80 -90 % of the civil cases. Some reasons should be mentioned: the district courts apply simple procedure in dispositions since most of the cases are simple and easy in fact-finding and application of law. The less complex these cases, the more time is saved for disposition. Further, *the Regulation on Strict Implementation of Time Limit in Jurisdiction (2000)* has had a strong impact on the judges in the lower courts.

Court delay is still a problem concerning cases filed in the High Courts and the Supreme People's Court, although the cases filed in these courts share around 10% of the total filings in the country. The duration of the court is longer when the hierarchy of the court is higher due to the complication and difficulty of the cases filed in the higher courts.

Court delay is obvious when cases are disposed under retrial procedure. This can be contributed to no restriction in times of trial and the time limit for retrial cases and a long tradition of Chinese legal culture in which people are more concerned about substantive justice and ignore the time limit in procedure.

Due to the different levels in economic development, efficiency of the courts in the eastern regions is higher than those in western regions due to the advantage in budget, court facilities, human capital, management and law enforcement etc.

Furthermore, the empirical study also implies that long duration exists in the execution of court orders/decrees and a high rate of exceeding time limit in enforcement of court orders/decrees. Chapter 5 is thus an endeavor to address this problem by presenting the problems and reasons behind that.

Part II: Critical Evaluation of Functioning of the Court System

– Restructuring the Court System

I. Introduction

The reduction of court delay cannot be achieved simply by an increase of judges and time available for judgment. An acute reform is necessary with respect to improvement of human capital, reform of the procedure, reducing litigation cost and improving the accessibility of the courts, together with the availability of legal aid to the poor. Meanwhile, the ADR mechanism shall be reinforced in jurisdiction to reduce the caseload of the courts.

Part II will provide a critical evaluation of the functioning of the courts based on the empirical study undertaken in Part I. The evaluation will focus on how to restructure the court system in China and how judicial reform, starting from procedural reform, can remove its obstacles and improve 'access to justice' by reducing costs and court delay.

II. Critical Assessment of Court Efficiency

Justice and efficiency are the goals of the judiciary. Low judicial efficiency is similar to corruption, which damages the people's confidence and trust in the judicial system.[357]

In China, there is an external impetus and growing expectation from the general public for an efficient judiciary. Such desire not only comes from the bottom, but also from the top. As addressed by the President of the Supreme People's Court, "The object of the People's Court in the new century is justice and efficiency"[358] The reform is aimed at reducing court delay and improving the efficiency of the courts, as well as the enhancement of substantive and procedural justice.

The assessment of the efficiency of the courts in China shall take the following criterion into

[357] Zhang, Wen Xian, The Jurisprudence,China University of Politics and Law Publication, 1993, p. 273.

[358] Xiao, Yang, in an interview during National People's Congress 2001, in: (China) Legal Daily, 09.03.2001.

consideration: the settlement ratio, the quality of settlement and the related human capital, and the average disposition of cases etc.[359]

1. Critics on Settlement Ratio and Duration of the Courts

Settlement ratio is the main criteria for assessing judicial efficiency to see how many cases are disposed or dismissed within the time limit. Time limit, in civil process, is stressed by the Supreme People's Court. In its *Regulation on Strict Implementation of Time Limit (2000)*, it requires the courts to abide by the regulation on time limit and reduce court congestion and court delay. [360] The previous study in this chapter based on the secondary data indicates a high settlement ratio of 90% ~ 95%.[361] Courts reduced court delay dramatically after the *Regulation on Strict Implementation of Time Limit (2000)* was promulgated by the Supreme People's Court in 2000. According to statistics, the settlement ratio for civil cases was around 92.90% in the year 2000, among which 79.61% of the cases were disposed by the application of simple procedure and settled within 3 months. 18.43% of the cases were settled by regular order within 6 months 1.96% of the cases were disposed in more than 6 months. By comparison, the survey based on secondary and primary data indicates that the duration of courts is almost as good as the duration in Germany.[362]

It is important to define the concept of settlement. In China, a case is seen as 'settled' when a court decision/order is made by the respective court. The Supreme People's Court adopts such criteria in its annual statistics; consequently the settlement ratio is reflected as being high from the statistics made by the Supreme People's Court. The ratio will be lower if a case is considered as 'settled', only when a final court decision/order is made.

However, it must be pointed out that such a settlement ratio does not reveal the real picture in China. In interviews with judges in the Supreme People's Court and the lower courts, it was

[359] Judicial efficiency can be measured quantitatively by the resource consumed in judiciary, namely the number of judges assigned for jurisdiction and the time consumed for disposition of the cases. It can also be measured by the output of the judicial work, in concrete it means the quantity of the disputes resolved by the courts. In this context, judicial efficiency shall be based on the assessment of settlement ratio, total dispositions and the duration of the courts.

[360] The Supreme People's Court: Regulation on Strict Implementation of Time Limit, 2000 Art. 12.
According to this regulation, the normal time limit for the normal proceedings in the first instance is 6 months; it can be extended for another 6 months under special circumstances in which it is necessary to be prolonged, in total it shall not exceed 13 months. The regulation has corrected the shortcomings in the old version, in which there is no limitation of the longest duration of the proceedings. Consequently, the efficiency of the courts is improved.

[361] As indicated in China Law Year Book, 1990 – 2000.

[362] See the previous empirical study made to the District Court of Huli and the Intermediate Court of Xiamen.

admitted by some judges that there existed many improper practices of the courts in order to seek a high settlement ratio. For example, each court has a time bound program for settlement ratios and judges should fulfill the task. To satisfy the time bound program, many judges treat the filings in October of that year as new filings for the coming year so that there will be no backlog in the courts; in many cases, especially at the end of the year, the litigants are asked to postpone the filings until the coming year, withdraw the filings, or settle the cases quickly by court-arranged mediation.[363] In the statistics, data related to disposition were even altered to meet the time bound settlement ratio. Therefore, based on these interviews, it was implied that the legal system does not work properly and even may sacrifice the interest of the parties by pursuing high settlement ratio at the cost of procedural and substantive justice.

In this context, the efficiency justification of the Chinese legal system cannot be merely based on the settlement ratio,[364] rather on the inclusion of additional factors such as average disposition and quality of judgment.

Though there has been an obvious enhancement of court efficiency since the 1980's when the legal system was established, it is still low compared to some Western countries. For example, in 1989 there were around 120,000 judges and 3,182,194 cases settled. The average disposition was 26.5 cases per judge; in 1998 the number of judges increased to more than 170,000 and there were 5,864,274 cases settled. The average disposition was 34.5 cases per person.[365] In 1998, the number of judges increased by 41.67% and the number of cases increased by 84.28% compared with the number in 1989; in the meantime the disposition has also increased 30.19%. It reveals that judicial efficiency has been improved. However, the average disposition by each judge is still very low compared with judges in the US and Germany. For instance, in 1997 each judge in China settled 21 cases[366] on average per year, such a figure is only one fortieth of that of American judges, or one fiftieth of German judges,

---

[363] In an interview with judges in the Supreme People's Court, judges doubt the authenticity of the statistics provided by the lower courts. In interviews with one judge who is responsible for statistics in the district court and interviews with lawyers, they all confirmed such practice in jurisdiction.

[364] Some judges in the lower courts and the Supreme People's Court drew conclusion based on the high settlement ratio as calculated from the China Law Yearbooks and regarded that the efficiency was high in the courts. I think it is too simple to make such conclusion given the fact that the statistics does not reveal the real world scenario and high cost (error cost, moral cost and miscarriage of justice) may incur because of speedy and rough dispositions. Compare: Huang, Song You, An Analysis of Judicial Efficiency, in: People's Judiciary, (11) 2001, p. 21.

[365] See Table 3.4.

[366] Statistics of disposed/dismissed cases in 1997, in: People's Judiciary, (4) 1998, p. 13.

or 1% of Macao judges.[367]

The above analysis and comparison reveal that the courts shall focus on disposition and shall enhance the human capital and assign more qualified judges in jurisdiction while reducing the number of judges in administrative matters within the courts. The pros and cons of a speedy disposal shall be considered; a time bound program in the courts shall consider some measures like granting reasonable adjournments so as to frame a more effective criteria in respect to court delay in order to avoid fraudulent behavior in statistics and speedy disposal at the cost of procedural justice and substantive justice.

2. Enhancement of Efficiency by Improving Human Capital

In the current Chinese legal system, a mixed and variety of regulations have affected the uniform rule of law and judicial efficiency, both the complexity of law and the lag of legislation may cause court delays. The lack of human capital in the legal system makes it more difficult to properly understand the law and the application of the law. On the one hand, many judges lack the necessary legal education and professional training. Still, other qualified judges are occupied by administrative matters and have little engagement in jurisdiction. In some courts, only around 50% of the judges are responsible for disposition of cases. All of these factors shown in the previous empirical study have affected the judicial efficiency.

Although the number of judges is big in China, for example, in 2002 the number was round 270,000, it must be admitted that many judges do not have legal education before admission and short term legal training simply cannot help.[368] In fact, many judges are not competent or qualified enough to deal with complicated disputes. On the other side, many judges who have legal education and legal training hold administrative positions in the courts and do not engage very much in jurisdiction. *The efficiency of the courts will be considerably enhanced by improving human capital, optimal assignment of jurisdiction, and judicial administration within the courts.* Further, the problem of the low average of disposition in Chinese courts cannot simply be concluded being attributed to low efficiency in every court, as the previous

[367] Li, Xiao Bin, How to Improve Judicial Efficiency, in: People's Judiciary, (10)1998, p. 17.

[368] Compare V. 2 in Chapter 2.

study indicates that the workload, budget and human capital differ from court to court and region to region. Some courts may have higher efficiency and some may have lower efficiency, but the average efficiency is still low.

III. Court Delay and the Trial Committee

1. The Trial Committee – 'Super Collegial Panel' and its Problems

According to the regulation of People's Court Organization Act, all courts shall establish a Trial Committee.[369] The main goals of the Trial Committee are to summarize experience in jurisdiction, discuss and decide complicated and big cases and discuss other important issues relating to the judiciary.

In practice, the Trial Committee has too much discretion in adjudication. The Trial Committee often instructs the tribunals to make judgment according to their views. In many cases the Trial Committee even overturns the decisions made by the tribunals, although the scope of work of the Trial Committee is defined by the Supreme People's Court and each local courts[370] according to the social and economic situation in each region. The trial Committee has excessive interference in tribunals.

According to statistics collected by the High Court of one province,[371] the Trial Committee of the court held 138 meetings (138 days) to make decisions on 1,011 cases, which is more than 1/3 of the total cases disposed by this court. The average cases adjudicated by the Trial Committee in each year are more or less 1/3 of the total cases disposed by the court. In another words, in every three cases, one is disposed by the Trial Committee rather than by the tribunals. To ensure that these cases can be disposed as quickly as possible, the court decides

[369] The establishment of the Trial Committee is based on the following laws and regulations: Art. 10 of the People's Court Organization Act, 1954, stipulates that "all courts shall establish a Trial Committee. The main task of the Trial Committee is to summarize judicial experience, discuss big or complicated cases and other issues relating to judicial work"; Art. 11 of the People's Court Organization Act, revised in 1983 and 1986, regulates that "all courts shall establish a Trial Committee, which shall be based on collective democracy. The main task of the Trial Committee is to summarize judicial experience, discuss big or complicated cases and other issues relating to judicial work". However, it is interesting that the current Civil Procedure Code (1991) has deleted the clause relating to the discretion of the Trial Committee over "trial and instruction on cases"; moreover, the Administrative Procedure Code (1989) keeps silent on whether the Trial Committee has the discretion to make decisions on cases. From the legislation point of view, the law intends to reduce the influence of the Trial Committee in trial activities.

[370] For example: Regulation on the Work of the Trial Committee of the Supreme People's Court, issued on 02.03.1999; Interpretation to Some Problems in Enforcing Civil Procedure Code, issued on 29.06.1999.

[371] See Zhang, Wei Ping, Review on Judicial Reform, Vol. 3, China Judiciary Publication, p. 52.

that the Trial Committee will spend 2 working days as regular time for discussion and decision on cases; this means that 40% of the working time in 5 working days shall be spent on discussing the cases. As the members of the Trial Committee consist of president of the court, presiding judges of the court, the heaviest amount of work is shifted from the tribunals to the Trial Committee. Many judges complained that the backlog of the cases has much to do with the time spent in the Trial Committee. Sometimes, the meeting was canceled due to absence of some members at the meeting;[372] in some cases, decisions were made even when the number of members was not enough to hold the meeting simply because the tribunals were urged to make a quick decision on cases within the time limit. The Trial Committee is therefore called the "super collegial panel".[373]

Further, the division of work between the tribunals and the Trial Committee is ambiguous. According to the law, the Trial Committee is only responsible for resolving problems concerning complicated cases or cases with big dispute value. In fact, many cases are complicated in nature; these cases are submitted to the Trial Committee only because the judges in the tribunals are not sure about some points. It causes a repeat of the trial and such a trial consumes additional time.

2. Pros and Cons of the Trial Committee

The existence of the Trial Committee is an issue of dispute in China. There are different views on whether or not to keep the Trial Committee in the courts. Some argue that the Trial Committee shall remain in the court because the Trial Committee can provide guidance and supervision in trial and help to solve problems in the application of law, especially when the substantive law and procedure law are not fully realized in China. Meanwhile the Trial Committee can provide better remedy and justice to the parties by taking advantage of collective decisions when the judges are not competent enough in terms of knowledge, legal training, and experience. Furthermore, the Trial Committee can be used as a shield against local intervention and used as an excuse by some judges not to follow the instructions of the

372 According to the regulation, at least half of the members shall be present in the meeting.
373 See Wang, Li Min, Research on Judicial Reform, China Law Press, 2000, pp. 195 – 200.

local administration in the name of the Trial Committee.[374] In one investigation, it was found that the existence of the Trial Committee helps to improve the quality of the judgment and curb corruption and inequality in judgment. Bribery is more difficult since each member of the Trial Committee has a deterrence effect on the others.[375] The existence of the Trial Committee is therefore rational when taking the legal environment into consideration.

But many others opposed the existence of the Trial Committee in the courts. As the tribunals have to report the cases to the Trial Committee, the duration the cases is extended simply because most of the members of the Trial Committee do not have a basic idea of the cases and it takes time for them to read through the files, evidence, etc. Further, the members of the Trial Committee often have bias that follow the opinion of the president of the court, therefore the goals of the Trial Committee often deviate from what is written on paper. The Trial Committee often abuses its discretion and interferes with cases. The trial Committee is therefore seen as an obstacle of justice and should be abolished.[376]

3. Comment

Despite the different opinions on whether to keep or abolish the Trial Committee, in the long run, it is in the interest of the judiciary to abolish the Trial Committee to enhance judicial efficiency and accommodate judicial reform based on several considerations. First, regarding the court decisions made by the Trial Committee, the People's Court Organization Act specifies that the main function of the Trial Committee is to discuss cases rather than make decisions on cases. Both the Civil Procedure Code and the Administrative Procedure Code do not specify the function of the Trial Committee and keep a distance from such legislation of law. Therefore, trial of cases by the Trial Committee is not specified by the Civil Procedure

---

374 Chen, Guang Zhong, Directives of Criminal Law of UN and the Criminal law in China, China Law Press, 1999, p. 93.

375 Su, Li, An Investigation and Re-thinking of the Trial Committee in the Lower Courts, in Beijing University Review, 2nd Collection, Vol. 1, pp. 361-363. The author argued that the quality of judges in the lower courts in general could not be improved considerably in the short run due to the lack of professional knowledge and training. Furthermore, individual judge is vulnerable to resist the interference from the administration and the higher courts, therefore the collective decision made by the Trial Committee could be a good means to resist the pressure from the outside interference.

376 Zuo, Wei Min, Comment on the Existence of Trial Committee, in: South Weekly, on 12. 03. 1999.
Judge Huang, Song You of the Supreme Court holds a modest view of the Trial Committee. It is regarded that the Trial Committee still has great value with respect to judicial supervision and it serves as the last guarantee of justice, despite heavy criticism. It is argued that the Trial Committee is competent to make correct judgment based on the analysis of evidence and fact-finding, therefore it is not urgent to abolish the Trial Committee in the short run, but to improve it until the time is ripe for abolishment. See Huang, Song You, Progress and Transition: Thinking on the Reform of Civil Jurisdiction, in: Contemporary Law, 4th ed., 2000.

Law. Second, in Art. 11 of the People's Court Organization Act, it is specified that the decision of the Trial Committee should be based on "Collective Democracy". In practice, decision-making is based on majority rule. There is no specific regulation on the procedure of the Trial Committee and no liability in the event of violation of the law by its members. Third, the Trial Committee is not responsible for its mistakes. Some discussions are based on the oral report of the presiding judges and it is difficult for the Trial Committee to make an accurate judgment in such a short time. A detailed review of cases would consume more time and lead to court delay. Fourth, the discussion by the Trial Committee is not a public hearing, but a closed door discussion. In such circumstances, the procedural right of the parties is violated. Fifth, there is no time limit and limit on times of trial for the cases brought to the Trial Committee. Though there is no specific statistics about the duration of cases decided by the Trial Committee, court delay is more likely to happen when the case is under review by the Trial Committee.

As the original purpose of the Trial Committee is to discuss complicated cases, which cannot be solved by incompetent judges, it is therefore essential to the success of the reform of the Trial Committee that the qualifications and competence of the judges be enhanced.

IV. The Application of Simple Procedure

Often, it is a waste of judicial resources when simple cases cost the time and energy of the judges and the parties. Take as an example, a passenger filed in the court against the Railway Administration of Zhengzhou City since he was charged 0.3 Yuan for using the toilet in the waiting room.[377] The case was brought to the appellate court by the litigant after the trial in the court of the first instance, though 0.3 Yuan was paid back to the litigant, the judicial cost for the case burdened by the state was too great. It is therefore not economic wise or efficient to have 2-tier judicial hierarchies for such simple cases, likewise it is meaningless to address justice when the social cost is high for such simple cases. To solve the dispute more quickly, it would be very practical to establish summary courts. For instance, in the rural area where many simple cases are uncomplicated and have small dispute value, it would be not necessary

[377] Quote from: *Newspaper Abstract, 3rd edition*, 27.09.2001

to have an appeal procedure for these cases; instead, summary courts or tribunals would be much more efficient in dealing with these kinds of cases.

According to the statistics, the personnel in the lower courts, namely the District Court/County Courts and the Intermediate Courts, share more than 80% of the total personnel of the courts in China and 80% - 90% of the civil cases are disposed by the lower courts, namely, the District Court/County Courts and the Intermediate Courts. The efficiency of the lower courts consequently has a great impact on the functioning of the court system in China.

According to current practice, cases filed in the District Court shall apply simple procedure first. The cases will be turned into normal procedure only when the judges find out that more time is needed to apply the law for these cases. However, no summary (or small claims) court has been established in the Chinese courts. It has been proven in many countries that small claim court is very efficient in providing speedy redressal and saving litigation cost for the parties. In many western countries, small claims courts are established to deal with piling of cases and to have a speedy trial. Some countries have enacted procedure law with respect to small claim cases. In America, the trial court can settle small claim case with only one judge after obtaining consent from the parties. Some judges are specially selected to deal with the cases filed in the small claim court. In Germany, there is a special and detailed stipulation about the application of simple procedure and small claims cases in its civil procedure law (ZPO). These regulations have the same common goal: to have speedy redressal.[378]

1. Problems Concerning Simple Procedure

The lower courts in China face the conflict of the availability of judges and increasing cases. In some courts, judges are overloaded by cases and thus many cases are not able to be resolved in time.[379] The duration of many cases is too long and therefore causing backlog and delay. Some cases are settled after a repeat hearing, whereas few cases are settled by just one hearing. Some easy cases are disposed in regular order and waste time and judicial

---

[378] In Germany, after the enactment of "Gesetz zur Vereinfachung und Beschleunigung gerichtlicher Verfahren" in 1st July 1977, cases are disposed very quickly. Under the new law, the case should be disposed within one sitting of the court; the judgment should be made within three weeks and the compensation is possible before final verdict of the case (Erleichterungen in Fallen vorläufiger Vollstreckbarkeit). Compare Rottleuthner, H. and Rottleuthner-Luther, M., Die Dauer von Gerichtsverfahren: Evaluation der ZPO Vereinfachungsnovelle, Nomos Verlagsgesellschaft, 1. Auf., Baden-Baden, 1990, pp. 248 ff.

[379] Bo, Min, Small Claims Tribunal: a new practice of justice and efficiency, in: People's Judiciary, 1st ed. 2002, p. 39.

resource.

Concerning cases filed in the District Courts and County Courts, 70% -80% of the cases are disputes involving small claims, family matters, physical injuries and/or tort, there is no need to apply regular order for the adjudication of these cases. In the sample study and through reading of the files of the District Court in Huli, Xiamen, it was found that the dispute value of 49.80% of the cases was below 50,000 Yuan, among which 35% of the cases were concerning credit and debt. The facts of most of these cases were clear and it was easy to apply the law. Meanwhile, due to the clear facts and small claim, few of theses cases engaged lawyers. These cases could have been settled quickly if simple procedure had been applied.

It is meaningful for the lower courts in China to establish small claim courts to deal with the increase in cases. Due to the rough definition of simple procedure, in practice, some problems exist in the application of simple procedure: first, judges are both responsible for complicated and easy cases. Judges apply simple procedure for all cases in the beginning and may turn simple procedure into normal procedure when the cases are found to be complicated.[380] In some cases, some judges turn it into normal procedure just to avoid exceeding the time limit of 3 months for simple procedure. Secondly, due to the reason that there is no separation of simple and normal procedure, some cases were under simple procedure at the beginning but normal procedure was applied in the hearing stage. The lack of standards for applying the simple procedure and normal procedure causes disorder in the jurisdiction of cases in the lower courts. On one hand, many simple cases cannot be solved in time because simple procedure is not applied. On the other hand, complicated cases cannot be adjudicated properly with care, due to no division of the work amongst judges. If a small claims court or a small claims tribunal can be established in the District Court, it would provide speedy settlement of cases and avoid the waste of judicial finances.

2. The Prospect of Small Claims Tribunal in China

To reduce the duration of cases and litigation costs, many countries apply simple procedure in

[380] In the interview, some judges admitted that simple procedure should be first applied. In fact, many cases were turned into normal procedure because the cases could not be settled within 3 months as established for the cases under simple procedure, thus, the cases were tried in regular order which allowed a time limit of 6 months.

disposition of cases. In the UK, US, and Japan, more than 90% of the cases filed in the District Court are disposed by simple procedure. In China, the courts have already realized the use of a small claims tribunal or small claims court can speed up the civil process and enhance accessibility of the courts.

One example based on an empirical study[381] indicated that the establishment of a small claims tribunal has improved efficiency of the courts by increasing settlements and reducing the duration of litigation. In the South District Court of Qingdao, one tribunal was established to specialize in disposition of small claims cases. From Oct. 2000 until Sept. 2001, the tribunal consisting of 4 judges disposed 1,313 small claims cases 1,247 were settled in a short time and the settlement ratio was 95%. In this tribunal, each judge disposed 28.3 cases on average per month and the number of dispositions was 50% more than the other tribunals in the court. The duration, from filing until settlement, was obviously shortened to an average duration of 38 days.[382]

Among the 1,247 settled cases, 349 cases (28%) were settled through mediation, 187 cases (15%) were withdrawn, 167 cases (13%) were dismissed by the tribunal, and 118 cases (9.5%) were settled during hearing. 90% of the cases were disposed by one hearing in the court. Moreover, only 64 cases were appealed and only 2 of court decisions were revised by the Intermediate Court of Qingdao. The appellate rate was only around 5%.[383]

Another example offers strength and support for the establishment of a small claims court or tribunal in the District Courts in China. The District Court of Huangpu, Shanghai, selected 6 judges from its 20 judges in the civil tribunals for disposing small claims cases. In 1999, 6 judges disposed 80% of the total cases filed in court by applying simple procedure; each judge disposed 74.7 cases on average per month. The establishment of small claims tribunal, as referred to in the summary report of the court, relieves the workload of the court and thus the collegial panel can concentrate on the complicated cases according to normal procedure and dispose these cases with high quality.'[384]

The establishment of a small claims tribunal is a good reform measures in the District Court.

---

[381] Bo, Min, Small Claims Tribunal: a new practice of justice and efficiency, in: People's Judiciary, (1) 2002, p. 39 ff.
[382] Ditto.
[383] Ditto.
[384] He, Bin, Restructuring the Mechanism of Dispute Resolution, in: Peking University Law Journal, Vol. 14, No. 1 (2002), pp.15-16.

For the court, it separates easy cases from complicated and improves efficiency. The parties view that the small claims tribunal can resolve disputes quickly in an easy way. Many of them are relieved from traveling, absences from work, time consumption, etc. It also reduces the litigation cost and saves time for the parties; on the other hand, it makes it easier to get access to the court.

V. Restructuring Supervision Procedure: Reducing Court Delay

1. The Aim of Retrial Procedure

The supervision procedure is defined in Art. 177 – 188 of Civil Procedure Code. The purpose of the supervision procedure is to guarantee substantive justice. However, in practice, the functioning of the supervision procedure deviates from the spirit of legislature contributing much to the defects in the design of the procedure. The current supervision procedure is based on the belief that all errors shall be corrected based on the facts; thus, court orders/decrees shall be corrected whenever a mistake is found. The supervision procedure is to provide justice and equality to the parties through retrial procedure. The Chinese procedure law, including the civil procedure code, criminal procedure code, and the administrative procedure code, has set up a retrial procedure to correct mistakes contained in the court orders/decrees even when they are already binding and effective to the parties. However, the retrial procedure faces strong critics due to the problems of lengthy process and the high cost incurred.

2. The Major Problems in the Retrial Procedure

Under the supervision procedure, the parties may apply for retrial under the supervision procedure if they are not content with the courts' orders/decrees.[385] The court can initiate the retrial procedure if it finds that the court orders/decrees might be wrong in fact finding and

[385] Art. 179 of Civil Procedure Code; "The court shall retrial the case if the application by the parties fulfills the followings: i. new evidence, which is sufficient to overturn the original court order or decision; ii. the major evidence is not sufficient to affirm the fact-finding, as well as supporting the court order or decision; iii. wrong application of law in the original court order or decision; iv. violation of procedure by the People's Court, which may lead to a unlawful court order or decision; v. corruption, miscarriage of justice by the judges during disposition of the case".

application of law.[386] Furthermore, the procuratorate can challenge the court orders/decrees and require the court to retry the case.[387] There are no specific regulations on time limit of evidence and times of disposition in retrial.[388] The finality of law and the legal relationship between the parties have again an unstable status.[389] The society should minimize the litigation cost and error cost caused by mistakes in judgments.[390] The overstressing of error-correction is not efficient from an economic point of view.

a) Retrial Procedure and Court Delay

The duration of the retrial procedure is much longer than that of normal procedure in the court of the first instance and the appellate court. According to the empirical study, the duration of the cases from the original court orders/decisions until the final jurisdiction made by the retrial court is more than 2-3 years in the Intermediate Court and in the Supreme People's Court. Retrial procedure can be repeated again and again.

To the parties, it means he/she can apply for retrial within 2 years if he/she thinks that the judgment or decree contained errors or mistakes, or when he/she has new evidence. Under such a broad definition for retrial, the parties can easily have access to retrial. Furthermore, for economic reasons, the parties may save costs by applying for retrial rather than appealing to a higher court since no litigation fee is required in a retrial procedure. Some parties may have another chance to win the case even when the probability of reversing the decision might be small when the case is brought back to the same court because the reason for retrial is not strong enough to overrule the original judgment. In some circumstances, the parties may even exhaust the other side by making use of the retrial procedure, namely, some

---

[386] Art. 177 of Civil Procedure Code: "The president of the court in all levels shall present the cases to the Trial Committee to decide whether to retry the cases when mistakes are found in the effective court orders or decisions. The Supreme Court can retry the cases by itself, or can authorize the local court to retry the cases, when mistakes are found in the effective court orders or decisions made by the local courts".

[387] Art. 185 of Civil Procedure Code: "The Supreme People's Procuratorate can challenge the court orders or decisions made by all of the courts; the higher procuratorate can challenge the court orders or decisions made by the lower courts and appeal for retrial according to the supervision procedure, if: i) new evidence is sufficient to overturn the original court order or decision; ii) the original major evidence is not sufficient to affirm the facts and make the court order or decision; iii) wrong application of law in the original court order or decision; iv. Violation of procedure by the People's Court, which may lead to the legitimacy of the court order or decision; v) corruption, miscarriage of justice by the judges during disposition of the case".

[388] One case was even under retrial for 12 times. See Zhang, Ai Zhen, Some Suggestions on Restructuring the Judicial Supervision in China, in: People's Judiciary (10) 2001, p. 21.

[389] Sheng, De Yong, Some Problems in the Reform of Judicial Supervision, in: People's Judiciary (8)2001, p. 16.

[390] Posner, A. Richard, Economic Analysis of Law, Little Brown Publication, Boston, Toronto, 1992, 4th ed. pp. 550 - 552; also see Posner, A. Richard, An Economic Approach to Legal Procedure and Judicial Administration, in: Journal of Legal studies 2 (1973), pp. 396 – 400.

evidence is hidden during the initial trials and are presented for application for retrial at a later time. In general, the procedure becomes too lengthy and exhausting to the other parties. For the courts, it means that they should correct the errors or mistakes in the judgment at any time when mistakes are found. The retrial procedure is thus referred to as the 'final jurisdiction that never ends', as court orders/decisions are in a state of uncertainty for long periods of time and the finality of the law is questioned.[391]

Besides, most of the courts treat retrial cases as new cases (filings) for statistical reasons. Since the promulgation of *Regulation on Strict Implementation of Time Limit (2000)*, many courts treat retrial case as "filings" in official statistics, consequently the settlement ratio is higher and the duration of the 'new' case does not take as long between filing and settlement of retrial, though the total duration is very long if retrial procedure is seen as the continuation of the original trial.

b) Retrial Procedure and Judicial Cost

According to the statistics, 20-25% of the appeal cases were further filed for retrial in the higher courts under judicial supervision procedure.[392] For instance, in the total filings of 1,376 cases at the High People's Court of Hainan, there were 311 retrial cases, accounting for 22.6% of the total filings.[393] This indicates that retrial cases represent big proportion of the caseload in the higher courts.

From an economic point of view, the goal of litigation shall minimize the costs of error and litigation costs.[394] The retrials not only cause longer duration of the courts, but also incur more litigation costs and time for the parties and consume judicial resources; consequently it is not in conformity with the goal of judicial efficiency and justice.

Table 3.15 shows the rate of unchanged court orders/decisions in each year from 1994 until 1999. With respect to retrial cases, during 1994 -1999, the rate for maintaining the original judgment made in the trial courts is 45%, 42.3%, 38.5%, 35.3%, 28.1%, 26.6%. Though the rate shows a continuing decline of retrial, the absolute number of cases is still big.

[391] Yu, Lei, Analysis on Some Problems in the Civil Retrial Procedure, in: People's Judiciary, (1) 2002, p. 37.
[392] China Law Year Book, 1991-2000. Besides, very few trial cases were filed for retrial, according to statistics, only 0.68% of the retrial cases were the trial cases. See Fu, Yu Lin, The Principle of Structuring the Judicial Hierarchy: a comparative analysis, in: China Social Science, (4) 2002, p. 84.
[393] Zhang, Ai Zhen, Some Suggestions on Restructuring the Judicial Supervision in China, in: People's Judiciary (10) 2001, p. 19.
[394] Posner, Richard A., Economic Analysis of Law, 4th edition, 1992, pp. 550 – 552.

Table 3. 15 Rate of maintained Judgments in Judicial Supervision Procedure (Retrial)

1994	1995	1996	1997	1998	1999
45%	42.3%	38.5%	35.3%	28.1%	26.6%

Source: compiled from statistical data issued by the Supreme People's Court. In: China Law Year Book, 1995 - 2000

As civil cases and economic cases share more than 80% - 90% of the total caseload, the quality of the judiciary is very dependent on the quality of judgment of civil and economic cases. The high rate of revision of the court orders/decisions indicates that the quality of judgment made by the court is low. This leads to an overwhelming consumption of time, which should be allocated to other cases. On the other hand, long duration of retrial impedes the dispute resolution and increases the cost to the parties.

3. Restructuring the Retrial Procedure

Due to the problem of long delay in the retrial procedure and for cost consideration, it is necessary for the legislature to reconsider the guiding principle of civil procedure law on the issue of supervision procedure. In Western countries, especially in continental European countries, the law imposes strict conditions on retrial in respect to time limit and times of disposition. In common law countries, the appeal procedure is mainly set up for correcting the errors in judgments.[395] For the Chinese civil process, it would be more efficient for the legislature to impose stricter conditions for retrial procedures. Some suggestions, as put forward below, might be recommendable in the future reform.

a) Canceling the Courts' Discretion in Retrial

According to the Civil Procedure Code, the courts have the responsibility to supervise adjudication and correct errors in judgment. Despite the goodwill of legislature, retrial procedure initiated by the courts would violate the neutral principle of the courts in litigation.

[395] Some scholars debated whether the trial system should be revised from two-tier system to be three-tier system in China and the current supervision procedure for retrial thus should be the third and final trial. See Wang, Li Ming, Judicial Research on Judicial Reform, 2000, P. 176, 479; Fu, Yu Lin, The Principle of Structuring the Judicial Hierarchy", in: China Social Science, (4)2002, p. 84.

Furthermore it would violate the principle of separation of litigation and trial, since retrial procedure initiated by the courts is likely to generate double function of the courts: on the one hand, the court acts as a judge and on the other side it acts as a litigant. Moreover, the intervention of the court goes against the principle of private autonomy in the civil process. Even if there may have been some errors in judgment, the parties may choose not to go through the retrial procedure and accept the trial so as to save time and cost. A retrial procedure started by the courts thus violates the principle of private autonomy. In civil law countries, it is stipulated in the civil procedure code that only the parties can initiate and apply for retrial procedure, but not the courts. From this viewpoint, the courts in China shall not have the discretion to imitate the retrial procedure.

b) Restricting Discretion of the Procuratorate in Retrial

Art. 185 and Art. 186 of the Civil Procedure Code delegate the power to the procuratorate to supervise the judicial work of the courts. The procuratorate can challenge the court rulings and ask for a retrial procedure in case of discontent. In practice, such discretion faces resistance from the courts and gives rise to the discussion of whether or not to abolish such functions of the procuratorate. In principle, the procuratorate shall not intervene with the judgment when the parties are able to be redressed by the courts and the procuratorate shall be restricted to those cases concerning public interest.

c) Limiting the Rights of the Parties

According to Art. 178 – 180 of the Civil Procedure Code, the parties can apply for retrial when one of the following conditions is fulfilled.

- The composition of members of the tribunal is not in conformity with the procedure.
- The judgment is based on fake evidence, groundless facts and is unlawful.
- The trial violates the procedures.
- New evidence is found and a retrial is necessary.

Under such a broad definition for retrial, the party can apply for retrial in the trial court or a higher court whenever there is new evidence found. The retrial procedure has no restriction with regards to time limit, times of dispositions and judicial hierarchy,[396] therefore the parties can further apply for retrial to the higher court or even the Supreme People's Court after retrial in the lower courts. Such an irrational system is against procedural justice of the modern legal system and leads to the repeating of judicial work as well as high litigation costs.[397]

The reform of retrial procedure shall regulate specifically the scope of evidence, which is allowed for the purpose of retrial and time limit for new evidence. Secondly, the retrial procedure shall consider more narrow standards for the application of retrial procedure in respect of the time limit since the current time limit of 2 years[398] is too long compared with the retrial procedure in other civil law countries like Germany.[399] Thirdly, all the conditions and reasons for the application of retrial shall be detailed rather than broadly defined.[400] Fourth, the times of disposition of retrial shall be limited only to once. Retrial shall only be conducted by a higher court and the jurisdiction of the higher court shall be final.[401] Under such arrangement for retrial, in fact, 3-tier jurisdiction would be applied with respect to retrial cases. In this way, the quality of retrial will be higher and the burden of the parties will be reduced.

VI. Evaluation of the Appeal

The social justification for the appeal process is to correct the errors made by the trial courts and is to grant the parties the right to be redressed by the higher tribunal.[402] The appeal process requires society to devote a greater magnitude of resources and increases the cost to the society. The more frequent the appeal, the more cost will be incurred by the society. In the US, about 16% of cases were appealed in 1992[403] and in Germany, about 16% of cases were brought before the regional courts (Landgericht) for appeal in 1991.[404] By contrast, in China,

---

[396] Sheng, De Yong, Some Problems in the Reform of Judicial Supervision, in: People's Judiciary, (8) 2001, pp. 16-19.
[397] Gu, Tao, Rethinking and Suggestions to the Civil Retrial Procedure in China, in: People's Judiciary (3) 2000, p. 24.
[398] Art. 182 of Civil Procedure Code.
[399] Compare Art. 517 of German ZPO, the time limit is 30 days after the party involved is aware of his right for retrial, nevertheless it cannot exceed 5 months after the original trial.
[400] Compare Sheng, Huang Wei, Basic Thinking on Restructuring the Judicial Supervision in China, in: People's Judiciary (7) 2002, p. 26.
[401] Gu, Tao, Rethinking and Suggestions to the Civil Retrial Procedure in China, in: People's Judiciary (3) 2000, p. 23.
[402] Shavell, Steven, The Appeals Process as a Means of Error Correction, in: Journal of Legal Study, 1995, p. 381.
[403] Reports by Administrative office of the US Courts, Federal Judicial Workload Statistics 10, 19, 34 (1993).
[404] See Metzler-Poeschel, Statistisches Jahrbuch 1993 fuer die Bundesrepublik Deutschland (1993).

the rate for appeal and retrial in 1995 was around 7.6%.[405] In the previous empirical study based on 63 appeal cases, it was revealed that these cases consumed 217.6 days in appeal. Such duration is comparatively long and exceeds the time limit of 90 days for appeal cases according to the Civil Procedure Code.

There are some findings based on the statistical data with regard to appeal process. Almost 50% of the appeal cases are reversed or revised, or mediated by the higher courts in the judgment.[406] Take the statistics of 1995 as an example, as indicated in Table 3.16, 50.7% of the appeal cases[407] still retained the original court decisions made by the trial courts. 49.3% of the court decisions were made by the trial courts are reversed, revised, mediated, were under retrial procedure, or were withdrawn by the litigants. Regarding civil and economic disputes, there was settlement of 208,263 cases concerning civil and economic disputes (138,585 civil cases and 69,678 economic cases), in which 44.6%[408] (66,759 civil cases and 26,211 economic cases) of the original court orders/decisions remain unchanged. This reveals a low quality of judgment by the trial courts given that the appeal courts were more competent.

Table 3. 16 The Judgments made on the Appeal Cases in 1995

	Filing	Settlement	No. of cases and the type of settlement					
			Maintained	Reversed	Retrial	Withdrawal	Mediation	others
Total	272792	**271741**	**137842**	54595	21368	19802	24085	14049
Criminal	53576	53942	38786	7989	4140	2127	------	900
Civil	139298	**138585**	**66759**	29865	10865	11313	16418	3365
Economic	70224	**69678**	**26211**	15333	5687	5704	7667	9076
Maritime	201	176	66	35	12	17	26	20
Administration	9694	9536	6086	1408	676	658	-----	708

Source: from China Law Year Book, 1996

Table 3.17 reveals the ratio of maintained judgment of all appeal cases from 1994 until 1999. 52.1% (1994), 50.7% (1995), 51.5% (1996), 50% (1997), 50.6% (1998), 52.4% (1999) of the judgment made by the courts of first instance remained unchanged as shown below.[409]

405 In 1995 there were 4,545,676 trial cases, 272,792 appeal cases and 70,885 retrial cases.
406 Based on China Law Year Book, 1991-2000.
407 The calculation (according to Table 6.2) is: 137842 / 271741 = 50.7%
408 (66759 + 26211) / ((138585 + 69678) = 44.6%
409 Calculation based on the statistical data issued by the Supreme People's Court, in China Law Year Book, 1994 -2000.

Table 3. 17 Rate of the maintained Judgments in the Appellate Courts

1994	1995	1996	1997	1998	1999
52.1%	50.7%	51.5%	50%	50.6%	52.4%

Sources: compiled from statistical data issued by the Supreme People's Court, in: China Law Year Book, 1995 – 2000

On average, 51% of judgments remained unchanged in the appeal phase, among the remaining 49% cases, 8% were withdrawn by the complainants; 40% of the judgments made by the trial courts were cancelled or regarded as void by the appellate courts, therefore it can be roughly concluded that 40% of theses judgments made in the trial courts consisted of legal problems or mistakes in fact-finding. Such a rate is very high. It reveals the fact that many cases were not correctly solved in the first place and continued to consume judicial resources and waste the time and energy of the parties involved. Meanwhile, it may also imply that the quality of the judges in the lower courts were not professional enough, as indicated before.

Compared to the investigation conducted in Taiwan, in the appeal cases, 70% of the judgment made in the trial court remained unchanged, showing that the quality of judgment was higher than that of Mainland China.[410] The high rate of change of the verdict in appeal reveals that the quality of judgment in courts of the first instance (mainly lower courts) is low due to the low quality of judges and corruption.

Further procedural reform with respect to appeal shall also be conducted. The appellate courts in China has the discretion to conduct full reviews of fact-finding and application of law,[411] consequently it increases the workload of the appellate courts and affects judicial efficiency. Thus the courts shall constrain themselves only to the appeal of the parties rather a full review of facts and application of law, except that the cases have impact on public interest. Furthermore, there is a different understanding about the evidence which is allowed to be presented in the appellate courts.[412] The law does not regulate clearly the validity of the evidence,[413] and new evidence is allowed to support the appeal by the parties. Compared with Germany and the US, in principal, new evidence is not allowed to be presented in

410 Su, Yong Qin, Reform of Judicial Reform, Yue Dan publication 1998, pp. 312, 313.
411 Art. 180, *Some Opinions on the Application of Civil Procedure Code*, issued by the Supreme People's Court.
412 It is the same problem confronting the retrial procedure.
413 Compare Cao, Shou Yue, A Discussion of Reform of Appeal in Civil Litigation, in: People's Judiciary (3) 1999, pp. 4, 5.

appeal.[414] The reform of appeal procedure shall strictly regulate the validity of new evidences. For instance, only those evidences which cannot be collected due to force majeure or objective difficulties can be admitted and accepted by the courts, whereas those evidences which are hidden on purpose for appeal and evidences which could not be collected due to negligence shall not be accepted. With such regulation, the courts can reduce the burden of the parties and avoid waste of judicial resources; furthermore it will reduce the high rate of change of trial in appeal, as well as reducing filing for appeal, retrial, and the re-opening of the procedure. The stability of the law can be more effectively guaranteed and court efficiency can then be improved.[415]

VII. Accessibility of the Court

1. Litigation Cost

Accessibility of the court can be enhanced by reducing litigation cost; but on the other side, the reduction of litigation costs would increase the financial burden of the courts and affect its functioning. In China, due to the lack of budget from the state, the courts rely heavily on the income from court fees. In some provinces, more than 60% of the total budget of the courts comes from court fees. To the parties, various fees are charged in the civil process, the total litigation costs in lawsuits share 15 – 20% of the amount claimed by the parties (for more details, see Chapter 4 about the study of litigation cost). Beside this, corruption is still a severe problem and the charge of corruption adds the costs of using court service implicitly. Furthermore, the race to find a 'relationship' with the courts or the local governments to influence the outcome of the judgment exhausts the time and energy of the parties. The quality and the role of lawyer as middleman for bribery further impede the confidence of the general public to utilize the legal services. Considering these factors, the using of court services to resolve disputes is an expensive process.

Frequent changes in the outcome of the judgment in appeal and retrial procedure increase

---

[414] See Art. 511 ff. of German ZPO, new evidence might be accepted only with the consent of the other party and his/her lawyer; Art. 16 the American Federal Rules of Civil Procedure.

[415] Compare Cao, Shou Yue, A Discussion of Reform of Appeal in Civil Litigation, in: People's Judiciary (3) 1999, pp. 4, 5

uncertainty and cost to the parties. The lack of predictability of the outcome in litigation reduces the willingness of the parties to solve disputes within the courts. Furthermore, the low probability of law enforcement frustrates the parties in pursuing justice within the courts, as it means the cost of using the court service is too great when the court orders/decisions cannot be enforced or need a long duration for enforcement.

2. Legal Aid

In broad terms, legal aid refers to a reduction in or exemption of lawyers' fees, court fees and/or notary fees, etc. The aim of legal aid is to provide accessibility of court to the poor who are unable to pay the various fees involved in pursuing a case. Legal aid thus helps to provide court remedy and justice to such parties.

In China, legal aid was introduced to improve accessibility of justice at the beginning of 1994, at which time it was proposed by the Ministry of Justice. In 1996, the basic principle and framework of legal aid was written in the Criminal Procedure for the first time in legislature; in 1999 regulation of legal aid to civil cases was issued by the Supreme People's Court and the Ministry of Justice.[416] According to the law, women, elderly, young people and the handicapped have priority in obtaining legal aid. According to statistics of legal aid cases, 16.1% of legal aid was extended to young people with low income. From January to May of 2000, 21% of the legal aid was extended to women.[417]

However, due to the lag of legislature in legal aid, there are some problems in practice. First, the lack of coordination among the courts, judicial administrations and bar associations leads to loose administration of legal aid. Secondly, there is no unified administration at the national level. Third, the application for legal aid is not easy. Due to the lack of time and funds, some organizations can only provide limited legal aid to the parties; as to legal aid provided by the lawyers, due to the lack of lawyers in China,[418] and increasing demand for legal aid, lawyers first consider providing services to big firms, government organizations and those who have financial capacity.

---

[416] See: Notification on Legal Aid to Civil Cases, May 1999, by the Supreme People's Court and the Ministry of Justice.

[417] See: Periodical Report of Legal Aid in China, in: China Lawyers, (8) 2000.

[418] The average number of lawyers per person in China is only 5% of that in the US.

Legal aid should be further enhanced to provide service and assistance to those who are in urgent need of legal assistance but are financially poor so that their legal rights can be protected. Furthermore, legal aid from lawyers will help the parties to protect procedural rights in litigation. For example, evidence can be collected more effectively and efficiently with the help of lawyers. In China, due to the weak legal consciousness among the public, legal education and legal aid will thus play an important role in accessibility to the courts and provide remedies for the weak parties. Since the laws and regulations with respect to legal aid are too diversified and lack systematic summary, it is important for the state to promulgate a law specifically for legal aid with practical regulations and rules.[419]

VIII. The Role of Mediation and Arbitration

1. Mediation

a) Mediation by People's Arbitral Committee

Mediation as an alternative dispute resolution mechanism plays a very important role in the judiciary. According to statistics in 1998, there were 983,700 People's Arbitral Committees[420] in China and there were a total of 9,175,300 arbitrators. 5,267,200 cases were brought to the arbitral committees and 5,049,400 cases were successfully resolved, which is 95% of the total cases.[421] These cases mainly relate to heritage, neighborhoods, private debt, property, personal injury and other small disputes.

The People's Arbitral Committees resolve, on average, 6 ~ 7 million cases yearly, which are 3 ~ 4 times the cases filed in the courts of the first instance.[422] This indicates that mediation by arbitral committees has considerably relieved the burden of the courts and helps to alleviate the problem of backlog and court delay by reducing filing in the courts substantially.

However, most of these arbitrators lack education and necessary knowledge in dispute

---

419 Qi, Shu Jie, Research on Reform of Civil Procedure Law, Xiamen University Press 2000, p. 309.

420 The People's Arbitral Committee is defined as an organization which is under the guidance of the local government and the local court. It is established to solve general civil disputes and some small penalty cases. Normally the Arbitral Committee is under the administration of the district or the Resident Committee of the district in the city. In the countryside it is established in each village. The People's Arbitral Committee normally consists of 3 to 5 mediators.

421 Source from China Judiciary Administration Year Book (1999), China Law Press, 2000, p.17.

422 In an empirical study, it reveals that the high rate of mediation is due to the difficulty and fear of court procedure by the parties, especially in the countryside. See, Liu, Guang An and Li, Cun Bang: Civil Mediation and the Protection of Rights, in: Xia, Yong, Towards an Age of Rights, China Law and Politics Publication, 2000, p. 273.

resolution. It is necessary to provide training to these arbitrators so that the quality of the resolution will be improved and the number of filings in the courts will be reduced.

b) Mediation by the Courts

To a startling degree, the costs that matter are the costs of the cases that reach trial. In fact, a majority of the cases filed in the lower courts, especially in the District Courts are settled voluntarily before trial and relatively little court time is required. Mediation and reconciliation by the courts therefore would reduce the amount of cases waiting for trial and save time for the minority of cases, which take up the overwhelming majority of judges' time.[423]

According to Art. 10 of Civil Procedure Code, the courts shall first consider other means of mediation to solve the disputes.[424] In case of failure of mediation, the case shall be disposed in time by trial. Compared with trial, court mediation enables the judges to dispose more cases in a shorter time and to avoid court delay. On the other side, appeal or retrial is not allowed in cases settled by mediation; therefore it is no surprise to see that judges in China have preference to settling the cases by mediation when the workload of cases is heavy on them. In practice, some judges even force the parties to accept settlement through mediation and ignore the procedural rights of the parties. As mentioned in the previous study, the judges use mediation to have a speedy settlement and avoid exceeding the time limit. To realize the time bound program, the procedural and substantive rights of the parties are often sacrificed. In procedure reform, it should be stressed that the priority of mediation as dispute resolution should be based on the willingness of the parties rather than the judges' will.

Nevertheless, the importance of mediation shall not be ignored. For instance, in 1997, among 3,242,202 cases settled by the court of first instance, 50.9% of the cases (1,651,996) were settled by mediation; in 1999, among the 3,517,324 cases settled by the trial courts, 42.7% of the cases (1,500,269) were settled by mediation.[425] Mediation plays a very important role in reducing the duration of courts and the litigation costs. The procedure reform shall further

---

423 Zeisel, Hans, Kalven, Harry, Jr. and Buchholz, Bernard, Delay in the Court, Little, Brown and Company, 1959, p. 5.

424 In China, the process of mediation is controlled by the judges, therefore, mediation is considered as trial activity in China. It is very unique compared to the legislations in other countries. See Qi, Shu Jie, Research on Reform of Civil Procedure Law, Xiamen University Press 2000, pp. 156, 157,166.

425 Sources compiled from China Law Year Book, 1998, 2000.

enhance the quality and quantity of mediation, as well as the enforcement.[426]

2. Arbitration

Arbitration as an alternative dispute resolution can provide lower costs and speedy remedies to the parties. Moreover, as the arbitrators are professionals and the rule of arbitration is fair to all the parties, arbitration can provide a binding resolution for the parties.

As of June of 2000, there were 150 arbitration organizations in China, including the International Economy and Trade Arbitration Committee under CCPIT (China Council for International Trade Promotion) and Maritime Arbitration Committee, with more than 2100 members, 1300 employees and more than 17,000 arbitrators. In reality, these newly established arbitration organizations did not function well as it was expected. From the enactment of Arbitration Act in 1995, the number of total cases disposed by all arbitration committees was around 170,000 cases, with a value of 25.7 billion Yuan. The disposition of cases by arbitration increased in 1999 only with 6,353 cases relating to contract disputes.[427] Compared with the data from 1992, the Industry and Commerce Bureau in 29 provinces and cities, the number of cases disposed in 1999 declined sharply. The number of cases disposed by Economic and Contract Arbitration Committees in 1992 was 279,617, among which 283,368 cases were settled through mediation of the arbitrators and 5520 were settled by award.[428]

There are some obstacles to apply arbitration: first, many corporations, economic organizations and individuals know little about arbitration. In an investigation made by the Arbitration Committee of Nantong City/Jiangsu province, only 4% of the investigated firms expressed that they knew much about arbitration. Secondly, in the case of enforcement of arbitration award, the courts often use it's discretion to review the arbitration award and even cancel the award. Thirdly, the arbitration award is not stable, since the Civil Procedure Code allows the courts to choose not to enforce the award in case of disagreement. Furthermore, the Arbitration Act allows the arbitration committee to cancel the award in case mistakes are

[426] Qi, Shu Jie, Research on Reform of Civil Procedure Law, Xiamen University Press, p. 173.

[427] Sources from the report: "The Fifth Arbitration Conference on Exchange of Experiences Held in Kun Ming (City)", in: Arbitration and Law, 2000.

[428] China Law Year Book, 1993, p. 154.

found. Thus, an award may be challenged and lead to instability of the legal status.

In fact, many cases can be shifted from the courts to the Arbitration Committees, which have more than a few cases nowadays in China. In China, due to the lack of goodwill of the courts in enforcement of award, the arbitration committees try to find cooperative measures within the courts. Some court presidents, especially those who are in charge of enforcement, are invited to have a position on the arbitration committees, by such arbitration award can be more easily enforced.

Due to the above mentioned problems, it may be practical to incorporate arbitration into the court system, as court-annexed ADR has proved to be very efficient in many western countries.[429] Under the court-annexed ADR, cases can be shifted from the courts to arbitration organizations, which do not have many cases nowadays. Moreover, the confrontation with respect to enforcement of awards and review of awards by the courts will diminish. Consequently, the parties are more willing and confident to submit the cases for arbitration to save time and cost when enforcement will not be confronted with resistance from the courts. However, the role of arbitrators and judges shall be strictly separated.[430]

IX. Lawyers' Engagement and Court Delay

Lawyers' engagement in the civil process has its importance in speeding up the pretrial process and realizing justice. The engagement of the lawyers can reduce the workload of the judges with respect to evidence-collection and fact-finding. In many Western countries, legal service is very developed. For instance, in the mid 1990's, the number of American judges was around 46,000, whereas the number of lawyers amounts to more than 800,000,[431] this highly developed sector of legal service has helped to reduce the time of judges in pretrial activities like collecting evidence and fact-finding. It is almost the same in the UK and Germany. By contrast, the legal service in China is still in its infancy. Lawyer, as a profession,

---

[429] Since 1970's, the courts in the US introduced ADR into its traditional dispute resolution mechanism and enriched the reform of Civil Procedure Rule; Art. 16 of Federal Civil Procedure Rule allows judges to consider the possibility of reconciliation and out-of-court dispute resolution before pretrial meeting. The new UK Civil Procedure Rule in 1999 has explicitly incorporate ADR into court system and ADR is taken as an effective means for case management. Court-annexed ADR is accepted by the courts in Canada, Australia, New Zealand and Germany. It is evident that almost all forms of ADR can be incorporated into court system, fro example, court annexed arbitration, court annexed mediation etc..

[430] He, Bin, Restructuring the Mechanism of Dispute Resolution, Peking University Law Journal, Vol. 14, No. 1 (2002), pp. 30, 31.

[431] See Qi, Shu Jie, Research on Reform of Civil Procedure Law, Xiamen University Press 2000, pp. 128, 129.

was recognized in the beginning of 1980's and since then the number of lawyers has steadily increased: in 1993, the number of lawyers was 68,834; in 1999, there were 101,220 lawyers and around 170,000 judges in China.[432] However, the proportion of lawyers is still comparatively too low. Such allocation of judicial resources is not possible to change in the short run. Consequently, procedural reform will be affected since judges often have to take over the work of evidence-collecting and even fact-finding in the absence of lawyers' participation.[433] Judges still have to take time for pretrial preparation since many people lack the capability to collect evidence and the competence to participate in the civil process actively.

In this context, lawyers' engagement will help reduce the workload of the judges and enhance the efficiency of litigation despite some tactical practices used by the lawyer's in delaying the process. Furthermore, judicial reform, especially the procedural reform with respect to the burden of proof and other pretrial preparations shall consider current legal resources in China.

X. Procedure Justice and Judicial Reform

Procedure is the heart of the law;[434] In Rawls's formalistic theory, legal procedure is the basic requirement of justice. The rule of law is dependent upon the formalistic process that is mainly realized by formalistic procedure. Law should minimize the moral costs in the course of enforcement and reduce losses arising from mistakes in judgment, which deprives one's rights. According to Dworkin, it is necessary to design procedural right so as to reduce the moral cost and realize substantive justice.[435] According to Max Weber, formal justice is the requirement of judicial formality. Posner argued that law should consider efficiency and should minimize the social cost by reducing the direct and indirect cost.[436] In these viewpoints, procedure is regarded as a tool for substantive justice and reduces consumption of resources. Justice is the most important value in the society.[437] Furthermore, a just procedure will guarantee the stability of law, continuity of the procedure and the predictable

---

[432] Sources from China Judiciary Administration Year Book, 1993 and 1999. and China Law Year Book, 1999.

[433] Qi, Shu Jie, Research on Reform of Civil Procedure Law, Xiamen University Press 2000, p. 129.

[434] Song, Bing, Procedure, Justice and Modernization,China University of Politics and Law Publication, 1998, p. 363.

[435] R.M. Dworkin, A Matter of Principle, Clarenden Press of Oxford, 1985; R. Aduff, Trial and Punishment, Cambridge University Press, 1986, p. 110 – 114.

[436] Posner, Richard, Economic Analysis of Law, Little Brown Publication, Boston, Toronto, 4th edition 1992. p. 541 – 551.

[437] Rawls, John, A Theory of Justice, Harvard University Press, 1997, p. 3.

outcomes of the law.[438] The judgment can only be legally justified when the judge follows the procedure, since judgment is not just an arbitrary decision. The outcome is easily accepted by the parties when the procedure is followed.

Unlike Western countries, the concept of procedure justice does not exist in the Chinese judicial history and leads to a dim view of procedural justice. In the current legal practice, the courts stress more substantive justice and despise procedure justice. Furthermore, under the current inquisitorial system,[439] judges enjoy a great amount of discretion and dominate the process of trial in respect of inquiry, evidence-collection, etc. The procedural rights of the parties are often ignored and violated by the judges.

In this context, procedure reform shall stress the importance of procedural justice. A just procedure provides a security mechanism for the application of law, and it is also the foundation of the rule of law. For instance, court-arranged mediation has been one of the most important dispute resolution mechanisms by the courts. On the one hand, it has been proved that mediation as a means of ADR can improve litigation efficiency and reduces court delay and costs, but many civil cases are settled by 'compulsory' mediation by the courts, especially at the end of the year when the courts speed up disposition of cases and ask the parties to agree by mediation rather than by trial. In such cases, substantive justice would be sacrificed if there were no procedural guarantee. A just procedure ensures that trial will be undertaken systematically since the procedures are rules based on judicial principles and experiences. The cardinal order from filing, acceptance, public hearing, and judgment to enforcement cannot be changed by the arbitrariness of the judges. The practice of internal communication and *ex ante* conclusions drawn before the trial, or collusion between the judges and the parties, will only lead to the miscarriage of justice. Therefore, a just procedure can restrict the arbitrariness of the judges and can effectively deter the abuse of power in judgment. The design in judicial hierarchy, time limit of disposition, public hearing and judicial supervision is to restrict the discretionary power of the judge properly. The more proper of the restriction of arbitrariness in jurisdiction, the more rational the procedure will be.

---

438 Jiang, Ping, "Summary on the Seminar of Civil Judicial System", in Law Research, (5) 1998.

439 Inquisitorial system refers to the litigation pattern applied by the judges in the civil law countries like Germany, where judges have big discretion in evidence-collecting, inquiry, fact-finding etc. The so-called "Super" inquisitional system is a term to describe the current Chinese civil process in which the judges enjoy too big discretion throughout the process. See Wang, Li Ming, Research on Judicial Reform, China Law Press, 2000, p. 312 – 315.

On the contrary, justice will not be secured and the judges may be corrupted easily if the judge is allowed not to follow the procedure and make an arbitrary judgment, or not to follow the procedure of evidence-collecting and meet privately with the parties and the lawyers. Miscarriage of justice is likely if a decision is made in advance through closed-door discussion before the trial, or allowing *ex ante* communication. Moreover, justice may also not be realized if the cases are not open for public hearing and legal reasoning is not sufficient to justify the adjudication. Procedural reform shall be further aimed at restricting the judges from making judgments simply based on his/her understanding of the facts, without listening to the statement of the parties, or simply based on the evidence collected by himself/herself and disregards the evidence from the parties. At the same time, the procedure shall treat all parties equally, irregardless of the social status of the person.

Procedural reform shall also stress the efficiency of the courts. From the view of society, justice means efficient allocation of social resources and reduction of the waste of economic resources. A stable, predictable legal system will create a better investment environment for the investors and increase their confidence in property exchange with good faith and expectation of future profit. From this viewpoint, procedure justice will maximize social welfare and enhance economic efficiency. On the other hand, efficiency does not mean simplifying the procedure to reduce appeal costs in some cases. Although appeals may incur higher litigation costs to the parties, the procedure is necessary to guarantee justice will not be abused.

Procedure justice should reduce court delay and reduce the costs borne by the parties and the state. Litigation cannot be endless and must be settled within a certain time limit. The time limit shall be applied for trial and appeal, as well as for retrial. The current Civil Procedure Code does not make it clear what the time limit is for providing evidence and the exact time limit for settlement of case by mediation. With respect to retrial procedure, there is no time limit for trial and no restriction on times of disposition; consequently, the retrial process is long and unbearable. The endlessness of a trial challenges the finality of law and increases the workload of the judiciary. The procedural reform therefore shall touch on these issues and a workable framework both for justice and efficiency shall be established.

Furthermore, current legal reform in China needs to transplant those successful and practical experiences from other legal systems in Western countries. For example, in civil law countries, it is regarded that the civil process emphasizes less on the facts and evidences, and lacks the feature of "discovery" process. The appellate court has to review all the facts and legal points again. This may result in low efficiency compared to the American civil process in which the dispute of facts cannot be taken as a reason for appeal.[440] However, the civil process of common law is dominated by the lawyers and leads to lengthy debate, which may also cause delay; the jury's participation is also not in line with the efficiency principle. Compared with the judge-dominated system of civil procedure, the lawyer-dominated procedure is regarded as less efficient.[441] Strictly said, the adversarial system (Common Law) is much rational in restrains the arbitrariness of the judges and is more likely to realize substantive justice. The two legal systems are continuing efforts to enhance efficiency; for example, a jury system is not applied in civil cases in Britain and more emphasis is put on mediation before the trial, while civil law countries are reforming the regulations on evidence. These practical experiences are useful for domestic reform.

XI. Summary

In this part, critical assessment has been made to the functioning of the court system in China addressing the problems existing in the judiciary and factors affecting court delay.

The efficiency of the courts is heavily influenced by number of cases settled, settlement ratio, duration of the cases and size of backlogs, etc. The efficiency analysis of the legal system in China cannot merely rely on the settlement ratio and duration, other factors like the average disposition and human capital shall be taken into consideration. The time bound program for time limits and settlement ratios is good in consideration of reducing court delay and congestions, but it must be designed to guarantee the procedural rights of the parties and quality of the judgment and it needs to take into account some measures such as framing

440 Kerameus, Konstantions D., "A Gvilian Lawyer Looks at Common Law Procedure", in Louisiana Law Review, Jan. 1987, 47 La. L. Rev. 493; also see Wang, Li Ming, Research on Judicial Reform, China Law Press, 2000, p. 78.
441 Langbein, John H., The German Advantage in Civil Procedure, 52 Chicago Law Review, 1985.

more effective criteria in granting adjournments.

Secondly, the Trial Committee has a great amount of discretion in jurisdiction and its interference has heavily affected the independence of judges and has even lead to lengthy duration of cases. The abolishment of the Trial Committee in the courts should be coupled with improvement of human capital in the courts.

Third, as most of the cases filed in the lower courts are simple in fact-finding and application of law, the courts should establish summary courts or small claims tribunals to deal with these cases. The principle of 'one trial as final' rather than a 2-tier jurisdiction should be also applicable so as to reduce the time of disposition and cost.

Fourth, the supervision procedure shall be restructured so as to improve court efficiency and reduce court delay. Measures shall be taken to deter the strategic behavior of the parties in conducting long litigation; for instance, time limits shall be applied for evidence and liability shall be imposed in case of hiding evidence in the previous trial. Furthermore, since the courts and the procuratorates are given too much discretion to initiate retrial procedure and interfere the private autonomy, the reform shall restrict the discretion of the courts and the procuratorates and the retrial procedure can only be initiated by them, and only when the civil cases are related to public interest.

Fifth, the error cost is high due to the fact that a high proportion of court orders/decisions of the trial courts are canceled reversed or revised by the appellate court; therefore, reform shall be aimed to improve the quality of the trial in the courts of the first instance. The time bound program should be workable and reasonable adjournments shall be allowed to avoid mistakes due to speedy disposition. Meanwhile, it is very important to improve the human capital in the lower courts (district / county courts and intermediate courts) since these courts dispose 80 – 90% of the total civil cases yearly in China.

Sixth, the accessibility of the court can be enhanced by reducing the litigation cost, simplifying filing procedures, and the availability of legal aid for the poor.

Seventh, an ADR mechanism can effectively reduce court delay and cost. The tradition of mediation shall be strengthened while respecting the procedural rights of the parties for trial. Furthermore, due to the high quality of arbitration in China, some cases, especially economic cases, can be transferred from the courts to arbitration committees so as to relieve the caseload of the courts. A court-annexed arbitration mechanism may improve efficiency in respect of law enforcement.

Further, lawyers' engagement in the procedure will provide more protection to the parties given the fact that many individuals have a dim view of law in the society. Lawyers' engagement can further reduce the problem of court delay since the shift of burden of proof and pretrial preparation will relieve the workload of the judges. Reform of procedure law shall also consider the current judicial resources in China; meanwhile, a reasonable cost scheme shall be designed by the judicial administration so as to foster the use of legal service and access to justice.

Finally, the current reform in China focuses on procedure reform, which is aimed at improving procedural justice and court efficiency. Judges in China have the tradition of stressing on substantive justice and dim view of procedure justice, and they enjoy big discretion in civil process. Procedural rights of the parties are often ignored and violated. Thus, the current judicial reform shall put stress on procedural justice since a just procedure will provide a security mechanism for the application of law and ensure substantive justice. Furthermore, procedural reform shall also take the efficiency and cost into consideration. Procedure reform shall reduce delay in the courts and enhance accessibility of justice.

Chapter 4

A Survey of Litigation Costs, Court Budgets and Access to Justice

The charge of various court fees has impeded the accessibility to justice. Under current administration of court fees, which are transferred to the local administrations and then reimbursed proportionately to the courts, the courts have more incentive to increase income by charging excessive fees. Meanwhile, the lack of budget autonomy leads to the interference of the local governments as well as the longer duration of the trial. To guarantee budget autonomy under current situation, it is practical to establish a two-tiered budget supply, namely, the remuneration of the judges and operational costs of the courts shall be guaranteed by budget of the state, whereas the costs for court facilities shall be borne by the locals. Under such budget allocation, the judiciary will be less dependent on the locals and the worries of the judges will be relieved.[442]

I. Introduction

The cost of a judicial system consists of mainly 2 parts. One is the public cost which is borne by the state in establishing the judicial system; the other is the private cost which is charged by the court such as litigation cost and lawyers' fees which are borne by the parties.[443] The functioning of the court system in a country is heavily affected by the burden of these costs. In economic terms, costs will affect the demand. The burden of the litigation cost of the parties will influence the decisions of the parties on whether or not to go to the courts for remedy under a certain constraint such as the probability of winning their case and enforcement of judgments. Additionally, delay and backlog will increase the price to the parties implicitly; consequently, people will react to this added cost by reducing their filings and not redress their grievances within the court system.[444]

In China, lawyers do not monopolize all of the litigation cases since the Civil Procedure Code

[442] Summarized view from different literatures with respect to budget autonomy for the courts.
[443] See Fu, Yu Lin, The Nature of Litigation Fees and the Burden of Litigation Costs, Peking University Law Review, Vol. 4, No. 1, 2001, pp. 239-243.
[444] Supra note 29.

allows a non-lawyer to represent the parties; consequently the parties involved depend less on the lawyers to plea their case. Besides cost considerations, non-engagement of lawyers in litigation has much to do with the fact that lawyers are not trustworthy nowadays because of bribery, lack of necessary legal training and substandard professional knowledge. If lawyers' roles are only seen as mediators and middleman in bribing judges, this will only increase the additional costs of litigation rather than increasing quality legal service as expected. In the past years, the moral hazard has been a hurdle for the development of the service sector of lawyers.

Furthermore, the court budgets will also affect the functioning of the court system. The lack of financial support to the judiciary could lead to a dysfunctional judicial system. In other words, if the courts lack financial support in office facilities, highly skilled personnel and other infrastructures like vehicles, communication equipment, etc., the filing and disposition of the cases will be affected and a prompt disposition is unlikely in such a situation. In Germany, litigation costs have arisen dramatically as a result of savings policy, which shifts the fees to the litigants.[445] Should the state save money and let the litigants pay more litigation costs or should the litigants simply sway from the courts and seek justice through other means or just bear the cost of possible court delay?

In this context, this chapter will discuss how these costs affect the efficiency of the court system in China. It also attempts to give policy suggestions on how the state could invest in the court system, and whether or not the state should reduce litigation costs or shift the burden of costs to the litigants. At the same time, how to regulate lawyers' fees and build a modern, well functioning law profession is also essential to the success of judicial reform. To answer these questions, first, a general review of cost composition will be made and some examples will be discussed to demonstrate the burden of litigation costs for the parties. Secondly, an investigation based on secondary data with respect to judicial costs incurred in the courts of Jiangxi province will be made in an attempt to show the accessibility of the courts and the necessity of the state to provide sufficient financial support to the courts.

---

445 Schaefer, H.-B., „Kein Geld für die Justiz – Was ist uns der Rechtsfrieden wert?“, in DriZ, 1995, p. 461.

II. An Investigation of Litigation Costs in China

1. The Burden of Judicial Costs and Litigation Costs

Civil process has incurred various litigation costs from its beginning. These costs can be summarized as the total amount of all consumed human resources, material cost and monetary expenses arising from litigation. Civil litigation costs are unavoidable to the parties, such a "cost of producing justice"[446] is divided into 2 parts: the "litigation cost" or referred to as *private cost*, borne by the parties involved in the civil cases and "judicial cost", referred to as *public cost*, borne by the state. Public cost in terms of the judiciary means the budget from the state in order to establish a judicial system for resolving civil disputes, and investment in judicial resources such as operational expenditures, court facilities and personnel etc. The litigation cost mainly includes:

- Litigation fees / court fees,
- Lawyers' or representation fees,
- Travel costs,
- Costs relating to litigation like evidence collection, time and energy spent for the hearings, and other expenditures in relation to the claims, etc.
- Costs arising from security of title and measures for compulsory enforcement of court orders.

The second part of the cost is the judicial cost borne by the state to guarantee the functioning of the judiciary with respect to judgment, prosecution and enforcement, etc.. This part of cost mainly includes:

- Salary and welfare of court personnel
- Facilities: office buildings, equipment, vehicles, etc.
- Investigation costs
- Hearing of cases
- Enforcement

Besides these two types of costs, there could also be error costs[447] in judgment due to

[446] Supra note 171.
[447] Posner A. Richard, An Economic Approach to Legal Procedure and Judicial Administration, in Journal of Legal Studies, 2 (1973), pp. 399 – 400.

mistakes of judgment, or moral costs, namely an unfair judgment leads to a waste of economic resources.[448]

The functioning of judiciary incurs costs to the state and the parties involved. To guarantee social justice and the functioning of the court system, the state should provide an adequate budget to the courts. The budget from the state (public cost) is consumed in the course of judgment, and part of the budget is spent in the filing and administration of the courts, whereas the litigation fee charged to the parties is used to cover part of the judicial cost and serves as a function for taxation to the court-users.

However, there are pros and cons regarding litigation costs. Those who are against court fees hold that: first, the state is responsible for providing adequate court remedies and court fees shall be burdened by the state; secondly, court service shall be public goods provided by the state, therefore the charging of court fees would mean a double taxation; third, in a state of rule of law, people have the right to get access to justice, charging of court fees would impede accessibility of justice to the poor; consequently, the state has the responsibility to provide court remedies and shall not charge court fees. Whereas the opposite view holds that court fees shall be burdened by court-users, such cost shall not be borne by the state and the people who never use court services. The charging of litigation fees will prevent those who may misuse court services and in a way force them to abide by the law.

Distribution of judicial costs between the state and the parties would have a strong influence on the functioning of the courts and accessibility to justice. The state can shift part of the public cost to court-users by raising the court fees or relieving the burden on court-users by taking over the work of investigation, collection of evidence and thus bear part of the private cost. The allocation of these costs will influence the number of filings since cost distribution may hinder or enhance some people's capability to get access to the courts, for instance, a rise in litigation cost will reduce meaningless filings and the workload of the courts, but likewise such reform shall not impede the accessibility to justice; therefore, a reasonable and well-designed judicial policy also takes the mechanism of legal aid into account.[449]

The current reform in respect to litigation cost in China faces two problems. On one side, the reform shall reduce the burden of the parties and lower the cost in consideration of the

---

448 R.M. Dworkin, A Matter of Principle, Clarenden Press of Oxford, 1985.

449 Qi, Shu Jie, Research on Reform of Civil Procedure Law, Xiamen University Press, 2000, p. 371.

income level of the people; on the other hand the state shall provide adequate budget to the courts so as to guarantee and improve the salaries of the judges and invest in the facilities of the courts.

2. Litigation Costs

In the civil process, the parties have to pay various fees to the courts. These court fees mainly include: (1) case disposition fees/litigation fees;[450] (2) fees for inspection, verification, public announcement (3) costs arising from transportation, accommodation, food, verification and translation of materials, and compensation to the witness due to their absence from their workplace (4) fees for applying for security of title and relevant costs arising thereof; (5) fees for execution of court decisions, arbitration awards and mediation agreements; and (6) other litigation costs which should be borne by the parties according to the view of the court.

There has been a shift in court fees. The losing party has to bear not only legal costs on his/her own but also the litigation fee of the opposite party.[451] In case of expert's advice or witness hearings, the loser has to bear the costs of the services of the experts. Conversely, in case of winning, the prepaid court fees can only be recovered from the losers rather than by a direct reimbursement from the courts; furthermore the winner has to bear the risk that they might not be able to collect the compensation and the legal costs such as court fees etc.[452]

Table 4.1 illustrates the budget of litigation cost which may incur to the parties according to the *Regulation on Litigation Cost (1989)*.

[450] Case disposition fee or litigation fee is charged according to the amount of the claim, namely, the dispute value. The litigants must prepay the fee in each case. Judges can decide the proportion of the court fees borne by each party according to the liability in causing the disputes. This is similar to the Austria ZPO, see Hans Zeisel, Harry Kalven, Jr. and Bernard Buchholz, Delay in the Court, Little, Brown and Company, 1959, pp. 292, 293, 294.

[451] According to Art. 107 of Civil Procedure Code, the litigant shall pay the litigation fee in advance to the court.

[452] In China, judges can decide sharing of the court fees among the parties involved according to the liability of each party causing the disputes. There is no regulation about the shift of lawyers fee. Normally, each party bears his own cost for lawyers' engagement. Supra note 450.

Table 4. 1 Budget of Litigation Cost

The standard for charging Case Disposition Fee		Supposed 'Dispute Value'	Fee	Security Fee		Execution Fee		Inspection, verification		Lawyers Fee		Total Amount	Percent
The corresponding amount	Rate			Rate	Fee	Rate	Fee	Rate	Fee	Rate	Fee		
<1000	50Y*	1000	50		30		50	1%	50	4%	40	270	27%
1000-50,000	4%	20,000	800	1%	200	0.5%	180	1%	200	4%	880	2100	10.5%
50,000-100,000	3%	60,000	2310	1%	600	0.5%	300	1%	600	3%	1800	5610	9.3%
100,000-200,000	2%	150,000	4510	0.5%	750	0.5%	750	1%	1500	3%	4500	12010	8%
200,000-500,000	1.5%	210,000	5560	0.%	1050	0.5%	1850	1%	2100	3%	6300	16060	7.6%
500,000-1,000,000	1%	800,000	13010	0.5%	4000	0.5%	4000	1%	8000	2%	16000	45010	5.6%
>1,000,000	0.5%	1,100,000	15510	0.5%	5500	0.5%	5500	1%	11000	2%	22000	59510	5.4%

* For dispute value below 1000 Yuan, 50 Yuan will be charged.

Some remarks to Table 4.1:

a) The calculation of case disposition fees/litigation fees is based on the accumulative amount of each corresponding amount times the rate as indicated in the second column of the table. For example, if the supposed 'dispute value' is 600,000 Yuan, the calculation will be as follows:

For the part below **1000**: 50 Yuan

The part above 1000 up to 50,000: **49,000** x 4% = 1960

The part above 50,000 up to 100,000: **10,000** x 3% = 300

Thus, the case disposition fee is equal to the accumulative amount, namely 2310 Yuan.

In case of appeal, the same fee amount must be paid to the appellate court.

b) There is no uniform regulation regarding lawyers' fees. Normally lawyers are allowed to charge fees according to the local economic level and the financial status of the parties.

c) Fees in respect to inspection/verification/public announcement may not be incurred in any case and there are no uniform standards for charging this fee.

Table. 4.1 reveals the normal expenditure for the parties and shows that the parties have to pay high litigation costs in the civil process. The costs are regressive; higher claims do not demand proportionate costs. The average litigation cost amounts to about 10% of the 'dispute value' of the case.[453] For instance, in a case with a 'dispute value' of 600,000 Yuan, the litigant has to pay 5610 Yuan if he wins the case; furthermore he has to consider the risk of failure of enforcement. Additionally, under the current procedural reform, the burden of proof is mostly shifted to the litigants and therefore the parties have to consider a cost increase in witness fees and travel costs for investigation.[454] These additional costs are sometimes charged by the courts at 5% or 6% of the 'dispute value', or even higher, possibly up to 10%.[455] Thus, the total litigation cost would be 15% ~ 20% of the 'dispute value' or even higher in case of more factors being involved.

One example[456] illustrates the high litigation cost incurred in the legal action against its debtors during the court of the first instance in 1997 and 1998 by KT Company (hereinafter called "KT"). The company is a state owned financial institution located in city A. In 1997 and 1998, KT lodged claims against 20 debtors for refund of loans. Table 4.2 presents a record of litigation fees incurred in the court of the first instance for 13 cases. In 8 cases, the debtors had no objection to the amount of loan and interest accrued thereof, as well as the time to repay the loan, therefore for these 8 cases the creditor could apply to the court and order the debtor to pay the money back under the non-litigation procedure[457] and there would be no need to pay litigation fees to the court according to the Civil Procedure Code. Though KT has applied to the court to do so, the court rejected applying the non-litigation procedure and the cases were handled under the litigation procedure. If KT could succeed in applying for a court order to pay debts due, then it would save up to 99% of litigation costs.

[453] In small claims it would not be economic to have lawyer's engagement and to appeal, otherwise the costs would even be higher than the claims. This is also the case in German Civil Process, in which the costs could be even many times of the claims, see Franzen, Hans, Was kostet eine Richterstunde? In: NJW1974 Heft 18, p. 786.

[454] In reality, the courts in China shift most of the costs to the litigants, even the cost for Xerox, printing and the postage. In case of traveling for investigation, the parties have to bear the cost of the courts.

[455] See an investigation conducted by two lawyers about the litigation cost in civil process. Liu, Tong Hai and Zhu, Xiao Long, Is the Court Fee Reasonable? In China Lawyer, (12) 2002, p. 40.

[456] This example is based on the one presented by Fang, Liu Fang, Research on Litigation Cost, in: China Social Science, (3) 1999, pp. 141-142.

[457] Non-litigation procedure is regulated in Chapter 17, 18 and 19 of the Civil Procedure Code. In a simple debtor and creditor relationship, the creditor can file the case in the court and the court will issue a court order to the debtor.

Table 4. 2 Court Fees paid by KT in the first Instance against its 13 Debtors from 1997 to 1998

Trial Court	Value of the claim (Yuan)	Case-disposing fee (Yuan)	Fee for security of title	Fee for execution of court orders	Lawyers Fee*
1. No.1 Intermediate Court of City A	28,217,000	151,100	164,450		
2. Ditto	5,148,000 USD	223,670	0		
3. Ditto	834,000 USD	44,640	35,160		
4. Ditto	58,338,000	301,701	292,220		
5. Ditto	21,485,000	117,440	107,950		
6. Ditto	2,840,000	24,210	14,720		
7. Ditto	12,299,000	75,510	0		
8. Ditto	6,746,000	43,740	34,250		
9. Ditto	5,061,000	35,320	0		
10. Ditto	14,856,000	84,300	74,810		
11. No.2 Intermediate Court of City A	2,985,000	24,839	0		
12. District Court in City A	649,000	11,510	0		
13. Intermediate Court of City B	18,176,000	100,892	0		
Sum	0	1,238,881	723,560	486,560	1,238,881
Total amount for all items	**3,687,882 (Yuan)**				

Source: from a case study presented by Fang, Liu Fang, Research on Litigation Cost, in: China Social Science, (3) 1999, p. 141-142.

*since in this case lawyers fee is almost equal to the case-disposing fee, the mount shown above is treated as same as the amount of case-disposing fee.

In fact, the total cost paid by KT is far more than the amount shown in Table 4.2, since besides these fees, KT must pay other fees like investigation, travel, etc. In case of appeal, KT must pay an additional case-disposal fee to the appellate court; additionally, KT must pay travel costs, accommodation and food expenditures for the judges if the defendant is located in a different city.[458]

In Table 4.2, the court asked KT to pay 486,560 Yuan as a compulsory execution fee as the court viewed that the assets of the debtor should be assessed according to the relevant

[458] According to the Civil Procedure Code, if the defendant is located in another territorial jurisdiction, the local court of the defendant will have the priority of jurisdiction of the case. In this case, KT company must file the claim in City B to sue the defendant who is located in this city.

regulation and law. The assessment company charged 0.8% based on the value of the assets and deducted the amount from the income of the auction. In this case, the assets were still not sold as of January of 1999. According to KT's accountant, the execution fee of 486,500 Yuan was not reimbursed by the court.

Though KT has won all the cases, the possibility to be compensated through the application for compulsory execution of the assets is small, since the debtors were all state-owned firms that were heavily indebted; there were few assets available for liquidation. In Table 4.2, 7 cases, namely items 1-5, 8, 12 were settled by compulsory execution of court orders. The total amount of the claims applied by KT were 171.70 million Yuan, but only 430,000 Yuan was liquidated through execution, whereas KT paid 1,380,310 Yuan in court fees and execution fees for these 7 cases, therefore, KT company could save a loss of 950,310 Yuan if it gave up litigation.[459] Even if the company is successful in redress, this case indicates that high litigation costs which are often incurred are beyond the limit of burden of many big firms.[460] If the litigation has no value in terms of economic meaning, then it loses its legal value. As it is known, law enforcement has become an obstacle of the judiciary. There are large amounts of cases which cannot be executed and in which the parties are unable to be the compensated for even if the cases are judged in their favor, especially cases with economic disputes.[461]

[459] Why KT Company took legal action against its debtors although he knew that he could save the litigation cost if he gave up? The explanation is much to do with the ownership and governance of the state company. As KT is a state-owned financial institution, KT should prove that the company had no engagement of corruption in the loan business; to prove that, it needs a court document for accounting purpose to offset the debt. Of course, the reason behind this case is not purely for justice or repayment of the loan. If KT were a private firm, then it would never pay such high cost for a court document just for accounting purpose.

[460] There are many cases with litigation fee over million Chinese Yuan. In the selective cases edited by the Supreme People's Court, civil litigation is a very costly game. For some examples: the first example concerning a real estate dispute, a firm in Hainan province paid 0.6 million Yuan for Case Disposition Fee, security of title in the first instance and case-disposing fee in the appellate stage. The litigation was estimated to be 1.5 million Yuan taking the lawyers fee, traveling cost and other expenditure into account. In the second example concerning dispute of leasing contract, United Leasing Company paid 0.57 million Yuan as court fee to the trial court and appellate court respectively, besides, court fee for counter-claims was 241,059 Yuan. In the third case concerning bond business, the South Portfolio Company paid total amount of 999,440 Yuan to the trial and appellate courts for a simple case with a debt value of 27 million. Details refer to "Selective cases of economic disputes with appeal and retrial disposed by Supreme People's Court", pp. 331 – 335, 423.

[461] According to statistics, more than 50% of the court orders relating to economic and contract issues cannot be executed and the creditors have no chance to be compensated even they win the cases. See Zhang, Wei Ying / Ke, Rong Zhu, "The adverse selection in civil litigation and its interpretation – an empirical study", in (2) 2002 China Social Science, p. 31.

III. Critical Assessment of the Current Cost Scheme in Civil Process and Accessibility of Justice

1. The Problem in Prepayment and Reimbursement of Court Fee and Litigation Risk

a) Prepayment and Procedural Right

The parties may be allowed to pay the litigation fee at a later date or be exempt from litigation fees in case of 'financial difficulty".[462] In reality, the law neither indicates the responsibility of the courts in legal aid nor the rules on how to define "financial difficulty" and when the exemption shall be decided. According to current practice, it is difficult for the parties to apply for legal aid from the courts.

Civil Procedure Code stipulates that the courts must accept the filing if the filing complies with all legal conditions, prepayment of court fees is not mentioned.[463] However, in its legal interpretation in 1994, the Supreme People's Court further stated, "it is a precondition for the court to accept the case that the claimant or the appellant pay case-disposal fees or appeal fees. In the event that the parties does not pay the above mentioned fees, or does not pay the full amount, or does not pay if the application for deferred payment / reduction of payment / exemption is not approved, the court shall not accept the filing and dispose the case, the case shall not come into the litigation procedure".[464] Additionally, Article 12 of the *Regulation on Litigation Cost (1989)* promulgated by the Supreme People's Court stipulates if the litigant and the appellant cannot prepay the litigation fees, then the case will be treated as "automatically withdrawn". As for the claimant, he/she may continue to file with the court when he/she has enough financial ability, but for the appellant, he/she may lose the right since the time limit for appeal may expire. For the counter-claimant, he loses the time and ability to defend his right. The inability to prepay the litigation fee does not mean that the parties give up the right and withdraw the case; therefore, the court seems to deprive the claiming right of the parties only because the parties are not in a position to pay. With respect to the appellate case, the case will be treated as "automatically withdrawn" when the appellant cannot prepay the fee to the court and may lose the chance to win the case.[465]

---

462 Art. 107 of Civil Procedure Code. (1991).
463 Art. 108, 109, 111, 131, 140. of Civil Procedure Code (1991).
464 The Supreme People's Court: "Reply to Questions about Litigation Fee", 1994.
465 Among the 76 court decisions/orders from 1993 to 1996, 8 court decisions were regarded as "automatically withdrawn",

Such regulation on the collection of litigation fees reveals that the courts only bear public costs and that the courts do not take the risk of bearing the private costs.

The regulation and legal interpretation of the litigation fee by the Supreme People's Court has blocked those who are unable to pay the fee to the court. In the absence of other dispute resolution mechanisms like legal aid, ADR, mediation; such regulation would be a big loss to the society, as no remedies would be available to the parties.

b) The Risk of Losing Case Disposition Fees

Under current civil procedure, the litigant, or the appellant, must consider the risk of losing the litigation fee as the court and the parties are not aware of whether or not the amount of compensation will be equal to the amount of claim. If the compensation is smaller than the amount of claim, then the fee paid by the respondent will only be calculated based on the amount of compensation, thus the amount of the fee reimbursed by the respondent will be less than the prepaid amount, the rest is absorbed by the court. In such a situation, the compensation obtained by the litigant may not cover the litigation fee which was prepaid. For example, if the litigant claims 1,010,000 Yuan, and he has to pay a litigation fee of 15,059.97 Yuan in accordance with the cost calculation. It is possible that the compensation ruled by the court is however only 10,000 Yuan, then the respondent will only have to pay 410 Yuan based on 10,000 Yuan (compensation amount), the rest of the prepaid amount, 14,649.87 Yuan, will be kept by the court and will not be reimbursed to the litigant. Therefore, if the parties are unwilling to bear such unforeseeable risk, he/she may give up the right of being fully compensated to avoid paying additional costs to the court.

In another case, the litigant overestimated the "dispute value" and the compensation obtained was not even enough to cover the litigation fee.[466] The litigant drove a Toyota car into a wall, and the air bag failed to function at the time of the accident. The litigant sued the carmaker for 1 million Yuan in 1993. In 1994, the court ruled that the description of the air bag was not detailed enough and the defendant should pay 13,685 Yuan to the litigant. In this case the defendant paid the litigation fee of 557 Yuan and the litigant paid litigation fee of 14,403

see selective cases published by Economic Tribunal of the Supreme People's Court, No. 100 Economic Tribunal, 1994 and No. 159 Economic Tribunal 1995.

[466] See, "J.T.Zhang sue Toyota for compensation due to personal injury", in: Case collection selected by Supreme People's Court, China Politics & Law University Publication, 1997, pp. 98 – 104.

Yuan. In addition, the litigant paid 25,000 Yuan to the lawyer for representation. In such a case, the litigant could have avoided the loss of 26,302 Yuan if he had not lodged the claim.

The litigant may run the risk of being unable to recover the fee even if he/she wins the case. In accordance with the Civil Procedure Code, the litigation fee shall be borne by the losing party; consequently, compensation will include the litigation fee. In practice, the fee shall be prepaid to the court, but will not be returned to the winning party directly. The litigant has to recover it from the respondent, very often through compulsory enforcement, further incurring an execution fee to the parties when he/she applies for compulsory measures to be taken to liquidate the property of the losing party. In such a situation, the court shifts its responsibility to collect the fee from the losing party to the winning party. In the event that the losing party has no property available, or the court is unable to seek out the property of the losing party, the remedies for the prepaid litigation fee and the rights from the judgment will not be realized. Such practices by the courts face strong criticism in China. Since the 1998 reforms in some courts have been made to reimburse the prepaid court fee directly to the litigants who win the case, although it is still not common.[467]

In a case filed in 1994, the litigant filed a claim against the defendant for damaging his reputation. The litigant prepaid a 1,450 Yuan litigation fee. The defendant was found guilty, but the original court decision was reversed after the defendant appealed to the High People's Court; consequently the appeal fee should have been borne by the original litigant (the losing party), but as of 1998 the litigant had not paid the defendant the 1,450 Yuan court fee. The defendant thus has not been able to get reimbursement of the fee prepaid by him to the appellate court. Additionally, he had to bear the other costs which were incurred, such as transportation costs and losses due to absence from the work, which was around 1,000 Yuan. In this case, the duration in the court case of the first instance and the appellate court exceeded 2 years and the winning party was unable to recover the prepaid fee and compensation.[468]

These examples indicate that the design of collection of court fee is not rational and it should be revised to convenience the parties to have legal remedies within reasonable time limits.

---

[467] For relevant arguments, see H.Y. Jia, H.Y. Li, "Improper way to absorb court fees from the winning party", in People's Court Press, on 07.01.1998; "Method of Reimbursing Court Fees, Reform in Le Qing Court", in People's Court Press, on 16.06.1998.

[468] In: Selective Cases from People's Court, 17th edition, pp. 77-83.

The court should not shift the risk to the winning party for collection of the litigation fees since the courts are in a better position to recover the litigation fees by using its' discretionary power.

2. High Cost of Non-Litigation Cases

Non-litigation cases refer to those civil cases, in which there is only one party involved, or the other party cannot be identified, or there is no need to have the other party involved in the case.[469] The court fee for such cases is only approximately 2% of the litigation cases.[470] In Japan and Taiwan, the scope of non-litigation cases is wide. For example, it includes the compulsory execution of security titles,[471] dissolution of corporations, settlement and reorganization of corporations,[472] judgment on buy-back prices in case of disagreements on mergers,[473] confirmations and compulsory executions on promissory checks. Compared with litigation cases, the court orders in non-litigation cases provide another form of legal remedy besides civil procedure and reduce unnecessary litigation cost.

However, in China the scope of non-litigation cases is too narrow in legislation. In accordance with the Chinese Civil Procedure Code, there are only 4 types of cases defined as non-litigation cases as stipulated in the Civil Procedure Code, namely, cases concerning property with absence of ownership, debt, loss of check, and bankruptcy procedure are filed under non-litigation procedure. In reality, for bankruptcy settlement, a litigation fee still will be charged in accordance with the 'dispute value'. Although the Supreme People's Court regulates that only 100 Yuan is charged for each case filed under special procedure,[474] in practice the courts are not satisfied with such small fee amounts compared with the court fees charged in accordance with the *Regulation on Litigation Cost (1989)* based on 'dispute value' and therefore always charge additional court fees[475] and violate the regulation. Many

[469] The non-litigation procedure is regulated in Chapter 17, 18 and 19 of Civil Procedure Code.

[470] In Taiwan, for example, for a case disposed in the first instance with "dispute value" of 6 million Taiwanese Yuan, the court fee will be 60,000 Taiwanese Yuan; whereas for a non-litigation case disposed with the same "dispute value", the court fee amount only to 1,113 Taiwanese Yuan, which is approximately 1.8% of the court fee under litigation procedure. See, Art. 2, Taiwan "Litigation Fee Act for Civil Cases", Art. 102, "Non-Litigation Case Act".

[471] See, Art. 71, Art. 100, Art. 101 of Taiwan "Non-Litigation Case Act".

[472] See Art. 81-96 of Taiwan "Non-Litigation Case Act"; Chapter 1, 3rd Edition of Japan "Non-Litigation Procedure Law".

[473] Art. 187, 317 of Taiwan "Corporate Law", Art. 81 of Taiwan "Non-Litigation Case Act"; No. 3 of Art. 254 of Japanese "Commercial Law" and Art. 126 of Japan "Non-Litigation Procedure Law".

[474] Art. 132, 134 of "Opinion of the Supreme People's Court on Litigation Fee".

[475] In an example reported in "Shanghai Legal Press", two Bank checks were stolen and the firm announced publicly

non-litigation cases are converted into litigation procedure and court fees are collected according to the standard of litigation cases.

3. The Cost of Realizing the Right of Mortgage

A high cost is incurred in liquidating security of title. The effectiveness of the Security Act in October 1995 and the Auction Act in January 1997 is a further reform in the legal system in China, which was intended to promote economic exchange and economic efficiency, but the realization of mortgage rights incurs a very high cost to the creditor. According to the Security Act, it is not legally effective for both parties to agree in advance, that the ownership of the mortgaged subject will be transferred to the creditor if the debtor is unable to pay the credit back.[476] The disposal of the subject can only be made after the debtor is unable to pay the debt due. In case of the debtor's failure to pay the debt due and rejection of reaching an agreement with the creditor on how to sell and auction the mortgaged subject, the creditor must first go to the courts for litigation. The compulsory execution will then be made after the judgment.[477] The sale of the title will not be conducted by the court directly, it must be first assessed by a asset-assessment company appointed by the court and then put up for auction through an auction company. In such a long and complicated procedure, the creditor must pay a litigation fee, an assessment fee, an auction fee, and a fee for compulsory execution, thus the total cost of realization of the mortgage is great in this respect.

If the concerned title of the mortgage is a "state owned asset", the assessment must be done even before the mortgage, and it must be done again in case of auction. The procedure of assessment must go through complicated procedures by government authorities.[478] The fee paid to the assessment company is similar to the fee paid to the court based on the "property

through the court. The court fees, as per "Opinion of the Supreme People's on Litigation Fee", should be 100 Yuan for supervision, and 600 Yuan for the public announcement. But when the date for announcement expired, the court asked the firm to pay 20,548 Yuan according to *"Regulation on Litigation Cost (1989)"*, otherwise the bank checks would not be released. As a result, the actual court fees incurred were over 200 times of the court fees charged under non-litigation procedure.

[476] Art. 40 of Security Act.

[477] Art. 40, 53 of Security Act; Art. 207, Civil Procedure Code (1991).

[478] The procedure includes feasibility research, approval, and confirmation through the firm, the local government, and the State Assets Management Committee, asset-assessment firm. The work of assessment is a specially-approved business and it is very common to have more than 2 firms involved in the assessment, each firm may be only granted to assess some of the items such as patent, trademark, portfolio, real estate.

value".[479]

Such a complicated and lengthy procedure in the security business incurs not only a high cost to the creditor, but also delays in providing speedy redressal for he litigant.

4. High Transaction Cost in Bankruptcy Procedure

There exists a high transaction cost in the bankruptcy procedure with respect to duration and cost. The procedure of liquidation of the bankrupt firm is the same as the procedure for security of title. In case of liquidation, settlement fees shall be paid first.[480] In many cases, after deducting various fees, the remaining value is even insufficient to cover the cost incurred by the court, the law firm, audit firm, assessment firm and the auction firm.[481] The creditors (mainly the banks) have little possibility to be compensated. For example, 111 firms in Liao Nin Province went bankrupt during the years of 1995 and 1996, the creditors of the 88 firms did not have any cash available from the bankruptcy, only small proportions of the assets were available from the 23 bankrupt firms. The lowest proportion of assets available was 0.0075% of the amount of credit and the highest was 8.4%. Due to the various costs incurred in the process, the compensation available to the creditors is normally very small. As reported, in a bankruptcy procedure against a fertilizer firm in Hu Bei Province, the cost charged by authorities, mostly as mentioned above, was more than 1 million Yuan, which was 17% of the total value being assessed, 90% of the creditors (without priority in the compensation scheme) have little chance to be compensated after the cash or assets are distributed to the authorities and creditors with priority.[482]

Furthermore, in the case concerning security of title and bankruptcy, these non-litigation cases are often changed into litigation cases in case of disputes among the parties. The civil process is lengthy and incurs high costs to the parties involved. Following complicated assessment procedures in the name of strict administration by the local government, various

---

[479] For example, in a mortgage agreement of 1 million, the fee for assessment is around 15,000 Yuan.

[480] The fee paid for liquidation of the assets.

[481] It is therefore a contradict and an inefficient solution if the transaction cost for bankruptcy procedure is too high. On one hand, if the firm applies for bankruptcy, the remaining asset will be used up to pay different costs in bankruptcy procedure; on the other hand, if the firm does not apply bankruptcy procedure, the assets of the firm may fade out.

[482] See "Investigation Report on Merger and Bankruptcy in Some Provinces and Cities (1996)" by the State Economy & Trade Department & Bank of China: in: Handbook for Optimizing Capital Structure in Cities for Test, China Economy Publication, 1996, p. 291.

fees have to be paid to the relevant authorities such as the courts, the assessment firms, the auction firms and the law firms. Such complicated procedures and regulations can be explained as rent-seeking behaviors of these parties, as the assets should be used to compensate the creditors, mainly the banks. These regulations and complicated procedures will only increase transaction costs to the society and the market economy, but do no benefit the market itself.

5. Fees in respect to Application for Security of Title and Law Enforcement

In case of application for security of asset, the fee is calculated based on the value of the asset[483] and the fee must be prepaid, otherwise the court will take necessary measures to secure the asset. All costs incurred in the investigation, lien, safekeeping and the cost of the guarantor will be on the account of the applicant. Thus, the cost incurred will be far higher than the application fee.

With respect to execution of judgment, the fee is calculated based on the value of the asset as applied by the applicant. In practice, some courts collect the fee before the execution and some collect the fee after the execution. The actual cost will be much higher if the enforcement further requires assessment of assets and auction.

6. Lawyer's Fee

a) Legal Service in China

Lawyer's fees are a disputable issue in today's litigation process. On one side, there is a tendency of increased filings and as a result the need for legal service is increasing. As most of the people still lack adequate legal knowledge to conduct the civil procedure, legal service is therefore very important for the protection of the procedural and substantive rights of the parties; on the other side, lawyers' fees have scared poorer parties who simply cannot afford for the service.

In the civil process in China, lawyers' engagement is still low. In 1991, among the 2,448,200 cases filed in the courts of first the instance, only 9.4% (226,900 cases) were engaged with

483 Art. 8 of *Regulation on Litigation Cost (1989)*.

lawyers; in 1992, among the 2,601,000 cases filed in the courts of the first instance, 15.2% (396,300 cases) were engaged with lawyers; in 1993, the rate of cases with lawyers' engagement increased to 16%.[484] By contrast, in Japan, where people have also a traditional fear of litigation, 86.1% of the cases were engaged with lawyers.[485]

The low rate of demand for lawyers in China is affected by the quantity of the supply and the quality of the services, as well as the lawyers' fees. First, lawyer, as a profession, was reestablished in the beginning of 1980's and the availability of lawyers was limited. In 1998 the number of lawyers was 101,220 and among them only 51,008 was engaged in the profession on a full time basis.[486]. Lawsuits are often conducted without the engagement of lawyers. Secondly, the quality of legal services has also affected the attitudes of the general public towards the legal profession. High quality means high possibility for the parties to realize their legal rights, and parties will ask for legal service when they foresee the benefit from lawyers' engagement. Generally speaking, lawyers in China do not enjoy good fame. In litigation, lawyers' personal contacts and relationships with the courts is very decisive in many cases. Lawyers also serve as middlemen to bribe judges. As a consequence, if the lawyer is regarded only as a middleman for bribery, the engagement of lawyers will only increase litigation costs to the parties involved. The moral crisis, bribery, cheating and malicious competition among the lawyers have heavily hurt the reputation of the profession in the past few years. Third, lawyer as a profession does not monopolize the sector of legal service as all procedure law in China allows individuals to represent the parties in civil process,[487] thus the parties rely less on the legal service provided by the lawyers.

b) Method of Charging Lawyers' Fee

The method in charging fees against the parties involved in the cases can be summarized as follows:

a. Per case principle

b. Per hour principle

[484] Source compiled from China Law Year Book, 1995.

[485] Hirto Miyake, Comparative Analysis of the Reform of Civil Procedure, Japanese Report, in Conference on Civil Justice in the Era of Globalization, Japan 1992.

[486] Source: China Judicial Administration Year Book, 1999, China Law Press 2000, p. 579.

[487] Art. 56 of Civil Procedure Code (1991).

c. Fixed charge principle

d. Per value principle (2～8%)

e. Per agreement

f. Reasonable share of some costs when litigation takes place in other places.

The standard of lawyer's fees is based on the *Regulation on Lawyers' Fee* and *Standard of Lawyer's Fee* promulgated in 1990. The previous fixed rate is regarded as too low and would frustrate the legal service, thus in 2000, a directive was promulgated[488] to allow the local judicial administrations in the provinces to set their own standards according to the economic development of the regions and the demand/supply of the local market. Table 4.3 reveals local regulations on the standards of lawyers' fee in Fujian, Shanghai, Shengzhen, and Shangdong provinces. According to the new regulation, lawyers can charge fees based on the local standards and the economic status of the parties. The fees can be flexible but must be in line with the directive.
For example, in Fujian Province, a new regulation[489] has been effective from 1st of April 2002. Lawyers can charge lawyers' fees according to local regulations. The rate can be based on per case, 'dispute value', per hour, or in accordance with the agreement made by the lawyers and the parties involved. The fees shall be in line with the guiding rate as stipulated in the regulations. Furthermore, it allows the lawyers and the parties to negotiate the rate according to the market.

According to Table 4.3, lawyers can charge rates below the limit as stipulated by the local judicial administrations. However, high rate lawyers' fees are an obstacle for 'access to justice' since the cost is a great burden to the litigants. The charge of 1,000 Yuan (approximately US$121) or more per hour is unbearable for the litigants when taking the average income of most people into account.[490] For many people with incomes below 2,000 Yuan in China, such high rates are criticized by most of the people as too high and unacceptable. Therefore, a reasonable cost scheme should take the income level of the people

[488] See Notification on Temporary Standard of Lawyers' Fees to be regulated by the Local Administration, by the State Plan and Development Committee and the Ministry of Justice, 2000.
[489] Regulation on Lawyers' Legal Service and Fees in Fujian Province, on 1st April, 2002.
[490] Xiamen Daily, 'Today's Focus', p. 3, 22.08.2002.

into account and meanwhile legal aid should be granted to the poor to obtain legal service.

Table 4. 3 Lawyer's Fees regulated in Fujian, Shanghai, Shengzhen, Shangdong

Case / Type/ Region		Fujian	Shanghai	Shengzhen	Shangdong
Criminal cases (Yuan/Case)	Investigation Phase	< 3000 or per hour	< 2000	2000 – 10,000	50 - 1000
	Litigation Phase	< 3000 or per hour	< 4000	2500 - 12000	500 - 3000
	Judgment Phase	< 8000 or per hour	< 8000	3000 – 15,000	1000 - 6000
Civil Cases (Yuan/Case)	Non-Property related	500 - 3000	< 5000	2000 - 5000	500 - 5000
	'dispute value' under 100,000 Yuan	500 - 3000	< 2%	3000 - 5000	< 4%
	100,000 – 1 million Yuan	< 2.5%	< 1.5%	2.5% - 8%	3%
	500,000 – 1 million Yuan	2%	-	-	-
	1 million - 5 million	1.5%	< 1%		1%
	5 million – 10 million	1%	<0.75%		
	10 million – 50 million	0.5%			
	Above 50 million	0.25%			
Administration Cases (Yuan/Case)	Non-property related	500 - 3000	< 5000	1500 - 15000	500 – 3000
	Property related	As per the standards in civil cases (property related)			
Fee Per hour (Yuan/Per hour)		Min. 100 Max. 1000	Max. 3000		

Source: Comparison of Lawyers Fees, in: Xiamen Daily, 22.08.2002.

The above study indicates the high litigation costs incurred in the civil process and that the parties involved are burdened by the various cost of litigation. Lawyers' fees appear to be high considering the income level of the people in China, partly contributing to the shift of burden of proof to the parties in recent procedural reform by the courts in order to relieve workloads and expenditures in investigations. This raises the question: are the courts in a budget shortage and thus rely heavily on the income from charging the litigation cost? To answer this question, the following is an attempt to analyze the budget supply of the courts based on the data available from the High Court of Jiangxi Province.

IV. A Survey of Judiciary Budget in Jiangxi Province

The input of the state in its judicial system will strongly affect the efficiency and output of justice. To guarantee justice for the people, the state should invest more in the legal system.[491] The problem of budget autonomy in Chinese courts is serious. According to one investigation made by a people's representative, of 1,423 courts (39.98% of the total courts in China), most are county courts and District Courts, have problems providing a stable salary to personnel. 122,403 persons could not be paid their salary on time.[492] Many local administrations cannot provide enough of a budget to the local courts due to financial stress. The budget shortage is one of the reasons that courts always charge additional cost to the parties and create more rent-seeking and corruptive activities. Moreover, lower courts cannot undertake reform measures in administration, case flow management and establishment of computer systems, and personnel management due to the shortage of budget. The efficiency of the courts cannot be improved given the current conditions.

In this context, based on the data from the High Court of Jiangxi province, this part is to analyze the input of the state and to investigate whether or not the supply from the state is adequate to secure minimum justice and to what extent the judicial cost (in case of insufficient input) affects the duration of the courts.

A well-functioning judicial system will incur high judicial costs arising from judicial activities, investment in facilities of the courts, personnel and operating costs in connection with the jurisdiction. It has been a problem in China that the courts have to rely on the fiscal budget arranged by the local governments[493]. In reality, the budget appropriated by the local administration is normally insufficient for the operating of the court system. To cover the judicial cost, the courts have to rely on the income of court fees charged to the litigants. However, for most of the courts, the local budget and the income from litigation fees cannot

[491] Schaefer H.-B., „Kein Geld für die Justiz – Was ist uns der Rechtsfrieden wert", in DRiZ, 1995, p. 461.

[492] Investigation made by Gu, Zhao Sheng, Report from Lower Courts, in People's Court Daily, on 14.03.2002.

[493] According to the Chinese Budget Act, the local government in each hierarchy shall keep the balance of its budget. Therefore the local courts depend mainly on the budget appropriation of the local governments.

cover the expenditure of the courts. Such problems are obvious in many provinces where the fiscal income is low and economic development is still backward compared with the provinces in the coastal area.

The shortage of judicial costs strongly affects the speed of the trial and may lead to court delay and low quality of judiciary.[494] The following is to illustrate the problem of the judiciary budget from the central and local governments based on the data available from the High Court of Jiangxi Province and analyze how the judicial costs could affect justice and efficiency of the courts.

1. An Anatomy of Income: Budget, Non-budget Income and Expenditures

The income of the courts mainly comes from the appropriation of the local governments (budget income) and the charging of litigation fees (non-budget income).

As indicated in Table 4.4, during the 4 years from 1997 to 2000 the fiscal appropriation (budget income) for the courts in the whole province increased by an average of 28.63% annually, non-budget income (mainly litigation fees)[495] increased by an average of 3.71% annually, the average increase in total income was about 12.93% annually; compared with the annual average increase of 10.35% of the courts' expenditure, the increase rate of income was 2.58% higher than the increase in the expenditure.[496] However, the income still cannot cover the expenditure of the courts, in the four years from 1997 to 2000, expenditures and income had an average gap of 5.66% despite the increase in budget supply for the local governments and the non-budget income. The sum of the gap was normally the debts relating to construction of court buildings, vehicles and communication equipment. The creditors were normally the construction companies and the local banks.

[494] The cost-saving policy of the state in judiciary with respect to lower budget and less personnel would endanger the quality of judiciary and cause a longer duration of civil process. See: Franzen/Apel, Prozessaufwand bei Gericht und Anwalt – betriebswirtschaftlich und anschaulich – mit Folgerungen, NJW 1988, p. 1062.

[495] Such income mainly comes from the litigation fees, confiscations, fines, etc..

[496] The fiscal income increases 10% in average each year in this province.

Table 4. 4 The Operating Cost of the Courts in Jiangxi Province from 1997 to 2000

Currency Unit: million Chinese Yuan

Fiscal Year	Fiscal Appropriation / Budget Income	Other Income / Non-budget Income	Income Total	Operating Expenditures					The gap between the total income and total expenditure
				Personnel Costs	Administration Costs	Costs in Connection with judgment	Construction Costs	Total Expenditure	
1997	64.512	123.00	187.512	57.177	40.721	74.593	35.769	208.26	-20.748
1998	79.09	142.188	221.278	69.376	49.58	77.539	38.70	235.195	-13.917
1999	97.854	163.043	260.897	86.168	54.20	86.084	37.555	264.007	-3.11
2000	136.718	131.849	268.567	113.133	54.056	102.183	10.165	279.537	-10.97

Source: compiled from the data from the High People's Court of Jiangxi Province[497]

Non-budget income, mainly from the charging of litigation fees, plays an essential role for the functioning of the courts since this part of the income consists of a big proportion of the total income of the courts. Table 4.5 reveals the proportion of income in the courts of Jiangxi province.

Table 4. 5 The Proportion of Non-budget and Budget Income of the Courts in Jiangxi Province

Year	Budget income (million Yuan)	Non-Budget Income (million Yuan)	Total Income (million Yuan)	Percentage of Non-budget income	Percentage of Budget income
1997	64.512	123.00	187.512	65.6%	34.3%
1998	79.09	142.188	221.278	64.3%	35.7%
1999	97.854	163.043	260.897	62.5%	37.5%
2000	136.718	131.849	268.567	49.1%	50.9%

Source: compiled from data from High People's Court of Jiangxi Province[498]

[497] See Investigation Report of Budget Guarantee of the Courts in Jiangxi Province, by Xue, Jiang Wu and Zhang, Yong Ling (High People's Court of Jiangxi), in: People's Judiciary (8) 2001, pp. 37-40.
[498] Ditto.

The table shows that the non-budget income (mainly from litigation fees) had a big proportion in the total income. The proportion was 65.6% in 1997, 64.3% in 1998, 62.5% in 1999 and 50.9% in 2000 respectively. This result shows that the courts are heavily dependent upon the income from litigation fees for its daily operations, in the meantime, it reveals another problem, namely, that the budget from local governments is low and the litigants are heavily burdened in the civil process.

2. The Effect of Low Budget

The investigation in Table 4.4 and Table 4.5 shows that the fiscal budget cannot cover the actual expenditures. The courts sometimes even cannot pay salaries and other benefits to the personnel in time. In general, the fiscal arrangement from the local governments can only secure the basic salary, whereas the position subsidy and medical insurance have to rely on the non-budget income. At the end of 2000, of 112 courts of the province, 87 courts (77.68% of the total courts) didn't have enough money to pay employee salaries due; among which 77 courts (68.75% of the total courts) could not pay the subsidy and allowances due, 10 courts (8.9% of the total courts could not pay both the basic salary and the subsidy/allowances due; 3736 persons were affected by the shortage of budget in the lower courts of this province.[499]

In addition, due to the shortage of budget, the functioning ability of the courts is weakened. For example, normally the administration costs of the courts shall be higher than those of local administrations,[500] but in the fiscal budget this part is not sufficiently appropriated, especially in the lower courts like district courts and county courts. The average expenditure per person is around 34,000 Yuan/Year in High People's Court, 30,000 Yuan/Year in the intermediate courts and even less than 20,000 Yuan/year in the district/county courts (this average is far below the average level for the whole country). Among the 100 lower courts, only 9 courts have the average expenditure of more than 25,000 Yuan/year, with which the normal running of the courts can be guaranteed; 30 courts have an average expenditure of

---

[499] The courts lacked 13.98 million Yuan to pay these costs. See Xue, Jiang Wu and Zhang, Yong Ling, An analysis and thinking of the problem of court budget, in People's Judiciary (8) 1999, p. 39.

[500] Normally the administration cost shall double the cost of the local government administration body, since the courts have to deal with much more documents, mailing and organization etc..

nearly 20,000 Yuan/year and the operational cost is very tight in these courts. 61 courts have an average of less than 16,000 Yuan/year. The tight budget has impeded the courts' capability to dispose cases.[501]

Furthermore, the fund for the construction of court buildings and facilities for most of the courts does not come from the fiscal budget of the local governments, but from other sources of income (litigation fees, loans from banks). In the whole province, only 7% of the courts receive funds from fiscal appropriation by local governments.[502] Poor office facilities, insufficient court tribunals and backward communication equipment in most of the courts have affected the filing process and the judgment speed.[503] Insufficient fiscal supply to the courts with respect to office building, vehicles, communication systems, and uniforms is the main reason for the courts' debts. Most of the courts are unable to pay the costs of construction of court facilities (mainly the court buildings) to the construction companies. 90% of the debts of the courts are related to the construction of office buildings. According to the statistics, the court system the province owes a debt of US$120 million Yuan.

3. The Allocation Problem of Fiscal Budget and Non-budget Income

According to the regulation referred to as "income and expenditure in separated account",[504] litigation fees charged by the courts shall be turned over to the financial department of the local government and will be re-allocated to the courts according to the situation of the courts in combination with the fiscal budget, but in reality the fiscal budget is not enough to cover

---

[501] Supra note 499.

[502] Ditto.

[503] Some courts even had to rent office building. Many courts, especially the county courts, face great difficulties in judicial work due to the lack of office building. In the investigation, Xunwu Court rented office building for long time, although the architecture design for their office building was ready, no money was available for starting the constriction. The construction of the office building of the court in the Fuliang County has been undergone for many years, but it was interrupted due to the lack of money and debt owed to the constructing firms, amounting to 100,000 Yuan. The construction of office building of the court in Xishan County took 10 years and was completed at last with the collected money from the judges and employees, but the collected money could not be repaid yet. With respect to the court uniforms, 86% of the courts did not have the money to change the old uniforms in the year of 2000. The total debt of the courts (including lower courts and Intermediate People's Court) in Ganzhou City reached an amount of 11.13 million Yuan. On the other hand, most of the courts hadn't enough vehicles and communication systems. The backward facilities cannot meet the requirement of high efficiency required for the judicial work.

[504] This means that the income from litigation fees, the fines, and confiscations, etc., shall be turned over to the local financial department via the designated bank; this part of income will be under the capital management in special account and reimbursed to the courts proportionately; whereas the operational costs of the courts will be appropriated from the local fiscal budgets.

the daily operation cost of the courts. 74% of the courts in the province rely on the litigation fees re-allocated from local governments. The sum reimbursed by the local government will normally be 80% ~ 85% of the litigation fees originally received and transferred by the courts.[505] The sum of the budget and non-budget funds appropriated to the courts is not enough to cover the expenditure of the courts. There are some adverse effects as a result of a such scheme: first, to cover the gap, the courts try to find other sources of income by charging excessive fees which violate the regulations or even accepting donations; in case of travel, the costs are frequently paid by the parties involved; secondly, bribery and corruption happen very often and increase additional costs to the parties involved; thirdly, as the returned sum depends on the amount of litigation fees paid to the courts, thus the courts have the incentive to increase the amount by receiving more filings, on some occasions, judges even violates procedural and substantive legitimacy by looking for filings.[506]

Moreover, problems exist in the distribution of state subsidies. To balance the operation cost of the courts, the central government and the financial branch of the province increases special subsidies to the courts to cover the gap. In 1999 special subsidies totaling a sum of 8.10 million Yuan were appropriated to the courts by the central government and the province; in 2000 the sum increased to 9.60 million Yuan, with an increase of 18.52% compared with that of 1999. However, this appropriation is somewhat misused. The subsidy is appropriated by the central government first to the province and then from the province to the local governments, but at the provincial level, the subsidy is often mixed together with the fiscal budget as a bundle of appropriation, therefore the courts are not always properly informed about the time and respective amounts to be appropriated. In some counties, part of the subsidy is detained by the county governments for other purpose of financial arrangements. For instance, the courts in Shang Rao and Ying Tan City only received 1.86 million Yuan from the 2 million Yuan subsidy in 2000, whereas in Jiu Jiang City, only 4 counties received the full amount, the other counties did not receive the full amount of appropriation.[507]

505 According to the regulation issued by the Supreme People's Court, 70% of the litigation fees charged by the courts shall be turned over to the financial department of the local governments and should be repaid to the courts according to the situation of each court.

506 Zhang, Wei Ping, Review on Judicial Reform, China Judiciary Publication, 2002, Vol. 4, p. 154.

507 In the investigation, the subsidy for 3 counties were severely discounted, in one county (Xingzi) only 290,000 Yuan of the 600,000 Yuan was appropriated by the financial branch of the local county government.

4. Low Budget and Accessibility of Justice

From the empirical study it is obvious to see some consequences of the shortage of financial supply in judicial activities. The shortage of budget for the courts has affected the daily work of the jurisdiction. For those lower county courts and some village tribunals, due to bad facilities, simple offices, lack of personnel and travel fees, cases were often delayed or just settled without careful investigation. It is unlikely that quality of the jurisdiction can be guaranteed and justice be assured.

According to statistics, the courts in Jiangxi province had a deficit of 3.87 million Yuan in travel costs in 2000 and 2.2 million Yuan in medical insurance for the court's personnel. The low level of income coupled with disqualified social welfare and an overload of work have diminished the enthusiasm of the judges. Judges have different income levels in different provinces, regions, hierarchies of the courts. Low salaries in the poor provinces may increase rent-seeking or corruptive behavior.

The absence of budget autonomy further leads to localism of jurisdiction, since the courts have to rely on the budget from the local administration and the level of budget is dependent upon the development of the local economy, consequently, the courts are inclined to protect the local economic interest in its jurisdiction and on the other side the jurisdiction is easily and unavoidably interfered with by the local administration. Under such circumstances, it is very difficult to realize judicial independence and justice in the judiciary, as well as the uniform rule of law.

V. Findings and Suggestions

In this chapter an investigation was made of the problem of litigation costs, which includes various court fees and lawyers' fee, as referred to as private cost, and an empirical study on the problem of judicial cost, referred as public cost, based on the investigation of all of the lower courts in Jiangxi Province.

The civil process in China incurred high costs. In the litigation, the parties normally have to consider at least 15% ~ 20% of the claimed amount to pay court fees and lawyer's fees, etc. High process costs impede the accessibility of justice and diminish the value of judiciary.

The operation of the justice apparatus relies heavily on the income from court fees. As indicated in Table 4.5, non-budget income, mainly from court fees, shares more than 60% of the total income. In a state rule of law, it is necessary to reduce the burden of the litigation and enhance accessibility of justice, but under the current financial capabilities of the state and the local governments, it is very difficult to shift part of the litigation cost to the state by increasing the local budget and state subsidies. Reduction of litigation cost will affect the functioning of the courts since court fees are still the main source of income of the courts under the current budget arrangement.

Furthermore, low budget appropriated by the local governments and the reliance of budget on local governments result in a low level of income and social welfare. Low income levels of the judges further frustrates the enthusiasm of the judges. In such an environment, rent-seeking behavior, corruption and localism in jurisdiction are more likely to happen, for instance, the courts will have incentive to charge additional litigation costs from the parties and thus increase the burden of the parties. The shortage of budget may further have an impact on the daily judicial work of the courts and causes delay in the courts.

The reform should be aimed to provide sufficient budget to the judiciary and reduce the burden on the parties so as to improve accessibility of justice. It is necessary for the state to provide more financial support to the courts especially in provinces which have comparatively less fiscal income. Put concretely, more financial support and salary increases should be considered for the courts.

Chapter 5

The Problem of Enforcement of Judgments by the Courts

If substantive law is adapted and continued according to technical and economic growth, if approaching the courts is easy, and if the procedures are fair and fast and law enforcement is swift, then all these factors would lead to comparatively low costs in using the market and enable, in many cases, the emergence of markets which do not rely on trust and reputation, but are based on anonymous transactions. If these conditions are missing, the use of the market will be cumbersome and the decisions for allocation of goods have to be made to some extent by other institutions like hierarchies or political processes in which other forms of transactions costs will surface.[508] *(Schaefer)*

I. Introduction

Law enforcement, as the last stage of the civil procedure, not only directly affects the rights of the parties, but also the respect for law and the authority of the courts, as well as social stability and economic development. The goal of judgment is to define legal rights among the parties, whereas enforcement of court orders is to realize legal rights, from this point of view, enforcement procedure is the continuation of trial procedure. Law enforcement and its legislature forms an important part of the civil procedure law. The realization of legal rights by law enforcement not only concerns the functioning of the courts, but also the protection of legal rights and the authority of the judiciary.

This chapter investigates the problems existing in law enforcement in China. The study will first address the organization of law enforcement in China and the reasons for, as well as difficulties in, law enforcement. It is publicly known that law enforcement has become the most serious problem in the judiciary and has been a bottleneck for legal development in

[508] Schaefer, H.-B., The Significance of a Well-Functioning Civil Law in the Process of Development, Paper presented at the Conference of the Latin Americans Law and Economics Association in Quito (Ecuador) June 15th to June 17th 1998, Manuscript, 1998, p. 4.

China. As old and new problems overlap under the market economy, the problem of enforcement becomes a long-lasting and troublesome problem facing the courts. Often, people in China refer to those court orders/decrees, which are not able to be enforced or simply treated as 'settled' by the courts due to impossibility of enforcement, as legal "blank notes". Meanwhile, based on the investigation report of the High People's Court of Chongqing,[509] 45 civil cases[510] filed for execution by court orders/decrees were selected to show the average duration of enforcement and to illustrate that the level of economic development has a great impact on court efficiency in respect to enforcement of law. Furthermore, this chapter will make a critical evaluation of the current enforcement laws and regulations.

It shall be mentioned that the study of enforcement of judgment is based on information gained from different sources since the statistics about enforcement of judgments is fragmentary and not systematically recorded by judicial statistics.[511]

II. The Organization of Enforcement and Procedure

Before addressing the problems existing in law enforcement and the difficulties encountered, it is necessary to review the organization of law enforcement in China.

1. Enforcement Procedure

The procedure of enforcement of court orders/decrees is incorporated into the Civil Procedure Code and forms an important part of the code. The current Chinese compulsory enforcement mechanism is regulated in Section 3 of Civil Procedure Code and is divided into 4 chapters with 30 articles, which includes General Rules, Application and Assignment, Measures, Suspension & Expiration, etc. In 1998, the Supreme People's Court issued judicial

[509] This is an unpublished internal report provided by the Supreme People's Court. See *Investigation Report* about the implementation of *the Regulation on Strict Implementation on Time Limit (2000)*, by the Research Team of Chongqing High People's Court, 2001.

[510] In the investigation, 73 cases filed for enforcement were selected by the Chongqing High People's Court to study the duration of enforcement and for comparison. Among the 73 cases, 45 cases were civil cases.

[511] Only since 1993, the official statistics in China Law Year Book revealed the number of settlement in law enforcement, whereas no information was available in respect to filing and the settlement ratio.

interpretation[512] on enforcement based on summarized experiences.

According to the Civil Procedure Code (1991), the trial courts are responsible for the enforcement of court orders with respect to civil cases;[513] furthermore, the enforcement of judgments should be undertaken by executors.[514] In practice, the judges, who make the court orders or decisions, normally undertake enforcement of court orders/decisions.[515] 'Executor' is another name for the judge, who is also responsible for the enforcement, delivery of writ, court records, etc. The problem of enforcement arises when the workload of the courts increases, as was the case in the 1990's, due to the increased caseload, causing the filings for enforcement to pile up in the courts.

Besides, if the respondent is outside of the limits of the territory of jurisdiction, the trial court (principal court) can assign the court order/decision to be executed by the court where the respondent is located (agent court) and the entrusted local court shall assist in the enforcement of judgment within 15 days.[516] The regulation is to save on travel costs and reduce the burden of complainants when the execution of court orders concerns parties in different territories of jurisdiction.[517] Thereupon, the entrusted court (agent court) shall enforce court orders/decrees from the principal court in the same manner as if it was a court order/decree made by it's self.

By contrast, Germany operates a system within which specialized agents (Gerichtsvollzieher) have a certain degree of independence, and have responsibility for certain aspects of enforcement,[518] while other aspects of enforcement are entrusted to a court officer (Rechtpfleger).[519] The courts with territorial competence are the Amtsgerichte[520] for the place

[512] The Supreme People's Court: *Regulation on the Enforcement of Judgments, No. 15 (1998)* Legal Interpretation.

[513] Art. 207 of Civil Procedure Code.

[514] Art. 208 of Civil Procedure Code.

[515] According to the People's Court Organization Act 1954, the courts not only adjudicate the case, but also execute the court orders/decisions by itself due to the few filings in the 1950s. Most of the civil cases were settled by mediation or arbitration rather than by adjudication. The adjudication of cases and enforcement of court orders/decisions thus were under the same tribunal. See He, Lan Jie / Lu, Min Jian (eds.), Judiciary in Contemporary China, Contemporary China Publication, 1993, p. 297.

[516] Art. 209 II, Civil Procedure Code (1991).

[517] The Supreme People's Court: *Some Opinions on the Application of Civil Procedure Code, 1992.* Art. 254 - 265

[518] The Gerichtsvollzieher has primary responsibility for execution against movable property and negotiable instruments, and for obtaining the delivery up of possession of movable and immovable property. See §§ 808 ff ZPO, § 57 GVGA and §§ 883 ff ZPO.

[519] The Rechtpfleger has, *inter alia*, responsibility for the local and register, and for seizures of immovable property as well as authorizing garnishment of debts. He also plays a role in guardianship and succession cases, and has recently taken on extensive responsibilities in relation to insolvency proceedings. See German Rechtspflegergesetz (RPflG) § 2 and § 3.

[520] Amtsgerichte are the district courts in Germany, which deal with small claims and family matters.

where enforcement is to take place, i.e. the debtor has his domicile or where the assets are situated. Whereas in the US, the law enforcement body is not subordinated to the courts, instead, the State administration is responsible for the execution of judgments.

2. Enforcement Basis

The basis for enforcement is effective court decisions / orders, arbitration awards and notarized claim rights.[521]

3. Measures of Enforcement

The main measures of enforcement include:

- inquiry, seizure, and freezing of the assets of the debtor;
- transfer deposit of the debtor, detaining and distilling the income of the debtor;
- sealing, seizure, freezing, auction, and sale of the property of the debtor;
- searching for the concealed property of the debtor in their living space or other possible places;
- compulsory liquidation of real estate etc.

4. Major Enactments and Judicial Interpretation with regard to Law Enforcement

Since 1991 several regulations were promulgated by the Supreme People's Court to reinforce the enforcement of law. The increase of enactments and regulations reveals the necessity of enhancing law enforcement, but also reflects the difficulty behind legislation. Table 5.1 shows the relevant regulations related to law enforcement.

The interpretations in 1992 and 1998 from the Supreme People's Court have defined some new measures to cope with the problems existing in enforcement, but these interpretations have not had a positive effect and in some circumstances have even restricted the efficiency

[521] By contrast, under the relevant Spanish law, the categories of enforceable title are comparatively wide. Any private contractual documents can also be used as the basis for enforcement. In France, the French law recognizes a number of types of instruments that allow a creditor to proceed to enforcement. These includes bills of exchange, unpaid checks and unpaid rent arising out of a written contract for the lease of immovable property. See Kennett, Wendy A., Enforcement of Judgments in Europe, Oxford University Press, 2000, p. 69.

in enforcement, since current measures are too old and cannot adapt to social and economic changes in China

Table 5. 1 Main Regulations on Law Enforcement

1991	Civil Procedure Code, Section III, Article. 207-236
1992	Some Opinions On the Application of Civil Procedure Code
1993	Regulation on Authorization of Enforcement between the Courts
1998	Regulation on the Enforcement of Judgments
2000	Regulation on Reinforcing and Improving Agent Enforcement

III. The Problems and Reasons for the 'Difficulty in Law Enforcement'

1. The Problems

Law enforcement has become a bottleneck for the judiciary in China. The situation in the past few years in China can be identified as another form of judicial crisis[522] when large amounts of court orders are unable to be enforced. The public complains about the incompetence of the courts in enforcing judgments and satirize the judgments made by the courts as legal "blank notes".[523] The difficulties in law enforcement have not only become a problem of legal system, but also a problem to society.

According to the statistics of the High Court of Hainan Province, from January to October 1999, the total filings for enforcement in the province amounted to 11,170, with a value of 19.22 billion Yuan. Among the total filings, 3,311 cases were settled, with a value of 3.2 billion Yuan being fully or partly paid to the claimants.[524] There were 7,859 cases still pending. The settlement ratio was only 29.6%.[525] In one of its cities, Haikou,[526] the size of

[522] As Buscaglia defined, "specifically, a judicial crisis begins at the point where backlogs, delays and payoffs increase the cost (implicit and explicit) of accessing the system". Similar to the problem of court delay, piling of filings for enforcement means that the law is unable to provide adequate remedies to the parties. To some extent, the failure of law enforcement is more serious to the public, the public will lose their confidence in judiciary by reducing filing at the courts since the probability of being redressed is low and the costs are high in the civil process.
[523] Liu, Tong Hai and Zhu, Xiao Long, Is the Court Fee Reasonable? in: China Lawyer (12) 2002, p. 40.
[524] Only 16.7% of the claim was compensated. Source: Tan, Shi Gui, Research on Judicial Reform in China, China Law Press, 2000, p. 283.
[525] Ditto.

the backlog in the district courts and intermediate courts amounted to 4,579 cases, the total value concerned amounted to 11.5 billion Yuan, which was around 8 times that of the total fiscal income of the city.[527] These statistics reveal that the law enforcement has become a sharp point of social conflict. The failure of law enforcement led to severe grievances by the creditors. Some of the creditors were not able to support their families or continued the operation of their businesses, some factories even went bankrupt due to the failure of speedy redressal. Parties had to appeal to local governments for help, some even used violent means. The adverse effects are obvious, social stability is affected; the foundation of market economy – trust and safety in trade – is endangered. Furthermore, such 'legal blank notes' have also damaged the respect for the judicial system and the image of the courts.[528]

Similar to the target set for trial, most of the courts have a time bound program for the target settlement ratio[529] for law enforcement. However, achieving the target in law enforcement is very difficult. In official statistics,[530] an average of 23.8% of court decisions/orders cannot be enforced each year,[531] because cases are congested in the courts. For instance, more than 530,000 cases were filed for enforcement at the end of 1998 and the value of the disputes exceeded more than 100 billion Yuan. But this empirical study and interviews show that the situation is even worse in reality. One investigation indicated that at the end of 2000, a piling up of 870,000 court orders/decisions relating to economic disputes were still yet not enforced; the statistics show that around 50% of economic cases cannot be enforced.[532] The situation is much worse for lawsuits between banks and companies, one investigation indicates that the banks won 95% of the lawsuits, but only 15% of them can be enforced.[533] In several interviews, lawyers even reported that only around 20% of the judgments can be successfully

---

526 The Intermediate Court of Haikou city, Hainan province.

527 Tan, Shi Gui, Research on Judicial Reform in China, China Law Press, 2000, p. 283. The fiscal income of the city (Haikou) is around 1.4 billion Yuan in 1998.

528 Quoted from Tan, Shi Gui, Research on Judicial Reform in China, China Law Press, 2000, p. 283.

529 I was told by some courts that the normal targeted settlement ratio was around 65% to 78% of the filings for compulsory execution. Furthermore see Luo, Shu Ping (Director of the Enforcement Bureau of the High People's Court of Si Chuan Province), The Difficulties in Law Enforcement: Difficulties and Chaotic Situation, in China Lawyer, (12) 2002, p. 44.

530 China Law Year Book, 1996 – 1998.

531 Calculation based on China Law Year Book, 1991-2000.

532 Zhang, Wei Ying / Ke, Rong Zhu, "The adverse selection in civil litigation and its interpretation – an empirical study", in (2) 2002 China Social Science, p. 31.

533 Report from the 5th Bejing University New Year Forum on the topic of 'Economic Reform and Social Trust'. In: www.sohu.com 07.01.2003.

enforced[534] and it is believed that the average rate of successful enforcement in all the courts is supposed to be 25 ~ 30%.[535]

The understanding of successful enforcement may vary between the courts, the parties and the lawyers, but nobody can deny the fact that law enforcement has become the most troublesome task of the judiciary and a bottleneck for legal development. Enforcement of judgments, especially relating to economic cases, has become a tough task for the judiciary. As President of the Supreme People's Court. Xiao Yang, said in his address at the 9th People's Congress on 10.03.1999:

"The cases filed at the courts in recent years for enforcement has risen sharply and there is an increasing backlog in law enforcement. It has affected the functioning of the market economy and the realization of justice..."[536]

Due to difficulties in law enforcement, the year 1999 was defined as "Year of Enforcement", and rules[537] was promulgated by the Supreme People's Court to urge the courts nationwide to treat law enforcement as a priority in judiciary work. In 1999, the courts were required to concentrate their efforts to settle the pending cases for enforcement of judgments.

The consequence of failure to enforce the law has a negative effect. "A right without a remedy is not a right". If judgment cannot be enforced, it may induce more breach of contracts as one will conduct behavior opportunistically as not to abide by the contracts when he/she can benefit from a breach of contract or when penalty and legal sanctions would be small or the chances to be caught are weak. As already mentioned, the loss arising from the disorder in the economy and the lack of trust in market transactions causes a reduction in the quota of 10 ~ 20% of the GDP, with indirect and direct economic losses of 585.5 billion Yuan each year, which is equal to 37% of the fiscal income of the state.[538] On the other hand, the rights of creditors are damaged. In some cases it causes loss of property or bankruptcy to the creditors, when they cannot receive remedies for their grievances from the legal system. In

534 These interviews were conducted with several law firms in Xiamen, Beijing and Chongqing.
535 Liu, Tong Hai and Zhu, Xiao Long, Is the Court Fee Reasonable? in: China Lawyer (12) 2002, p. 40.
536 According to the Annual Report of the Supreme People's Court, 1999.
537 *Regulation on Enforcement of Judgments*, by the Supreme People's Court, 1998.
538 Supra note 86.

some instances, it results in a loss of trust in the judicial system by the people causing individuals to replace law enforcement with violent means. Furthermore, potential court-users may reduce demand, as he knows that there is no remedy available even when the judgment is in his favor. In this scenario, the rights of the parties cannot be protected. The social trust system, which is the foundation of the market economy, is in danger since trade is not secure, capital cannot be efficiently allocated, and the economic order is disturbed. It also impedes the uniform rule of law and pride in the law when judgments are satirized as legal "blank notes" of the law. Furthermore it violates the value of justice and equality and is contrary to the principles of rule of law. Thus, the problem of law enforcement not only affects economic development, but also affects social stability.

2. The Reasons behind the Difficulties in Law Enforcement

In practice, there are some obvious reasons behind the difficulties existing in law enforcement:

a) Absence of the Debtors

The debtors disappear during the litigation, thus the writ cannot be delivered. Some companies have no fixed offices and the authorities do not have effective administration in respects to company registration, company profiles, and activities of the company. For example, the debtors were not available in 30% of the cases filed for enforcement in a district court in Kun Ming City of Yun Nan Province; in Quan Zhou city and Zhan Zhou city of Fujian Province, judgments of 40% of the civil cases were made in the absence of debtors. It is difficult for the courts and creditors to find out where the debtors are located.[539]

b) Difficulty in Tracing Property

The current economic system does not function well enough to tackle the problems arising from law enforcement. For example, there are weak supervisory measures against the secret transfer assets by the debtors. Some debtors have several bank accounts. They often use private accounts to evade inquiry, or transfer cash. Some companies arrange artificial

[539] Tan, Shi Gui, Research on Judicial Reform in China, China Law Press, 2000, p. 285.

contracts of security or assignment agreements for their assets like vehicles or land to escape legal liability. Due to the problems existing in commercial administration and lack of cooperation from local banks, sometimes it is difficult for the courts to trace the property of the debtors and the enforcement will take a longer time. However, this problem not only exists in China, but also in Europe, obtaining the information about the debtor is very essential in enforcement of judgments.[540]

c) Non-availability of Assets

In some cases which are related to administration, financial sectors, and enterprises owned by the army,[541] it is difficult for the court order to be respected since the debtor can resist payment even when there are assets available. For example, a trust and investment company belonging to the provincial government rejected payment of the debts it owed, as a result the courts simply were not able to seize the assets and property of the company because of the government's intervention.

d) Rough Legislation and Regulations

In general, the difficulties in law enforcement have their roots in legislature, the economic system, the social environment and the political system.

The regulation on law enforcement is incorporated into the Civil Procedure Code and there is no special legislature with regard to compulsory enforcement. The rough regulations on law enforcement cannot meet the current situation. First, the regulation on law enforcement is not detailed enough and too rough, thus it causes differences in understanding and interpretations in practice; under a rough and ambiguous law, courts lack the necessary and tough measures to cope with repudiation of debts, escape from liability in the form of transfer and concealment property. Additionally, the law does not impose tough sanction on those debtors who resist compliance with the law enforcement. The sanctions are weak and not effective enough to deter unfaithful behavior of those debtors who reject declaration of their property

540 See Kennett, Wendy A., Enforcement of Judgments in Europe, Oxford University Press, 2000, p. 99 ff. It is recommended that, for tracing the immovable property, technological innovation like computerization may be of great help. Internet technology shall be introduced in future and registers shall be open to the general public so that they can get access to the information related to enforcement.

541 In the 1990's, enterprises with military background entered the market and caused disorder to the market economy because they abused their special power to escape taxes, smuggle goods and engage in illegal license trade etc.

or declare it in a fraudulent way. The courts and creditors have to investigate by themselves, sometimes even secretly, to find the property of the debtors. Secondly, there exist many vacancies and gaps in the regulation and many new questions with regard to law enforcement, it is difficult to find accurate answers in the current legislature and judicial interpretations and there are no countermeasures defined by the law.[542] Courts face many difficulties during the investigation of company registrations, business activities of the companies and compulsory seizure, and freezing of assets of the debtors. Also, there are no regulations on coordination among the courts, the administration, the banks and the taxation offices. This results in low efficiency and many restrictions in law enforcement. Moreover, the law contradicts itself in many circumstances, some public sectors reject complying with the law by the application of its' own regulation as an excuse; for instance, a state-owned textile factory may reject the following of the liquidation or reorganization procedure since all measures must be approved by the local governmental industrial bureau.[543] In some cases the governmental administrations will not allow the registration office to suspend or declare bankruptcy of its subsidiaries so as to avoid legal liabilities.[544] The courts simply cannot force them to comply with the law since these public sectors have much more influence in the local government, which often instructs the courts to behave in a certain manner.

e) Corporate System and Bankruptcy

Under a transition economy, the difficulty in law enforcement reflects conflicts of interest in the economy. Most of state-owned corporations experienced a low efficiency under a backward corporate system, which has resulted in large amount of debts. It is beyond the capability of state-owned corporations to liquidate their debts when they are faced with continuous loss. In some cases there are more than ten creditors against one debtor, the creditors would have little hope of being compensated if the debtor is bankrupt. In some cases the firms already had difficulties paying the salaries to its workers. The compulsory measures in these state-owned firms would trigger more unemployment for which the local government

---

542 Qi, Shu Jie, Research on Reform of Civil Procedure Law, Xiamen University Press, 2000, p. 257.

543 Law enforcement is extremely difficult with respect to bankruptcy proceedings, as the local governments very often use their administrative discretion to influence the courts not to enforce the court orders or delay the enforcement in fear of unemployment, or simply because of selfish departmentalism.

544 In China many firms were set up by the local industrial bureaus. Some years ago many firms were even set up by the local customs and the local army for economic purpose. This phenomenon is diminishing after the strong regulations by the government in the recent years.

would not like to see happen. In some cases the state-owned firms have received special funds from the state to resolve financial difficulties within a certain number of years. Capital is frozen under special management and the courts are not able to enforce orders against these firms.

The problems of enforcement also have to do with state policy in recent years, especially in real estate and land development. Thousands of building projects closed down during the crisis, which happened in 1999 as a result of excessive lending in the real estate market. It is much more difficult to enforce the judgments related to real estate due to its complexity and the ambiguity of property right.

f) Debtors' Resistance

Many debtors have a dim view of law and do not honor the court orders/decisions. Legal sanctions are not effective in forcing the debtors to obey the law. Repudiation of debt or denying payment is very common. Some debtors conceal or transfer property secretly, or even save the cash of the firm under private accounts to avoid detection by the courts.[545] As 'piercing the corporate veil' is not a rule in Chinese corporate law, it is difficult for the courts to secure assets which are transferred by the mother company to its subsidiaries strategically before the judgment is made. Some firms even arrange artificial contracts, security and bestowal to escape debts.

Under the current reform scheme of the modern corporate system,[546] many big state-owned firms take advantage of the reform and get rid of the burden of debts by separating the old firm from the new one. Many firms make use of defects in the accounting and auditing systems and leave debts to its old firm, which are valueless, whereas the valuable assets are incorporated into the newly formed entity. Some firms hang their debts on government administrations, which have no assets and will never pay the debts. In some cases, some private enterprises establish subsidiaries to play games with the courts and even escape the debts by means of bankruptcy.[547] In case of bankruptcy, other problems exist, for instance, under reorganization, special arrangement with regard to aftercare of the workers and debts

[545] Qi, Shu Jie, Research on Reform of Civil Procedure Law, Xiamen University Press, p. 250.
[546] The reform began in the early 1990's to restructure the corporate system of state-owned firms, mainly to build up an efficient modern corporate system. Under the reform scheme, many big state-owned firms were reorganized as stock companies, which were listed in the stock market in Shanghai and Shen Zheng.
[547] Qi, Shu Jie, Research on Reform of Civil Procedure Law, Xiamen University Press, p. 251.

will be made under the assistance of local governments. Debts are normally offset by paying a sum of compensation to the dismissed workers; whereas the creditors, like banks or other state-owned firms, have to follow the instructions of the local governments under special arrangements.

g) Localism

Localism is a problem not only in trial, but also in law enforcement. The enforcement of court order requires assistance and the coordination of land registration authorities, banks, taxation offices, and vehicle administrations. In practice, the local authorities like banks, taxation offices, vehicle administration and the local courts of the respondent are normally not active in providing assistance and cooperation if the creditors are from other territories. They typically have a strong bias to protect local economic interest and it is very difficult to enforce court orders.

Furthermore, interference of local governments increases the difficulties in enforcement of law. Some local governments press the courts not to take action against particular firms which are under special protection, especially for big state-owned firms, any liquidation and reorganization would be extremely difficult if there were no consent from the local governments.

h) Weak Sanction and Deterrence

The law is not effective enough to impose sanctions on those debtors who attempt to escape their liabilities by transferring assets before enforcement procedures; meanwhile, there are no effective measures to deter the behavior of the debtors.[548] Due to skepticism about the competence of the courts and the dim view of law, some creditors even use violent means for private enforcement.[549]

i) Organizational Problem and Qualification of the Executor

The courts do not treat the enforcement as a priority and focus much more on trial activities.

[548] Qi, Shu Jie, Research on Reform of Civil Procedure Law, Xiamen University Press, 2000, p. 257.

[549] Violent means against enforcement is also frequent. According to the report from the National Meeting of the Courts in 1999, there were 330 cases of violent resistance against enforcement and more than 400 executors injured from January until Sept. 1999. This is attributed to the dim view of law of the debtors, possible miscarriage of justice, or improper behavior and attitude of the executors in the course of enforcement.

First, most of the courts haven't set up a separate tribunal for law enforcement until only recent years. The Civil Procedure Law only stipulates that 'the District Courts/County Courts and the Intermediate Courts can establish enforcement bodies according to its 'necessity'.[550] Under such regulation, an enforcement tribunal within the court is seen as an option; besides, the law does not even regulate that the Supreme People's Court and the High Courts shall establish such professional institute. The organization of law enforcement differs from court to court, some have a special tribunal to deal with enforcement of court orders/decisions, but in many other courts, judges who adjudicate cases have to enforce the court orders/decisions.[551] Secondly, the position of executor is ambiguous. The management of personnel is according to the relevant regulations in the Judge Act. The executors are only seen as annexed personnel to the courts. Low quality personnel are not competent enough in law enforcement and are one of the main reasons for delay.[552] Some ignore the rights of the creditors and do not perform their duties, some are corrupted and even collude with the respondent. By contrast, in Germany, the qualification of Gerichtsvollzieher is based on a variety of laws; the Gerichtsvollzieher shall work within the court service for at least two years.[553] In Sweden, where the enforcement agency is a part of the State administration, the senior officers shall be qualified lawyers. In Sweden, the enforcement agency appears to operate very efficiently due to high qualification of the personnel and easy access to wide range of public records concerning debtors, although it has some of the problems inherent in bureaucracy. In France, a huissier de justice (the executor) must have a law degree, and in addition must undergo a training period of two years.[554]

Furthermore, organizational limitations with regard to administration and coordination of the courts affect the functioning of law enforcement in China. The courts lack good coordination due to their loose ties with each other and sometimes are even in conflict with each other

---

550 Art. 209 II, Civil Procedure Code (1991).

551 Compare Wu, Dong Yu and Hua, Shi, An Investigation and Comment on the Internal Setup and Categorized Personnel Management of the People's Courts, in: Zhang, Wei Ping, Review on Judicial Reform, Vol. 4, 2002, p. 463, under Footnote 1.

552 According to Mr. Luo, Shu Ping, director of the Execution Bureau of the High Court of Si Chuan province, due to the law quality of the personnel, cases are often delayed by the executors by excuses.

553 The relevant laws include the law on civil servants (Beamtengesetze) and the federal Gerichtsvollziehersordnung (GVO), as well as various state laws on qualifications, training, office management, and aspects of enforcement process. Organizationally, the Gerichtsvollzieher is attached to the Amtgericht, and subject to the direction and control of the President of that court. He is subject to the supervision, but not a direct management, of the court. Whereas the Rechtpfleger is a court administrator who has taken specialized legal training, but need not to have a legal training, as per Rechtspflegergesetz (RPflG) § 2.

554 Kennett, Wendy A., Enforcement of Judgments in Europe, Oxford University Press, 2000, p. 77 ff.

because of localism in the course of enforcement. At the same time, higher courts do not have effective supervision measures to enhance enforcement work in the lower courts, which is strongly influenced by the local administration.

IV. A Survey of Duration of the Enforcement of Judgment

1. Sample Study

In order to find out the average duration of enforcement of court orders/decisions, 45 civil case filings[555] for enforcement were sleeved to reveal the duration of the enforcement. Furthermore, comparison of enforcement among different regions and different hierarchies was made to see the impact of economic development on the success of law enforcement.

2. Average Duration of the Enforcement of Judgment

Table 5.2 reveals the average duration in each phase and the total duration in law enforcement based on random sample of 45 civil case filings. The average duration for enforcement of court order after filing is 105.9 days, 14 cases exceeded the time limit as regulated in Civil Procedure Code,[556] which accounts for 31.1% of the total sample.

Average time consumed for filing (from date of filing for execution till the date when notification was delivered) was 19.5 days; in the phase of preparation for execution (from the date of notification till the date of the first compulsory measure was taken), the average time was 47.1 days; in the phase of compulsory enforcement (from the first compulsory measure taken till the date of compulsory enforcement was completed), the average time was 17.5 days; in the phase of dispute resolution (from the date of dispute was submitted till the date of decision by the collegial panel), it took 0.98 days on average; in the phase of final settlement (from the date of decision made by the collegial panel till the date when the decision was delivered), the average time was 11.9 days.

[555] Supra note 509, 510.

[556] Art. 219 of Civil Procedure Code: 12 months if one of the parties or both are natural persons; 6 months when both parties are firms or organizations.

Table 5. 2 Average Time Consumption in each Phase and Average Duration of Cases. Sample: 45 Civil Case Filings for Enforcement of Judgments

Phase of Civil Cases	Filing	Preparation for Enforcement of Court Orders	Execution	Meeting of the Collegial Panel	Settlement / Court Orders Enforced	Average Duration	No. of Cases exceeding Time Limit	Percentage Of Cases exceeding Time Limit
Duration in Each Phase	19.5	47.1	17.5	0.98	11.9	105.9	14	31.1%

Source: compiled from unpublished internal report provided by the Supreme People's Court, *Investigation Report* about the implementation of '*Regulation on Strict Implementation on Time Limit*', by the Research Team of Chongqing High People's Court, 2001.

Graph 5.1 shows the average time consumed in each phase during enforcement of court orders/decrees

Graph 5. 1 Average Time Consumption in each Phase of Execution

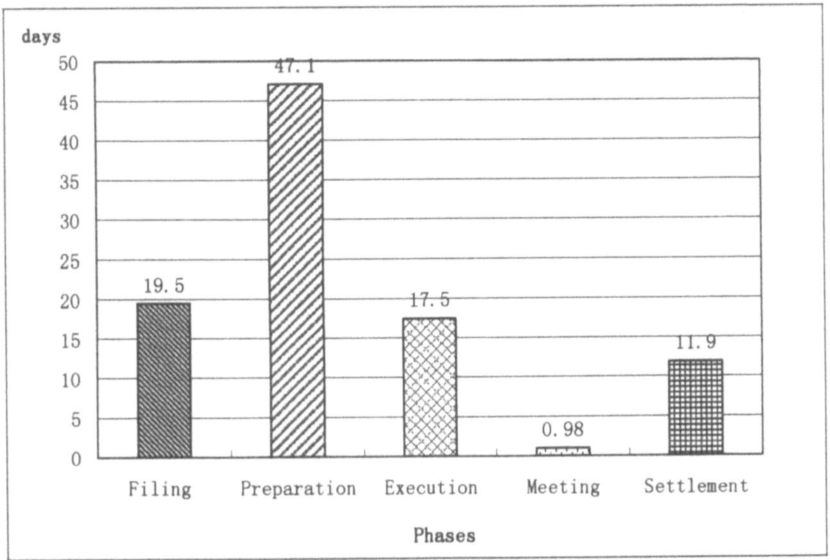

Source: compiled from unpublished internal report provided by the Supreme People's Court, *Investigation Report* about the implementation of '*Regulation on Strict Implementation on Time Limit*', by the Research Team of Chongqing High People's Court, 2001.

The empirical study shows that delays in the enforcement of court orders/decrees in civil cases were serious. Among 45 civil cases, 14 cases were delayed, some cases were 'settled' by the courts simply because the probability of enforcement was seen as being 'small ' or because the time limit was running out. Under the time bound program, judges or executors settle the cases according to the target of settlement ratio instructed by the higher courts.[557] Many lawyers say that only around 20% of their cases can be successfully enforced, whereas most of the cases are delayed or treated as 'settled' when the judges think that the probability of successful enforcement is low or the time limit is running out.[558] In most of the interviews, judges, court police, parties, and lawyers admitted that besides the problem of court delay, enforcement of judgments has become the toughest problem currently facing the judiciary in China.

3. *Comparison: Economic Development and Duration*

a) Comparison between Different Regions

Economic development in China differs from region to region. In the east region, economy performs better than that of the western part and the courts in the east region were functioning better due to a better capacity of the local budget supply, human capital, and people's attitudes towards the rule of law.[559]

Table 5.3 presents the average duration of enforcement of Court Orders in Chongqing Region (West) and Jiang Su Province (East).

Table 5. 3 Comparison of Enforcement of Court Orders in Different Regions

	Average Duration of Law Enforcement (days)	Percentage of Exceeding Time Limit
Chongqing (City)	126	27.3%
Jiang Su Province	76	14.3%

Source: compiled from unpublished internal report provided by the Supreme People's Court, *Investigation Report* about the implementation of '*Regulation on Strict Implementation on Time Limit*', by the Research Team of Chongqing High People's Court, 2001.

Table 5.3 reveals that in the east province of Jiang Su, the duration of enforcement of court

[557] The court can stop enforcing the court orders/decisions when the possibility for enforcement is very little and thus the case is regarded as settled in statistics.
[558] The interviews were made with judges and lawyers in Xiamen City.
[559] Due to the legal education, social and economic environment, people in different regions have different attitudes towards the enforcement of law. In China, the law enforcement further has to do with the effort of the local government. See Xiamen Daily (07.02.2003).

orders was far less than that of western region like Chongqing where economic performance was not as promising compared with the eastern provinces. This indicates that economic development has a strong impact on the duration of enforcement of court orders.

b) Comparison of Courts within the Same Jurisdictional Territory

Even in the same region, the duration of law enforcement differs from court to court under the same territory of jurisdiction. Take 2 regional district courts which are under the jurisdiction Chongqing High Court as an example. Table 5.4 reveals that in the Districts Courts of Bei Pei and Sa Ping Bei, where the economy has a higher development level than the districts of Peng Shui and Wu Long, the duration of enforcement of court orders was much less.

Table 5. 4 Comparison of Law Enforcement in Different District Courts under Jurisdiction of Chong Qing City

	Average Duration of Law Enforcement (days)	Percentage of Exceeding Time Limit
Peng Shui and Wu Long (districts with better economic performance)	74	1.2%
Peng Shui and Wu Long (districts with bad economic performance))	186	33.3%

Source: compiled from unpublished internal report provided by the Supreme People's Court, ***Investigation Report*** about the implementation of '***Regulation on Strict Implementation on Time Limit***', by the Research Team of Chongqing High People's Court, 2001.

In Peng Shui and Wu Long (districts with better economic performance) it took 74 days on average for law enforcement; whereas in Peng Shui and Wu Long (districts with bad economic performance), it took 186 days on average for law enforcement and the percentage of violation of the time limit was higher (33.3%).

The comparison revealed that in a more developed economy, law enforcement will have a higher probability of success because people may have better financial status and are more trustworthy.

V. Critical Evaluation of Current Law Enforcement Mechanism

The difficulty in law enforcement has become a bottleneck for the judiciary in China and there are plenty of reasons for it, as already illustrated previously in this chapter. The following makes a critical evaluation of law enforcement and it also attempts to find a better solution for a sound enforcement mechanism.

1. The Effectiveness of Enforcement Law

The enactment of the Civil Procedure Code in 1991[560] has increased some specific measures of enforcement, especially in tackling the transfer of assets, repudiation of debts, despising court orders, awards of arbitration, etc. The main legal consequences resulting from these unfaithful behaviors are primarily defined in Art. 227, 102 of the Civil Procedure Code and Art. 283, 285 of the 'Opinions'[561] issued by the Supreme People's Court;[562] however, in practice, these regulations contain some shortcomings: i) the clauses are not detailed enough and mainly consist of abstract and general principles, therefore the courts have different understandings and interpretations of these clauses during the course of enforcement. Furthermore, the lower courts have to ask the higher courts to coordinate and instruct them on how to do apply the regulation when they have doubts about these clauses. Consequently, the efficiency of enforcement is affected; ii) some measures for enforcement have little impact on the parties and lack feasibility; iii) the measures are not effective enough to tackle considering the newly emerging social and economic changes and judicial interpretations are not effective enough to fill in the gap. For instance, the courts normally put the properties of the debtors up for public sale so as to provide remedies to the creditors. In practice, the properties of the debtors cannot be auctioned or sold because of the absence of a market[563] and/or buyers. Furthermore, liquidation requires a strict legal procedure for the auction or sale of the assets. According to the judicial interpretation of the Supreme People's Court, the properties of the debtors can only be used to offset their debts directly, when both the

[560] The draft promulgated in1982 only contained some very simple measures.
[561] The Supreme People's Court: *Some Opinions on the Application of Civil Procedure Code*, 1992.
[562] These clauses and regulations mainly define the right of the courts and the legal consequences if the parties impede the judgment and enforcement, as well as the consequences of violation of the law by violent means.
[563] In many cities, there is no auction market or publicly recognized asset-assessment organization.

creditors and debtors agree not to undertake auction or sale of the property. Those unsellable assets of the debtors can only be transferred at a specific discounted value to the creditors with consent. Thus, enforcement becomes difficult under these conditions in which offset of debts by sale or transfer of assets is restricted. Enforcement law and judicial interpretations are not effective in providing applicable measures.

It is necessary for the courts to adapt to the emerging social and economic changes, by summarizing the problems existing in the enforcement of law, so as to find effective measures to tackle the problems. Meanwhile, it is considerable to enact a separate compulsory enforcement law to enhance the efficiency of the enforcement.[564]

2. The Social and Economic Environment for Enforcement

Difficulties in law enforcement are rooted in the social and economic environment of law enforcement. They can be summarized as follows:

a) Lack of Financial Ability of the Debtors

According to an investigation by the Execution Bureau of the High People's Court of Fujian province, the failure of enforcement contributes largely to the financial ability of the debtors.[565] In a survey of 3146 civil/economic cases filed in one district court, it was found that 2057 judgments could not be enforced simply because the debtors were not available. The remaining cases could not be enforced because the debtors did not have enough financial capability or the creditors agreed to postpone the payment.[566]

b) Local Protectionism

A strong local protection exists within local governments and administrations in the course of transit from a planned economy to a market economy. Localism exists not only in the local administrations, but also in the courts. Due to the dependence upon the budget in local governments and the social ties within local firms, the local courts sometimes lack the

---

[564] The Supreme People's Court has put forward "enactment of compulsory enforcement law" as a research subject in 2000.

[565] The Execution Bureau of the High People's Court of Fujian province, Impossible enforcement and the risk of the private and commercial exchange, in: People' Judiciary, (10) 2002, pp. 26, 27.

[566] Ditto.

goodwill to cooperate and assist in law enforcement when the court orders/decrees are made by other courts which are outside of its territorial limit of jurisdiction.[567]

c) Intervention from Local Administrations

The intervention of the local administrations has been an obstacle for law enforcement. The parties use their ties and "relationships" in the administrations to influence judges and executors, especially when the cases are related to local state-owned companies. The executors are strongly affected by the explicit or implicit instruction of the officers in the administrations. As a result, enforcement is often interrupted or delayed.[568]

d) Dim View of Law

Many people or firms are still not well adapted to the rule of law. Moreover, an unsound and infant legal system gives the parties the opportunity to escape liabilities. A lot of businesses still rely on soft constraints like morality, reputation and goodwill.[569] This leads to the difficulty of legal intervention and protection when the civil and economic rights of the parties are infringed upon.

e) Ad Libitum

Ad Libitum exists in economic activities and mismanagement in the Industry & Commerce Administration.

In the course of establishing and developing a market economy, law is still not effective enough because social norms and ethics are deeply rooted in the culture as a soft norm still plays a very important role in economic activities.[570] Law enforcement faces more difficulties when economic activities are not undertaken within the framework of law, because the judgment made in such a situation will not be effective. In many cases, litigants are not able to get compensation for litigation cost from the respondents, much less the remedies.

---

[567] Qi, Shu Jie, Research on Reform of Civil Procedure Law, Xiamen University Press, p. 250
[568] Ditto.
[569] Qi, Shu Jie, Research on Reform of Civil Procedure Law, Xiamen University Press, 2000, p. 250. Compare: Schaefer, H.-B., Die Bedeutung des Zivilrechts fuer den Entwicklungsprozess, Braunschweigische Wissenschaftliche Gesellschaft, J. Cramer Verlag, 2001, p. 135.
[570] Ditto.

Furthermore, mismanagement in the Industrial and Commercial Administration is also a cause leading to difficulties in enforcement. For example, some firms were in heavy debt but no bankruptcy orders were given; some firms did not meet the registration standard with respect to capital and personnel; some were leased out by the state firms to private firms and it has led to ambiguity of the legal entities; consequently, law enforcement against these firms or individuals is very difficult and the process becomes very complicated.

3. Short-term Deterring Effect of the Measures by the Central Government

The severity of law enforcement hinders, not only economic development, but also leads to stress and pressure on the courts. This problem was especially severe from 1995 to 1999. On one hand, the courts were unable to deal with the increasing workload from filings and piling up of civil cases, as well as the increase in filings for enforcement;[571] whereas on the other hand, the public lost confidence in the courts' competence in enforcement and sometimes the legal means were replaced by private settlements or even violent means.[572]

This serious problem in law enforcement affects the reform and development of economy of the country. In October 1999, the Central Government Discipline Committee and Ministry of Supervision jointly issued a notification requiring all its administrative branches to supervise and scrutinize any violation in law enforcement.[573] The importance of supervision and scrutiny are mainly an effort to deter and avoid the following problems, which are most troublesome and frequent in law enforcement.

- intervention by local government into the courts,
- unlawful regulations or instructions by local governments for the protection of local economic interest,
- transfer of assets by firms,
- lack of cooperation and assistance by local courts[574] when the enforcement of

[571] Tan, Shi Gui, Research on Judicial Reform in China, China Law Press, 2000, pp. 284, 285, 287.
[572] Ditto.
[573] Ditto.
[574] According to the regulation of the Supreme people's Court, all cases involved with debtors outside of territorial limit of the trial courts shall be assigned to the local courts for enforcement. The local courts (the agent courts) shall cooperate with the original courts, but the regulation does not define the responsibility and obligation of the local courts, as well as how to proceed and coordinate between the courts, it is very often that the local courts delay the enforcement or do not cooperate with the original courts when they are influenced by the respondents or the local governments.

assigned court orders/decrees (against the local debtors) are made by the trial courts outside of their territory limit,

- making use of current reform of state corporation asset reorganization to escape legal obligation and transfer corporate assets, or avoid paying debts and loans through fake bankruptcy and fake security of titles. (The reform of state corporations in recent years has allowed state-owned firms, which are de facto bankrupt, to undertake reorganization procedures with creditors. The reorganization normally separates the assets and debts of a firm. Debts will be converted into shares, and the creditors (mainly the banks) have to accept the reorganization scheme since they haven't got a strong influence on the reform of state firms.[575] The reorganization even allows a newly established firm to take over the assets and leave the debts to the old firm; in many cases, firms transfer assets to subsidiaries or branches so as to delay and escape debts. The old firm may go bankrupt quickly, in such a situation the creditors find it difficult to trace the assets of the new firm due to the complexity of the reform. In fact, the reform of state corporations is very tough and troublesome in China, the creditors find it difficult to have redressal by legal means since the law is weak in this field).

These emphases have touched on the central problems in law enforcement. Political intervention from the central government indicates that difficulties in law enforcement have endangered the social and economic order. A further deterioration would cause the loss of public trust in the legal system; meanwhile, it may also reveal that due to the current complexity of legal and economic reform, as well as the strong influence of local administrations, the problems of law enforcement cannot be solved simply by legal means, special means, namely political supervision and scrutiny is also necessary to deter the abuse of power under the current political system. Thus, the notification issued by the two central state departments can help to deter the abuse of power and intervention by local governments in the judiciary. Nevertheless, it must be addressed that in the long run the difficulties should be dealt with by legal means rather than by supervision from the standpoint of the rule of law.

[575] Local banks normally have to follow the orders of the local governments. The reform is controlled and dominated by the central government and the local administrations.

4. Assessment of 5 Year Reform Outline of the People's Court (Reform Outline)

While China is facing many obstacles in law enforcement, reform of enforcement law is considered to be the most necessary and acute. On 22.10.1999, the Supreme People's Court issued the *Reform Outline* aimed at establishing a sound legal system.[576]
The proposed organizational reform and the goal of reform with respect to law enforcement are put forward in Section 2 of the *Reform Outline*. The main contents are:

i) Before the end of 1999, judicial work with regard to law enforcement in each province or each autonomous region shall be under the administration and supervision of the High People's Court; the Supreme People's Court and the High People's Courts shall coordinate with each other to deal with problems arising from law enforcement;

ii) Reinforcing the personnel for enforcement, that is, unqualified personnel will be assigned to other work. The personnel for enforcement shall not be less than 15% of the total personnel in the each court and they shall be professionals and specialized in enforcement;

iii) After experimentation, a nationwide enforcement mechanism shall be established to supervise and coordinate enforcement work for all of the courts in China.

Furthermore, the Supreme People's Court requires that all of the High Courts should establish an Execution Bureau within the courts to coordinate and supervise enforcement work within its' territorial jurisdiction. Almost half of the High Courts in China have established Execution Bureaus within the courts.[577]

It is a good reform suggestion to conduct institutional and organizational reform within the court system. However, it has been criticized that the *Reform Outline* with respect to law enforcement is still too abstract and broad; there are no specific measures or enforcement law to follow and the courts still execute the court orders/decisions based on its' own

[576] Luo, Shu Ping, The Difficulties in Law Enforcement: Difficulties and Chaotic Situation, in China Lawyer, (12) 2002, p. 47. Compare: Tan, Shi Gui, Research on Judicial Reform in China, China Law Press, 2000, p. 288.
[577] Luo, Shu Ping (Director of the Execution Bureau of the High People's Court of Si Chuan Province), The Difficulties in Law Enforcement: Difficulties and Chaotic Situation, in China Lawyer, (12) 2002, pp. 43, 46.

understanding.[578] The reform shall focus on the improvement of personnel for execution and promulgation of Civil Compulsory Enforcement Law and relevant regulations, moreover, in all lower courts, execution tribunals shall be established within the courts so that the Execution Bureaus and the tribunals will have both the function of solving disputes arising from enforcement and the function of judicial administration.[579] Besides these internal reforms, it must be mentioned that reform shall also touch on external factors like the deterrence of intervention, localism, and corruption, since law enforcement is closely related to the political, administrative and economic environment.

5. The Coordination between Judgment and Enforcement

In some countries like Germany and Japan, the organization of law enforcement is established within the court. The executor is appointed by the court, and judges have a close coordination with the executors.[580] The enforcement of law will be assigned by the tribunals to different executors according to the nature of the civil cases. Each executor shall specialize in certain cases and thus enforcement will be easier. While in the US, UK and France, law enforcement bodies are established outside of the court, the judicial executor or judicial officer does not belong to the court but instead belongs to judicial administration; courts are only responsible for judgment, but not responsible for enforcement.

In China, the enforcement body is established within the court. According to Civil Procedure Code, the court of first instance is responsible for enforcement, and executors are assigned for law enforcement. The district courts/county courts and the intermediate courts may establish Execution Tribunals within the courts.[581] The Execution Tribunal shall be separated from the Trial Tribunal and is responsible for law enforcement in the civil cases.

Although the enforcement mechanism within the courts is not a critical reason for difficulties in law enforcement, the separation of trial and enforcement results in some difficulties in the law enforcement mechanism.

First, within the courts, the coordination between the executors and judges is very weak since

[578] Ditto.
[579] Ditto, p 47.
[580] In Taiwan, law enforcement body is established within the court, but it is separated from the tribunal and is an independent department of the court.
[581] Art. 208, 209 of Civil Procedure Code

they are under different departments of the courts and there is no hierarchical links; they care only about their own work and therefore it makes coordination difficult. Judges concentrate much more on adjudication but ignore the importance of enforcement, and judges seldom assist in law enforcement after the court orders/decisions are assigned to the executors (judges sometimes have to execute the court orders/decisions in case no executor is available in the courts). Meanwhile, it is regarded that the difficulty of law enforcement has also much to do with the low quality of personnel for execution, as the executors are not professional and competent enough for the task.[582]

Secondly, coordination and assistance among the courts is weak. According to a regulation[583] issued by the Supreme People's Court in 2000, most of the court orders with the debtors outside of the territorial limit of the original court (trial court) shall be entrusted to the courts where the debtors are located. Chart 5.1 shows the relationship between the courts under the current regulation when the debtors are out of the territorial limit of the principal court.

Chart 5. 1 The Pattern of Law Enforcement when the Parties are in different Territory of Jurisdiction

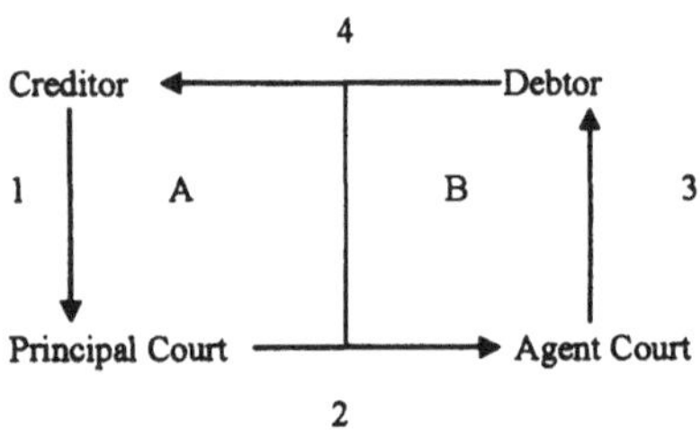

Remarks:

1. The Creditor in City A applies for compulsory measures against the debtor in City B based on the court judgment or other legal documents.
2. The Principal Court must assign the court order to the Agent Court in City B where the debtor is located and asks for enforcement.
3. The Agent Court shall enforce the court order made by Principal Court against the Debtor.
4. The Creditor will have its remedies in case of successful enforcement.

[582] There is no specific qualification requirement for executors. Some of the executors do not have systematic legal education and training before taking the work. They are assigned to the job after the calling for reinforcement of enforcement in recent years. See Luo, Shu Ping (Director of the Enforcement Bureau of the High People's Court of Si Chuan Province), The Difficulties in Law Enforcement: Difficulties and Chaotic Situation, in China Lawyer, (12) 2002, p. 47.

[583] The Trial Committee of the Supreme People's Court: Regulation on Reinforcing and Improving Agent Enforcement, passed on 24.02.2000.

The *"Regulation on Enforcement of Law" 1998* further regulates that the courts entrusted "have the right to take compulsory measures for enforcement and compulsory measures against any conduct which violates enforcement".[584] In practice, the efficiency of entrusted execution as shown in Chart 5.1 is very low due to the problems of localism, corruption and self-interest of the local courts. The entrusted courts have no incentive to enforce court orders since the judgments were made by others and the execution will take extra time and increase the workload of the courts. Meanwhile, there is no time pressure on the entrusted courts since there is no sanction against them if the court orders from other courts are not enforced. The regulation of the Supreme People's Court does not specify any responsibility and obligation[585] by the entrusted courts if they fail to perform their duty. Furthermore, the entrusted courts have a bias to protect local debtors and local interests, especially if there is a strong government intervention when the debtors are state-owned firms. The problem of localism is currently regarded as one of the most serious problems in execution in law enforcement.[586]

The efficiency of the enforcement is affected to a large extent by coordination between the courts and the organization within the same court. It is necessary for the reform to enhance cooperation between the courts and other departments under the same court.

6. Enforcement of Arbitration Awards

The law enforcement mechanism does not function well in respect to arbitration awards. According to Art. 207 of Civil Procedure Code, besides court orders/decrees, the courts are responsible for execution of other legal rulings like arbitration awards and notarized payment obligation. In practice, very few of such legal rights can be enforced in time or even successfully because the courts are unwilling to undertake responsibility when the workload for the enforcement of court orders/decisions is already very heavy; enforcement in case of arbitration awards is therefore put aside. Furthermore, the Civil Procedure Code allows the courts and the executors to undertake substantive and procedural review of the arbitration

[584] The Supreme People's Court, *Regulation on Enforcement of Judgments*,1998, Art. 113, 118.
[585] In Civil Procedure Code and relevant regulations it only regulates that the entrusted courts "shall not reject" any assignment by the trial courts (the principal courts), Art. 209 II, Civil Procedure Code (1991).
[586] Tan, Shi Gui, Research on Judicial Reform in China, China Law Press, 2000, p. 288; Qi, Shu Jie, Research on Reform of Civil Procedure Law, Xiamen University Press, 2000, p. 270.

awards and the notarized documents.[587] The executors very often reject enforcement of the awards made by arbitration committees and ask the parties to take court proceedings. Although the *"Regulation on Enforcement of Judgments" 1998* have reaffirmed the legal effectiveness of arbitration rulings and notarized documents for compulsory enforcement,[588] there are no signs of any improvement in enforcing the arbitration awards and notarized documents.

VI. Findings and Suggestions

1. Findings

Enforcement of court orders / decrees has been an obstacle of the judiciary in China. According to interviews and literature, the ratio of successful enforcement is very low. 25% ~ 30% of the court decisions/orders cannot be enforce.[589] According to the statistics of Hainan province, the settlement ratio was only 29.6% for cases filed for enforcement from January to October 1999.[590] The conclusion based on the statistics in the China Law Year Book also reveals severe problems in law enforcement in China,[591] and indicates that the judiciary in China is heavily affected by the failure of law enforcement.

The reasons behind the difficulties in law enforcement in China are complicated: first, the enforcement law and relevant regulations are too rough and lack practical measures. The regulations on law enforcement is written in the current Civil Procedure Code and only has 30 articles, which are mainly principles and lack workable measures, this leads to different understandings, and arbitrariness, in law enforcement. In the meantime, such rough regulations cannot solve the difficult and complicated problems arising from the reality of enforcement.[592] Secondly, the average quality of executors is low. They are not professional and not competent enough to deal with execution when disputes arise, to some extent, it increases the difficulty of law enforcement. Thirdly, these difficulties have also a lot to do

[587] Art. 216-217 of the Civil Procedure Code.
[588] The Supreme People's Court, *Regulation on Enforcement of Judgments*, 1998, Art. 2.
[589] Supra note 535.
[590] Supra note 525.
[591] Supra note 531
[592] See report from the National People's Congress Assembly, in www.sina.com.cn 10.03.2003.

with the current reform of the corporate system in China and debtors often make use of the reform to escape liability. Fourth, the coordination between judgment and execution within the court is weak; judges and executors do not communicate with each other closely; concerning enforcement outside of the courts of the territorial limit of jurisdiction. The local courts entrusted to enforce the law lack the incentive to cooperate and assist when their own caseload is already heavy or when they have a bias to protect local debtors or local interests. Fifth, the problem has much to do with the current social and economic environment in which localism has become a serious issue in jurisdiction, but also in law enforcement.

The sample study based on 45 cases reveals the serious problem facing the judiciary. The duration of law enforcement for these 45 case filings for compulsory execution was 105.9 days. The study also indicates that the level of economic development has had a great impact on the efficiency of law enforcement. In most of the interviews, judges, parties and lawyers admitted that the enforcement of court orders/decrees is the toughest and most troublesome problem in the judiciary.

2. Suggestions

a) Reinforcing and Improving the Enforcement Law

Currently there is no separate enforcement law in China. Section 3 of Civil Procedure Code defines compulsory enforcement procedures and specific measures to tackle transfer of assets, repudiation of debts, and consequences of despising the court orders of arbitration awards etc. Table 5.1 (see II. 5. in this chapter) illustrates enforcement law and relevant regulations. Since execution is different from judgment and has its own characteristics and tasks, it is necessary to promulgate a separate law for enforcement rather than incorporating it into the Civil Procedure Code. The enforcement law should be made to apply more effective practical measures for execution. A separate law[593] for compulsory enforcement can avoid a weak link between the civil process and the enforcement procedure;[594] furthermore, it will

[593] Compulsory enforcement mechanism is an important part of the judiciary. There are mainly 3 types of legislature in respect of enforcement law: the first is to incorporate the compulsory enforcement mechanism into the Civil Procedure Code, like Germany; the second is to promulgate a separate enforcement law, like Austria, Japan, Belgium and Taiwan; the third is to incorporate the enforcement mechanism into bankruptcy law and mix it with the bankruptcy legislature, like Swiss land and Turkey. See Liang, Shu Wen, Theory of enforcement and practicing, People's Court Publication, 1993, pp. 183, 184, 185.

[594] Qi, Shu Jie, Research on Reform of Civil Procedure Law, Xiamen University Press, 2000, p. 253.

help avoid the frequent application of the principles of civil procedure law in law enforcement due to the absence of practical regulations and specific enforcement laws.[595] A separate law will enrich workable measures compared to the abstract principles and simple measures of enforcement law, which are incorporated into the Civil Procedure Code.

Besides a detailed and workable law, there should be strict regulations on asset assessment, auction, sale, suspension and expiration of execution, enforcement procedures and supervision procedures in the short term.

b) Elimination of Localism and Local Intervention

Interference by the administration is a big obstacle in law enforcement, especially in case of disputes between parties in different regions. Localism focuses only on the local interest and damages the national interest in the long run. The enforcement of law therefore shall find ways to tackle this serious problem in the judiciary within the current framework of administration and partisan influence. Under the current political framework, it is important for the local governments to reinforce supervision and scrutiny for any violation of the principle of the rule of law.

c) Professionization of the Executors

Considering the low quality of human capital for law enforcement in the courts, the reform shall stress the importance of improving the quality of executors. Meanwhile, the executors shall be more professional in dealing with complicated cases. In some countries like Germany, the executors are more professional and specialize in specific cases. This will help to resolve the problems arising from execution more efficiently and effectively. Professional and qualified personnel are essential to enhance the efficiency in law enforcement.

As more than half of the High Courts in China have set up Execution Bureaus within the courts, execution tribunals are recommended for establishment in the lower courts and these execution tribunals shall be under the administration of the High Courts. The High Court in each province shall be responsible for administration and supervision, while the lower courts

---

[595] Ditto.

shall be responsible for execution.[596] Some have also suggested to the establishment of a collegial panel in the courts for law enforcement,[597] under which the presiding executor is responsible for enforcement of court orders, the assistant executors are responsible for assisting in the work, but enjoy the right to express his/her opinion in case of disputes during the enforcement, such an organization would be more democratic and efficient.

Furthermore, the courts shall also reinforce enforcement by increasing the number of personnel for law enforcement according to the nature of the cases. In the 5 year *Reform Outline* of the Supreme People's Court, it is aimed to have more than 15% of the personnel in the courts to be responsible for law enforcement. In short, both the quantity and quality of personnel shall be enhanced to reinforce law enforcement. Moreover, an incentive scheme shall also be considered to promote work efficiency of the executors.

d) Application of Flexible Measures

Due to the change of circumstances, part of the enforcement law cannot adapt to current market economy.[598] In the short run the legislature is not able to fill the gaps of the enforcement law, therefore, before the new law and new measures are promulgated, it is also necessary to reform the inadaptable measures under the current legal framework. For example, many state-owned firms with heavy debt are striving to survive under the current corporate reform, and the enforcement may cause more difficulties to these firms, thus, flexible measures like reorganization instead of liquidation might be more efficient in some cases from an economic point of view, but to those firms which are de facto bankrupt and have no value in an economic sense, liquidation is necessary to provide due remedy to the creditors.

Additionally, other measures shall be also considered to supervise the parties and the execution procedure. For instance, media plays a very important role in supervision. Debtors are more disciplined under the supervision of media. Some cities use media like TV and newspaper to disclose the names of debtors, who have escaped from liability, and it has resulted in a good effect. Furthermore, a mechanism of declaration of property should be set up to trace the property of the debtors. And it is practical for the courts to arrange

[596] Luo, Shu Ping (Director of the Enforcement Bureau of the High People's Court of Si Chuan Province), The Difficulties in Law Enforcement: Difficulties and Chaotic Situation, in China Lawyer, (12) 2002, p. 47.

[597] Qi, Shu Jie, Research on Reform of Civil Procedure Law, Xiamen University Press, 2000, p. 275..

[598] Many measures regulated in the Civil Procedure Code were based on the plan economy.

coordination meetings or discussions to find effective procedures. In general, it is important to build up a sound social environment with respect to media supervision, coordination among the courts, banks, taxation offices, administrations, etc., as well as an effective legal mechanism for law enforcement.[599]

Enforcement is complicated work; it not only needs improvement in the legislature and the coordination within the courts, but also improvement of the social and economic environment. The compulsory enforcement law and legal reform should be aimed at protecting the rights of creditors and providing speedy redressal to them, and further guaranteeing the safety of economic transactions.

[599] Qi, Shu Jie, Research on Reform of Civil Procedure Law, Xiamen University Press, 2000, p. 286.

Chapter 6

Summary and Policy Recommendations

If the judiciary is to provide the impartiality and efficiency necessary for public trust, a well defined program for judicial reform needs to address the major causes of deterioration in the quality of court services. This reform effort must address the root political, economic and legal causes of an inefficient and inequitable judiciary and not simply deal with its symptoms. Basic elements of judicial reform must include improvements in the administration of the courts and case management practices; the redefinition and/or expansion of legal education programs and training for students, lawyers and judges; the enhancement of public access to justice through legal aid programs and legal education aimed at fomenting public awareness of its rights and obligations in the courts; the availability of ADR mechanisms, such as arbitration, mediation and conciliation; the existence of judicial independence (that is, budget autonomy, transparency of the appointment process and job security) coupled with a transparent disciplinary system for court officers; and the adoption of procedural reform where necessary. [600] *– Edgardo Buscaglia*

Legal System and Civil Process in Developing Countries

A well functioning legal system shall provide speedy redressal to the parties and easy accessibility of justice to the general public. However, court delay has been an obstacle of the judiciary in developing countries. Legislatures and judicial systems in developing countries still lack the autonomy, stature, resources and competence needed to carry out all of their constitutional functions fully. Courts are overburdened and their proceedings, both criminal and civil, are routinely delayed for years. Judges are, for the most part, poorly trained and low paid, and the courts lack the funding to conduct investigations and administer justice effectively. Furthermore, judicial decisions are heavily influenced by political considerations, intimidation, or outright corruption. Therefore, if the judiciary is to provide the impartiality and efficiency necessary for public trust, a well-defined reform program needs to address the

[600] Buscaglia, Edgardo, Law and Economics of Development, Encyclopedia of Law and Economics, Vol. II, de Geest and B. Boukkaert (eds.), 1999, pp. 585-586; Also see homepage (http://encyclo.findlaw.com/).

main problems affecting the current quality of and causing constant deterioration to court services. The reform should be a permanent commitment to implement a program to change the inefficient system. Moreover, the reform shall not only deal with the symptoms of an inefficient judicial system but also to address the political, economic, and legal roots of an inefficient and inequitable judiciary.

Civil process in China has more or less the same problems as other developing countries. The courts lack budget autonomy and rely heavily on local governments; in the meantime, strong intervention exists from local administrations and partisan influences within the courts. Internally, judges have to report cases to higher-ranking positions for instruction. Corruption and miscarriage of justice are still common in the courts. Furthermore, the legal system does not function well in respect to quality of judgment. Despite the high settlement ratio and the relative moderate duration of trial cases, the ratio for appeal and retrial is comparatively high in China and the increase of such instances leads to a lengthy and costly process.

Summary of the Empirical Work

- Research Design

The functioning of the court system in China with respect to court delay and its costs have been analyzed based on primary as well as secondary data. The primary data were collected randomly from the district court of Huli, Xiamen City and the Intermediate Court of Xiamen City, with a sample size of 287 and 213 filed civil cases, respectively. Among 287 trial cases filed in the district court of Huli, Xiamen, 63 cases were brought for appeal in the Intermediate Court of Xiamen. The Secondary data (107 cases) is mainly collected from relevant publications edited by the Supreme People's Court.

The overview of filing and disposition in all the courts in China is based on the secondary data collected from China Law Year Books; the analysis of duration of the courts in the High Courts and the Supreme People's Court is based on 107 trial cases filed in the High Courts. These cases are also appeal cases filed at the Supreme People's Court and are collected randomly from the case books edited by the Supreme People's Court.

The opinions of the parties, judges and lawyers were collected through the use of a designed questionnaire; a separate questionnaire was designed to collect opinions from court personnel in respect to court delay and the factors affecting duration. Meanwhile, oral interviews and personal observations were conducted to analyze the functioning of the courts.

The study of current litigation cost and its effect on the judiciary was based on current laws and cases; specific investigation of the budget in all of the courts of Jiangxi province was done to illustrate the importance of financial support from the state in enhancing the accessibility of justice.

The study of enforcement of judgments was based on statistics and secondary data. Furthermore, 45 civil cases filed for compulsory enforcement were collected to illicit the duration of execution and the impact of economic development on the efficiency of law enforcement. Specifically, the investigation of difficulties in law enforcement was based on oral interviews with lawyers, the parties and judges.

This empirical study is an effort to investigate the average duration of the courts and to find the reasons causing court delay. What are the problems existing in procedural law? What kind of reform measures are needed to improve accessibility of the courts and to provide speedy and inexpensive remedy to the parties involved?

- Findings based on the Empirical Work

In general, according to the empirical study, so far court delay has not been a big problem in the lower courts (district courts/county courts and the intermediate courts) in respect of trial cases. The problem of delay exists in appeal cases and retrial cases, which consume larger amounts of time, especially for retrial cases, it normally takes around 10 months on average for disposition in retrial court and 2 or 3 years to complete the whole process.

First, the empirical study based on the secondary data shows that the settlement ratio is high in China. The settlement ratio is more than 90% each year. This high settlement ratio has to do with the time bound program used in the Chinese courts. Under the time bound program, the courts are expected to realize the target established in the time bound program. The time bound program increases pressure on the judges to settle the cases within a certain time limit and to avoid delay in the courts. However, the justification of efficiency cannot simply be based on the settlement ratio. The average disposition of judges is still very low compared to judges in other countries, for instance, one judge only disposes 34.5 cases per year[601] on average, this indicates that in general the efficiency of the courts is still very low. Furthermore, the time bound program has had some adverse effects: due to the imbalance of disposition, caseloads become heavy at the end of the year, and judges have to make a speedy trial so as to reach the targets established in the time bound program.[602] Mediation is frequently arranged by the courts to speed up settlement. The procedural and substantive rights of the parties may even be violated.[603] Another side effect is the low quality of judgment arising from speedy and rough judgment: around 40% of the judgments made by the trial courts are changed in the appellate courts,[604] and around 20 - 25% of the appeal cases are further under retrial.[605] Under appeal and retrial procedure, lawsuits will be lengthy in the whole procedure and costly to the parties involved, as well as the state.

Secondly, the empirical study based on random cases collected from the district court and intermediate court in Xiamen City indicates that court delay in the lower courts, namely the district court and the Intermediate Court, is not a big problem. The average duration of 287 civil cases filed at the district court of Huli was 56.5 days for cases disposed under simple procedure and 155 days for cases in regular order. The short duration is due to the fact that many cases filed at the district courts are cases with small dispute values and are simple cases in respect to fact-finding and application of law. The average duration of 213 trial cases filed at the Intermediate Court of Xiamen was 261 days. The average duration of disposition in the High Courts and the Supreme People's Court based on 107 cases was 10.63 months and 9.51 months respectively. Due to the complexity of cases, the higher the judicial hierarchy the longer the disposition will be.

Interviews with involved parties, judges and lawyers shows that the statistics submitted to the Supreme People's Court do not reveal reality since many lower courts establish a target settlement ratio for the year and dispose the cases according to the time bound program. This leads to manipulation of figures and fraudulent reporting of disposition in the statistics when

601 See Table 3.4 in Chapter 3.
602 The promotion as well as the remuneration of the judges are based on the fulfillment of the target established in the time bound program.
603 See Chapter 3, Part II, VIII b).
604 See Chapter 3, Table 3.16 and Table 3.17.
605 Supra note 392.

judges face piling up of cases at the end of the year. As a result, a high settlement ratio cannot explain the social sentiment towards the efficiency of the courts. On the contrary, the time bound program for high settlement ratios and speedy settlements may lead to more miscarriage of justice. The empirical study based on secondary data reveals that judges tend to settle their entire caseload at the end of the year, either by asking for withdrawal first and for re-filing again in the coming year, or by speedy settlements such as simple trial and mediation. Furthermore, there are some links between the high settlement ratio and the miscarriage of justice, that is, the high ratio of judgment made by the trial courts were changed in the appeal stage and many cases were further filed for retrial after appeal.

Thirdly, as to the duration of appeal and retrial cases, the duration of these cases are is comparatively long, besides the complexity of the cases, the longer duration of these cases has much to do with the length of time taken for delivery of filing documents from the trial court to appeal court. The time consumed in delivery of filing documents is a 'blind' in calculation and judges may intentionally delay the delivery of documents; the time is not calculated in the duration of the case and is regarded as one of the major reasons for delay.[606] Retrial cases take a much longer time compared with trial and appeal cases. In this empirical work, it was found that retrial cases normally take 2 or 3 years on average from filing until settlement. The long duration is a result of defects in procedure law in which there is no restriction on length of disposition and time limit for retrial cases. Although the amount of retrial cases is not big compared with the total caseload filed in the courts, the proportion is large based on the caseload of appeal cases. Around 20 - 25% of appeal cases are brought for retrial under the procedure of judicial supervision.[607] It is these cases that frustrate the parties and the long duration of these cases has been one of the main reasons which have caused public sentiment and mistrust in the judiciary.

Fourth, the investigation of litigation costs indicates that the burden of these costs and the lack of budget for the courts has hindered the accessibility of the courts and impeded the

[606] In an interview with judge Wang, Yan Bin of the Supreme People's Court. Also see Wang, Li Wen and Wang, Yan Bin, Understanding and Application of Regulation on Strict Implementation of Time Limit, People's Judiciary, (1) 2000, p. 11 ff.
[607] China Law Year Book, 1991-2000. Supra note 287.

functions of judiciary. The study of the cases reveals that the litigants were burdened by various fees in litigation and in some cases the additional cost for bribery. In a lawsuit, the litigation cost is about 25% - 30% of the claim.[608] Due to insufficient local budgets and state subsidy, the courts in China rely heavily on the income of litigation cost for its' daily operations. More than 60% of the total budget comes from the income related to litigation fees, as shown in the study based on the statistics in the courts of Jiangxi province. The participation of lawyers in the civil process is still not promising, since lawyers charge too high fees and sometimes are considered as middlemen for bribery. In 1996, 84% of civil cases did not have the engagement of lawyers.[609] In recent years there has been a tendency for more lawyer engagement in the civil process. In another investigation by the High Court of Chongqing City, based on 445 civil cases in 2001, it was found that 45.2% of the cases involved a lawyers' engagement.[610]

Fifth, the central problem lies in law enforcement. It has been admittedly obvious that law enforcement has been an obstacle for the development of a market economy and a bottleneck for the judiciary. The study of enforcement of judgment is based on fragmentary information from different sources due to the lack of systematic records in judicial statistics. According to statistics issued by the Supreme People's Court, the settlement ratio for enforcement of judgment ranged from 60% - 80%[611] and the courts normally establish a target settlement ratio of 60% - 70% or even higher.[612] However, according to the statistics of the High People's Court in Hainan province, from January to October 1999, only 29.6% of 3,311 case filings for enforcement were fully or partly settled;[613] according to interviews with individual lawyers and literature, many lawyers believe that only 20 – 30% of judgments can be enforced. Furthermore, the study based on 45 samples reveals that the duration of law enforcement for these cases filed for compulsory execution is 105.9 days. The study also

[608] See Chapter 4, II, 2 and Table 4.1.
[609] Supra note 484.
[610] Source: from unpublished internal report of the High Court of Chongqing City 2002, provided by the Supreme People's Court.
[611] China Law Year Book, 1996 –1998.
[612] Luo, Shu Ping (Director of the Enforcement Bureau of the High People's Court of Si Chuan Province), The Difficulties in Law Enforcement: Difficulties and Chaotic Situation, in China Lawyer, (12) 2002, p. 44. This is also confirmed by interviewed judges who told that the normal targeted settlement ratio established was around 65% to 78%
[613] Supra note 525.

indicates that the level of economic development has a great impact on the efficiency of law enforcement. In most of the interviews, judges, involved parties and lawyers admitted that enforcement of judgments is the toughest and most troublesome problem in the judiciary.

Finally, the empirical work justifies the theory that rules are better than standards. For instance, the problem of court delay was regarded as serious before the Regulation on Strict Implementation of Time Limit (2000), which was promulgated by the Supreme People's Court to enhance the efficiency of the courts and reduce court delay. The regulation defines in details how to calculate the time for filing, disposition, prolongation of the judgment, time limit for collecting evidence, adjournments allowed in the process and the time for assigning the cases, as well as the time limit for law enforcement, etc. According to investigations made by the Supreme People's Court,[614] the detailed regulation has restricted the arbitrariness of the judges in calculating the time and has established a more workable program for trial.

Policy Recommendations

- Independence of Jurisdiction within the Courts

The interference of the court administration and the Trial Committee in consideration of quality control, is not persuasive. Only with the independence of judges in jurisdiction within the court, will the quality and efficiency of the judgment be finally improved. Interference from the Trial Committee and the higher courts not only causes delay, but also leads to reliance of judges on the decisions made by the court rather than by judges themselves. The quality of trial will be affected since the judges cannot make their own judgment, while those know little about the case make the judgment. Moreover, from an efficiency point of view, the decision process would be much longer if higher ranking officials or the Trial Committee interfere into cases. As experience shows, this is one of the reasons that many cases take a long time for discussion by the Trial Committee and result in delay.

Another problem with respect to independence of jurisdiction in China is interference from

[614] See the report made by the Supreme People's Court, by Wang Li Wen, and Wang, Yan Bin, Understanding and Application of Regulation on Strict Implementation of Time Limit, People's Judiciary, (1) 2000, p. 11 ff.

higher courts. According to the law, the higher courts can only supervise the lower courts according to legal procedure, for example, appeal and retrial procedures, higher courts are not allowed to interfere into the judgment of cases in the lower courts. In practice, it is very common for lower courts to ask for instruction from higher courts on how to make case decisions. In fact, it has changed the 2-tier jurisdiction into one trial. The procedural right for appeal and retrial is deprived by such practices, as the parties will obtain the same court decision when the case is appealed.

Thus, judicial independence in China not only means independence from external interference, but also independence from internal interference. According to the Constitution and the Civil Procedure Code, the courts shall undertake jurisdiction independently and shall not be interfered with by the administration. This principle should be further interpreted into practice within the courts: the judge and the collegial panel should be free from the interference of the presiding judge, president, Trial Committee of the court and all other departments or individuals within the court;[615] moreover, judicial independence shall also keep the courts free from any interference by higher courts.

- The Need to redesign the 2-tier Jurisdiction

Due to the differences in situation and background of legislature, the establishment of a jurisdiction system must take litigation efficiency and cost into consideration. A 2-tier jurisdiction is considered to be more efficient in China in consideration of its vast land and density of population. However, the 2-tier jurisdiction reveals some problems in practice: first, the 2-tier jurisdiction cannot guarantee the quality of some complicated cases since most of the cases are filed in the local courts for appellate jurisdiction which is final and binding on the parties. In practice the local courts very often ask for opinions from higher courts on how to apply the law to complicated cases and such practice violates the principle of independence of jurisdiction and the spirit of procedure law. Secondly, the parties often apply for retrial even after final jurisdiction is made by the appellate court. As there is no time limit on

[615] Such independence in jurisdiction can be referred as 'internal independence' within the courts.' External independence' refers to independence of jurisdiction which is free from the interference by any parties outside of the courts.
It is viewed that independence of jurisdiction in China refers to the independence of the courts rather than judges. According to the law, each Trial Committee can review the cases and make decision on the cases; in practice, judges have to report cases to higher official in the courts for opinions. See, Yang, Li Xin, Civil and Administrative Litigation, Supervision and Justice, in Law Research, (4) 2000, p. 16.

settlement and times of disposition, the parties can try again and again to gain from the generosity of the procedure. This results in a '3-tier' or '4-tier' jurisdiction *de facto* or even indefinite trials and lead to a vulnerable finality of law.[616] On the other hand, a 2-tier jurisdiction is a waste of judicial cost and resources to easy and simple cases. In practice, many cases with respect to small claims and family matters are frequenty brought for appeal. In China, a country with vast land, is it necessary to apply a 2-tier jurisdiction for large numbers of simple and easy cases, or cases with small dispute values, especially in the countryside? Experiences in Western countries may be useful in the design of a new Civil Procedure Code in respect of a summary court, in which one judge is selected for judgment of simple and easy cases. Appeal is only allowed when the parties make the statement of their intention to do so during filing.

In this context, the 2-tier jurisdiction may be revised as follows: for simple and easy cases, or cases with small dispute values, normally one trial of jurisdiction shall be final and binding on parties so as to speed up the process and reduce caseloads in the lower courts and reduce litigation cost, as well as judicial costs and resources. For complicated cases, cases with big dispute value or high level of difficulty in application of law, a 3-tier jurisdiction may be allowed. In order to save litigation cost and avoid court delay, the Civil Procedure Code shall allow a leap-frogging procedure[617] in case the parties who filed in the District Court or County Court are keen to resolve their dispute in an early manner and they agree on the facts of the case but only disagree on the law. Furthermore, to relieve the burden of cases in the High People's Courts and the Supreme People's Court, original cases shall not be filed in these courts. These courts shall only be responsible for appellate cases and supervision of the lower courts, and keeping the uniform rule of law of the county.

- Time Limit for Evidence Collection

The Civil Procedure Code has only some rough regulations on how to collect and provide evidence to the court during litigation. In practice some problems arise from this "roughness",

---

[616] Liu, Nanping, A Vulnerable Justice: Finality of Civil Judgments in China, Columbia Journal of Asian Law, Vol. 13, Spring 1999. Compare Sheng, De Yong, Some Problems in the Reform of Judicial Supervision, in: People's Judiciary (8) 2001, p. 16.

[617] In German Civil Procedure Law (ZPO), Art. 556 a allows the parties who file in the County Court or District Court to appeal directly in the Federal Supreme Court and bypass the Court of Appeal if the parties only disagree on the law.

which affects the efficiency of the courts.

With respect to burden of proof, the Civil Procedure Code does not exactly state the issue of burden of proof, and to what extent it must be proven. It does not regulate when the reversal of the burden of proof shall apply and when the burden of proof can be exempted, etc.[618] The law also does not have any regulations and rules for consequences to the parties in case of non-performance of the duty of providing evidence.

The regulation on time limit of evidence in Civil Procedure Code is not detailed and is not exact enough, causing frequent delay in the court, especially in the pretrial phase.[619] The parties may make use of this procedural defect to delay the hearing and the trial. Thus, very often it causes delay in the courts and incurs high litigation costs and judicial costs.

In some cases, the parties hide particular evidence from the court of the first instance but present it later in the appellate court deliberately as new evidences so as to win the case, or they simply apply for appeal or retrial when there is new evidence available. The consequence is that the parties are able to apply for retrial again and again whenever new evidence is available. It is inevitable that the duration of cases will be long and costs for all parties involved will be high. Therefore, the law should regulate that the appellate court can reject the evidence in case of intentional hiding of and the party who provides new evidence during appeal shall compensate the other party for their economic loss. Such regulation will guarantee the implementation of burden of proof and protect the interest of the innocent party.

Since the current regulation on burden of proof is too rough, has a heavy impact on duration of court proceedings and incurs a high process cost to the parties, it is necessary for legislature to enact new regulation on evidence.[620]

- Restructuring Mediation Mechanism

Mediation has a long tradition in China and has played a very important role in civil dispute resolution. In practice, the courts overstress the role of mediation and ignore the procedural and substantive rights of the litigants (creditors) whom are forced to accept mediation arranged by the courts since judges have bias in using meditation to solve cases. The

[618] Art. 64 (1) of Civil Procedure Code: "The Parties have the responsibility to provide evidence for his claim".
[619] As revealed in the investigation of court duration, the pretrial preparation is too long compared with other phases of trial.
[620] Evidence Act is under draft to solve some problems in legal practice.

acceptance of mediation because of pressure from the judges sacrifices the legal rights of the creditors. Many cases are settled in this way as it is quicker and more economic to solve the cases and avoid the application of law in complicated cases; moreover, mediation is used as a means to conduct a speedy trial to realize the target settlement ratio of the year.[621] In such situations, procedural and substantive rights are more likely to be violated.[622] Therefore, law should restrict the discretion of judges to mediate the cases and respect the private autonomy of the parties; meanwhile, lawyers should play an active role in reconciliation for the parties. In such circumstances, the settlement ratio by mediation may be lower, but the rate of settlement by reconciliation will rise.

Besides, according to Civil Procedure Code,[623] the parties are not bound to the consent made through mediation before receipt of the written form made out by the court and are allowed to ask the court to undertake proceedings. Such regulations seem to extend more substantive rights to the parties, but it is against the principle of efficiency and leads to an increase in litigation costs simply because the legal relationship is unstable when the parties still have the right to overturn the agreement already reached with mutual consent in mediation. On the other hand, court delay may occur when the parties are able to apply for retrial if new evidence proves that the mediation was made against the will of the parties or the mediation agreement violates the law.[624] The retrial procedure, after mediation, creates additional proceedings in the court and will increase the caseload. It contradicts the principle of free will in mediation and the basic purpose of mediation itself. Consequently, such retrial increases litigation costs and leads to lengthy process. In this context, the courts should not overuse mediation to settle the case, just for the purpose of speedy disposition and avoiding application of law.

---

621 Compared with trial, mediation has some benefits: first, there is low risk to the judges if the cases are settled by mediation since mediation avoids the possible mistake in the application of law if the cases are settled by court hearings and trials; furthermore, cases settled by mediation normally will not involve further proceedings of appeal and retrial; secondly, settlement by mediation will facilitate the enforcement; third, settlement by mediation save time and cost, judges do not have to spend time and energy to study how to apply the law if the case is complicated (mediation is preferred by judges especially under the current situation in which the quality of judges in China is low).

622 Jing, Han Chao and Lu, Zi Juan, Some Basic Problems in the Revision of Civil Procedure Code, in: Zhang, Wei Ping (ed.), Review on Judicial Reform, 3rd ed., 2002, pp. 18-21.

623 Art. 91 of Civil Procedure Code: "If agreement is not made after mediation, or one party pulls back from the agreement before receipt of written documents, the court shall make judgment in time".

624 Art. 180 of Civil Procedure Code.

- The Need to Restructure Retrial Procedure

Retrial Procedure plays a very important role in the Civil Procedure Code and in legal practice. However, this empirical study indicates that retrial procedure is the main cause for long delay in the courts since there are no restrictions on time limits and times of dispositions in retrial procedure.

Since retrial procedure is stipulated in Supervision Procedure – Chapter 16 of the Civil Procedure Code and most of the cases filed for judicial supervision are retrial cases, it would be better to revise the Supervision Procedure as Retrial Procedure so as to be aligned with reality[625] and general practice in civil law countries.

Law should be relatively predictable and stable. However, under the current design of retrial procedure, the finality of law is challenged. The original purpose of the legislature for retrial procedure is to correct any mistakes based on facts and to protect the substantive rights of the parties. But, law is being used as a means to adjust social relationships and to seek balance in social order. Legal procedure is regarded as the last available remedy for the parties and therefore the court orders/decisions shall be final and binding on the parties in litigation. Stability and safety will be diminished if the court orders/decisions are frequently changed through retrial procedure. Further, from an efficiency point of view, law should find a balance between correcting mistakes, cost savings, and reducing court delay.

As already discussed in detailed previously, the scope of the retrial procedure is too broad and excessive. The parties, the courts, and the procuratorates can start the procedure if 'they think there are mistakes contained in the court orders (which are already effective)'; besides, the losers have a strong incentive to misuse the procedure since no fees are required for retrial. Consequently, the number of retrial cases will be great and the workload of the courts will increase. The long process of retrial will lead to an increase in litigation costs and the waste of judicial resources, diminishing the confidence of the public in the judiciary.

Compared with retrial procedures in other countries, the definition of retrial procedure in Chinese Civil Procedure Code is too rough and broad, even cases settled by mediation can be filed again under retrial procedure. The broad definition in conditions for retrial and the elastic stipulations of the articles has damaged the seriousness, stability and finality of law.

---

[625] Cases under judicial supervision are called retrial cases in China.

In this context, the Civil Procedure Code should redefine the conditions for application for retrial and narrow the scope for retrial. The law shall also stipulate time limit and times of disposition for retrial procedure so as to avoid delay and endless trials. It might be practical to undergo only one disposition for retrial case, and only a higher court can have jurisdiction of retrial cases. Moreover, as private law, private autonomy shall be respected; in principle, retrial procedure shall only be initiated by the parties involved whereas a third party, like the court, should not be allowed to intervene and initiate the retrial procedure only when it is related to public interest.

- Human Capital and Quality of Judgment

As the District Courts and Intermediate Courts settle more than 80% of the cases in China, the quality of judges in these courts are very important to justice. The training of judges in lower courts has affected the quality of judgments and leads to a high rate of appeal and retrial in the higher courts. Therefore the reform shall address the importance of human capital. If the lower courts are equipped with judges who lack proper training, the courts will not be competent to provide speedy redressal to the parties since low quality of judgment will cause an increase in appeal and retrial cases and result in long duration of process as well as an increase in litigation costs and judicial costs. Obviously, the functioning of the legal system and the quality of judgments will be affected when the courts lack human capital.

Furthermore, despite the large number of judges in China, many of them lack legal education and legal training, as well as practical experiences. Many judges came to the courts as retired officers from the army and their understanding of law is insufficient in the modern market economy. Some judges are admitted after only a short training period. Besides, many judges' time is occupied by administrative matters and the time available for trial is not sufficient for a heavy caseload. Therefore, reform should remove those unqualified judges from their positions and reallocate them to other supplementary positions in the courts. All judges must have legal education and pass the National Judicial Exam as already experimented with in 2002. An incentive scheme including a high salary should be provided to qualified judges to guarantee justice, as well as to deter corruption. In short, the quality of judges is decisive for the success of judicial reform since the quality of judgment cannot be guaranteed and the law cannot be properly enforced without qualified judges.

- Budget Autonomy and State Subsidy

Low budgets and state subsidies lead to high litigation costs and impede accessibility to justice. Many local administrations cannot provide enough financial support to the local courts due to financial stress. The budget shortages are one of the reasons that courts always charge additional costs to the parties and create opportunities for more rent-seeking and corruptive activities. Moreover, the lower courts cannot undertake reform measures in administration, case flow management and establishment of computer system, as well as personnel management due to the shortage of budget. Furthermore, the reliance upon the budget in local courts creates another problem: intervention of the local administration into judiciary.

Under the current situation in China, the reform may be more realistic if the budget of the courts is based on a 2-tier supply system, namely, the state shall provide sufficient budgets to the courts, especially those in poor provinces and regions to guarantee a certain level of budget autonomy. This part of budget will ensure the daily operation of the courts in respect of remuneration and operational costs of the courts. On the other hand, the local governments shall be responsible for the budget of court buildings and facilities. Meanwhile, the unqualified personnel shall be removed from the courts so as to relieve the financial burden of the courts and guarantee the salary of judges especially in the County and District Courts.

- Enforcement of Law

Law enforcement has been an obstacle of the judiciary in China. As the previous study indicated the main reasons behind the difficulties in law enforcement are: First, compared with law enforcement, courts put much more emphasis on the jurisdiction of cases and ignore the importance of enforcement of judgment. The quality of executors is not high and the facility for enforcement like vehicles and communication system is not well equipped in the courts. Secondly, the lack of coordination within the courts and the lack of coordination and assistance from other courts make it more difficult to enforce court orders/decrees in time, especially in case of existence of rent-seeking, corruption, interference and local protection.

Thirdly, due to backward administration in case flow, the speed of execution is strongly affected. Fourth, as a result of rough legislature of enforcement law, the general principles and abstract regulations lead to disputes and different understandings in the course of enforcement. Furthermore, the difficulties in law enforcement are strongly affected by the current difficulties in big state-owned firms in respect to liquidation and reorganization, as well as the social and economic environment.

It is necessary for the courts to enact reform measures to solve the problems existing in law enforcement. First, it is necessary to promulgate a separate enforcement law to summarize the experiences gathered from the past and tackle current problems in law enforcement. Workable and practical measures shall be introduced to replace abstract principles since the difficulties of law enforcement have much to do with the rough legislature of enforcement law. Second, it is recommendable to establish an Execution Tribunal in each court. The Execution Tribunal shall be equipped with professional executors and deal with all the enforcement of judgments; the coordination between the judgments and law enforcement shall be improved within the court. Additionally, these Execution Tribunals will be under the administration of the Execution Bureau established in each High Court in the provinces so as to improve coordination and quick dispute resolution in the course of enforcement.[626] Furthermore, case flow management shall be applied in enforcement of court orders in each court, which should also be under the administration of the High Court in each province. In case of enforcement of court orders in other places that are out of the territorial limit of jurisdiction, the entrusted courts shall do their utmost to assist in the execution and avoid local protection. Finally, the executor shall be given more training in enforcement. They should be professionals and specialize in this specific field of work.

Conclusion

In a transition economy, the legal system, especially civil law, plays a very important role in the market economy. Countries around the world, east and west, are undertaking profound judicial reform in order to reduce court delay and improve litigation efficiency. A judicial

[626] Compare Luo, Shu Ping (Director of the Enforcement Bureau of the High People's Court of Si Chuan Province), The Difficulties in Law Enforcement: Difficulties and Chaotic Situation, in China Lawyer, (12) 2002, p. 47.

system with 'Chinese characteristics' faces a grim challenge in respect to inequality, court delay, high litigation costs and difficulties in law enforcement. From the end of 1980's, judicial reform and justice itself have caught the attention of the general public. In the past years, it seems that the reform has made no big progress. There are various obstacles and impediments in the way of the realization of justice and accessibility to justice. Courts are often interfered with and cannot be independent from the local administration; judges cannot make their own decisions, as they have to report cases to higher rank officials; corruption in the judiciary is serious and leads to distrust by the public; the quality of judges in general is still very low and the pattern of trial is backward; case flow management and the supervision mechanism should be improved to adapt to the increase of burden of cases; difficulties in law enforcement impede the sound development of a market economy and the judiciary. All these problems behind court delay and high litigation costs, as well as law enforcement, indicate that the judicial system in China is far from the goal of justice and the modernization of law.

In this context, the current judicial reform should not only deal with the symptoms, but also the roots of political and economic reform. As commented by Edgardo Buscaglia: 'If the judiciary is to provide the impartiality and efficiency necessary for public trust, a well defined program for judicial reform needs to address the major causes of deterioration in the quality of court services. This reform effort must address the root political, economic and legal causes of an inefficient and inequitable judiciary and not simply deal with its symptoms. Basic elements of judicial reform must include improvements in the administration of the courts and case management practices; the redefinition and/or expansion of legal education programs and training for students, lawyers and judges; the enhancement of public access to justice through legal aid programs and legal education aimed at fomenting public awareness of its rights and obligations in the courts; the availability of ADR mechanisms, such as arbitration, mediation and conciliation; the existence of judicial independence (that is, budget autonomy, transparency of the appointment process and job security) coupled with a transparent disciplinary system for court officers; and the adoption of procedural reform where necessary'.[627] A country in transition, like China, needs an efficiently functioning judiciary to defend the legitimate, and correct the illegitimate, relations among citizens,

[627] Buscaglia, Edgardo, Law and Economics of Development, Encyclopedia of Law and Economics, Vol. II, de Geest and B. Boukkaert (eds.), 1999, pp. 585-586; Also see homepage (http://encyclo.findlaw.com/).

regardless of their income levels, and safeguard the reform of the market economy. By working together, the judicial system and ADR mechanisms can foster the much-needed balance between equity and efficiency in the provision of justice

Bibliography

Adams, Michael, Ökonimische Analyse des Zivilprozesses, Königstein/Ts., 1981, p. 80

Aduff, R., Trial and Punishment, Cambridge University Press, 1986, pp.110-114

Adrian A.S. Zuckerman (ed.), Civil Justice in Crisis, Oxford University Press, 1999, pp. 12-55

Baumbach/Lauterbach/Albers/Hartmann, Zivilprozessordnung, Verlag C.H. Beck, 61. Auflage, pp. 1549-1656

Buscaglia, Edgardo, and Maria Dakolias, Judicial Reform in Latin American Courts: The Experience in Argentina and Ecuador, 1996

Buscaglia, Edgardo Jr., Maria Dakolias, and **William Ratliff**, Judicial Reform in Latin America: A Framework for National Development, Stanford University 1995

Buscaglia, Edgardo Jr., Judicial Reform and Corruption in Latin America, Paper presented at the International Workshop on Law and Economics, Ghent, February 1996, pp. 2-13

Buscaglia, Edgardo, Law and Economics of Development, Encyclopedia of Law and Economics, Vol. II, de Geest and B. Boukkaert (eds.), 1999, pp. 564-588

Buscaglia, Edgardo Jr. and Domingo, Pilar, "Political and Economic Impediments to Judicial Reform in Latin America", in: Buscaglia, Edgardo, Ratliff, Willam and Cooter, Robert (eds), Law and Economics of Development, JAI Press, 1996

Coase, R., The Problem of Social Cost, Journal of Law and Economics, 1960, p. 1

Cooter, Robert, Decentralized Law for a Complex Economy: The Structural Approach to Adjudicating the New Law Merchant, in: 144 University of Pennsylvania Law Review 1996, pp. 1643-1696

Dworkin, R.M., A Matter of Principle, Clarenden Press of Oxford, 1985

Faundez, Julio (ed.), Good Government & Law: Law and Institutional Reform in Developing Countries, Macmillan Press Ltd., 1997, p. 3

Franzen/Apel, Prozessaufwand bei Gericht und Anwalt – betriebswirtschaftlich und anschaulich – mit Folgerungen, NJW 1988, p. 1062

Franzen, Hans, Was kostet eine Richterstunde? – Berechnung und Folgerungen, in: NJW 1974 Heft 18, pp. 785-786

Galanter, Michael, 'Why haves' Come Out Ahead: Speculation on the Limits of Legal Change, in: 9 Law and Society Review, 1974, p. 95 ff

Gerking, Wiebke, Die Wirtschaftlichen Folgen langer Verfahrensdauer, in: Schmitdtchen/Weth (Hrsg.), Der Effizienz auf der Spur, Nomos Verlagsgesellschaft, Baden-Baden, 1999, pp. 38-42

Gilles, Peter, Prozessrechtsvergleichung, Prozessrechtliche Abhandlungen, Prueting, Koeln-Berlin-Bonn-Muenchen, 1995, p. 50

Gottwald, Peter, The German Administration of Civil Justice, in: Civil Justice in Crisis – Comparative Perspective of Civil Procedure, Oxford University Publication 1999

Hirto Miyake, Comparative Analysis of the Reform of Civil Procedure, Japanese Report, in Conference on Civil Justice in the Era of Globalization, Japan 1992.

Kennett, Wendy A., Enforcement of Judgments in Europe, Oxford University Press, 2000, pp. 69-99

Kerameus, Konstantions D., "A Gvilian Lawyer Looks at Common Law Procedure", in Louisiana Law Review, Jan. 1987, 47 La. L. Rev.

Langbein, John H., The German Advantage in Civil Procedure, 52 Chicago Law Review, 1985.

Larkings, Christoper M., Judicial Independence and Democratization, in: 44 American Journal of Comparative Law, Fall, 1996, p. 605

Leubsdorf, John, The Myth of Civil Procedural Reform, in Civil Justice in Crisis, ed. by Adrian A.S. Zuckerman, Oxford University Press, 1999, p. 55

Louis Kaplow, General Characteristics of Rules, in G. de Geest / B. Boukkaert, International Encyclopedia of Law and Economics (http://encyclo.findlaw.com/)

Lubman, 'Studying Contemporary Chinese Law: Limits, Possibilities and Strategy', in: 39 American Journal of Law, 293 (1991)

Metzler-Poeschel, Statistisches Jahrbuch 1993 fuer die Bundesrepublik Deutschland (1993)

North, D., Institutional Change and Economic Performance, Cambridge Univ. Press, 1996

Posner, A. Richard, An Economic Approach to Legal Procedure and Judicial Administration, in: Journal of Legal Studies, 2 (1973), pp. 396-400

Posner, A. Richard, Economic Analysis of Law, Little Brown Publication, Boston, Toronto, 1992, 4th ed. , pp. 541-551

Rawls, John, A Theory of Justice, Harvard University Press, 1997, p. 3

Redishs, Martin H., Federal Judicial Independence, 46 Mercr Law Review, 1995, p. 707

Rene, David, A Civil Code for Ethiopia: Consideration on the Codification of the Civil Law in African Countries, Tulane Law Review, Vol. 37, 1963, p. 189

Rottleuthner, Hubert / Rottleuthner-Luther, Margret, Die Dauer von Gerichtsverfahren: Evaluation der ZPO-Vereinfachungsnovelle, Nomos Verlagsgesellschaft, 1. Auf., Baden-Baden, 1990, p. 248 ff

Schaefer, H.-B., Die Bedeutung des Zivilrechts fuer den Entwicklungsprozess, Sonderdruck aus Braunschweigische Wissenschaftliche Gesellschaft, J. Carmer Verlag 2001, Sonderdruck, p. 1 & pp. 135-144

Schaefer, H.-B., The Significance of a Well-functioning Civil Law in the Process of Development, Paper presented at the Conference of the Latin Americans Law and Economics Association in Quito (Ecuador) June 15th to June 17th 1998, Manuscript, 1998, pp. 1-16

Schaefer, H.-B., „Kein Geld für die Justiz – Was ist uns der Rechtsfrieden wert?“, in: DriZ, 1995, p .461

Schaefer, H.-B., Enforcement of Contracts, Comment given at the Workshop on Institutional Foundations of a Market Economy, World Development Report, 23 -25, Feb 2000 Berlin, Manuscript, p. 3

Seidman, Robert B., State, Law and Development, New York, St Martin's Press 1978

Shapiro, Martin, Courts: A Comparative and Political Analysis, the University of Chicago Press, 1981, p. 8

Sherwood, Robert M, Shepherd, Geoffrey and De Souza, Celso Marcos, "Judicial Reform and Economic Performance", in: The Quarterly Review of Economics and Finance, Vol. 34, 1994, p. 101

Shavell, Steven, The Appeals Process as a Means of Error Correction, in: Journal of Legal Study, 1995, p. 381

Sir Jacob, The Reform of Civil Procedural Law, in: The Reform of Civil Procedural Law and Other Essays in Civil Procedure, London, 1982, p. 1

Tubek, E., Towards a Social Theory of Law: ' An Essay on the Study of Law and Development', 82 Yale Law Journal, 1972, pp.1 ff

World Bank, Governance: The World Bank's Experience (Washington DC: The World Bank, 1994)

World Bank Technical Paper No. 350, World Bank, Washington D.C.

World Development Report 1997

World Bank, Ecuador: Constraints to Private Sector Development, Washington, DC, The World Bank, Trade, Finance and Private Sector Development Division, LAC Country Department IV, 1993.

Wright, J. Skelly, The Pre-trial Conference in American Court Systems, Readings in Judicial Process and Behavior, Sheldon Goldman and Austin Sarat, 1978, p. 120

van der Sprenkel, S., Legal Institutions in Manchu China, A Sociological Analysis, London, 1962.

Zweigert / Koetz, An Introduction to Comparative Law, Cambridge, 1999, pp. 286-292

Zeisel, Hans, Kalven, Harry, Jr. and Buchholz, Berhard, Delay in the Court, Little Brown and Company, 1959, pp. 5-10 & 293-294

Chinese Literature:

Bo, Min, Small Claims Tribunal: a new practice of justice and efficiency, in: People's Judiciary, 1st ed. 2002, pp. 39 ff

Cai, Hong and Li, Han Chang, Civil Procedure Code (Text Book), China Judiciary Publication, 1999, p. 32, 68

Cao, Shou Yue, A Discussion of Reform of Appeal in Civil Litigation, in: People's Judiciary (3), 1999, pp. 4-5

Chen, Guang Zhong, Directives of Criminal Law of UN and the Criminal law in China, China Law Press, 1999, p. 93

Chen, Gui Ming, Litigation Justice and Procedural Guarantee, China Judiciary Publication, 1996, pp. 113-123

Fang, Liu Fang, Research on Litigation Cost, in: China Social Science, (3) 1999, pp. 141-142

Fei, Xiao Tong, Native Soil of China (1st ed. in 1947), San Lian Book Publication, 1985, p34.

Fu, Yu Lin, The Principle of Structuring the Judicial Hierarchy: a comparative analysis, in: China Social Science, (4) 2002, pp. 84-98

Fu, Yu Lin, The Nature of Litigation Fees and the Burden of Litigation Costs, Peking University Law Review, Vol. 4, No. 1, 2001, pp. 239-243

Gan,Wen, Some basic questions with respect to justice, in: China Jurisprudence, 5th edition 1999

Gu, Tao, Rethinking and Suggestions to the Civil Retrial Procedure in China, in China Judiciary (3) 2000, pp. 23-24

He, Lan Jie / Lu, Min Jian (eds.), Judiciary in Contemporary China, Contemporary China Publication, 1993, p. 297

He, Bin, Restructuring the Mechanism of Dispute Resolution, in Peking University Law Journal, Vol. 14, No. 1 (2002), pp. 6-16 & 30-31

Huang, Song You, An Analysis of Judicial Efficiency, in: People's Judiciary (11), 2001, p. 21

Huang, Song You, Progress and Transition: Thinking on the Reform of Civil Jurisdiction, in: Contemporary Law, 4th ed., 2000.

Jiang, Hui Ling, The Condition and Ways to Realize Independent Jurisdiction in China, in: People's Judiciary (3), 1998, p. 16

Jiang, Ping, "Summary on the Seminar of Civil Judicial System", in: Law Research (5), 1998

Jing, Han Chao, Reform of the Pattern of Trial, People's Court Publication, 1997, p. 63

Jing, Han Chao and Lu, Zi Juan, Some Basic Problems in the Revision of Civil Procedure Code, in: Zhang, Wei Ping (ed.), Review on Judicial Reform, 3rd ed., 2002, pp. 18-21

Li, Xiao Bin, How to Improve Judicial Efficiency, in: People's Judiciary (10), 1998, p. 17

Liang, Shu Wen, Theory of Enforcement and Practicing, People's Court Publication, 1993, pp. 183-185

Liu, Guang An and Li, Cun Bang, Civil Mediation and the Protection of Rights, , in: Xia, Yong, Towards an Age of Rights, China Law and Politics Publication, 2000, p. 273

Liu, Nan Ping, A Vulnerable Justice: Finality of Civil Judgments in China, Columbia Journal of Asian Law, Vol. 13, Spring 1999

Liu, Tong Hai and Zhu, Xiao Long, Is the Court Fee Reasonable? In: China Lawyer (12), 2002, pp. 22, 40

Luo, Shu Ping, The Difficulties in Law Enforcement: Difficulties and Chaotic Situation, in: China Lawyer(12), 2002, pp. 43-47

Ma, Jun Ju and Lie, De Zhong, The existing problem in current Chinese legal system and the way for improving, in: Legal Comments, 6th edition, 1998

Qi, Shu Jie, Research on Reform of Civil Procedure Law, Xiamen University Press, 2000, pp. 11-19 & 128-371

Sheng, De Yong, Some Problems in the Reform of Judicial Supervision, in: People's Judiciary (8), 2001, pp. 16-19

Sheng, De Yong, Reform of Judicial System, in: Judicial Research 1996, 8th edition

Sheng, Huang Wei, Basic Thinking on Restructuring the Judicial Supervision in China, in: People's Judiciary (7), 2002, p. 26

Sheng, Zhong Ling, Research on Comparative Law, Beijing University Press, 1998, pp. 433-436

Song, Bing, Procedure, Justice and Modernization,China University of Politics and Law Publication, 1998, p. 363

Su, Li, An Investigation and Re-thinking of the Trial Committee in the Lower Courts, in: Beijing University Review, 2nd Collection, Vol. 1, 2000, pp. 361-363

Su, Yong Qin, Reform of Judicial Reform, Yue Dan Publication/Taiwan, 1998, pp. 312-313

Sun, Bo Sheng, Analysis of Retrial Cases, People's Court Publication, 1999, p. 23

Tan, Shi Gui, Research on Judicial Reform in China, China Law Press, 2000, pp. 235-288

Wang, Li Wen and Wang, Yan Bin, Understanding and Application of Regulation on Strict Implementation of Time Limit, People's Judiciary (1), 2000, pp.11 ff

Wang, Li Ming, Research on Judicial Reform, China Law Press, 2000, pp. 33-250 & 312-507

Wu, Dong Yu and Hua, Shi, An Investigation and Comment on the Internal Setup and Categorized Personnel Management of the People's Courts, in: Zhang, Wei Ping, Review on Judicial Reform, Vol. 4, China Judiciary Publication, 2001, pp. 336-447

Xia, Yong, Toward An Age of Rights: A Perspective of the Civil Rights Developments in China,China University of Politics and Law Publication, 1999 and 2000 revised edition, pp. 62 & 234-273

Xue, Jiang Wu and Zhang, Yong Ling, An analysis and thinking of the problem of court budget, in: People's Judiciary (8), 1999, pp. 37-40

Yang, Li Xin, Civil and Administrative Litigation, Supervision and Justice, in Law Research (4), 2000, p. 16

Yu, Lei, Analysis on Some Problems in the Civil Retrial Procedure, in: People's Judiciary (1), 2002, p. 37

Zeng, Xian Yi (eds.), The History of Chinese Legal Thoughts, China People's University Publication, 2000

Zhan, Shun Chu, "Correcting local protectionism to guarantee the uniform judiciary and the respect of jurisdiction", in: Jurisprudence Comments, 1st ed., 1991

Zhang, Ai Zhen, Some Suggestions on Restructuring the Judicial Supervision in China, in: China Judiciary (10), 2001, pp. 19-21

Zhang, Wei Ping, Review on Judicial Reform, Vol. 2/3/4, China Judiciary Publication, 2001

Zhang, Wei Ying / Ke, Rong Zhu, "The adverse selection in civil litigation and its interpretation – an empirical study", in: China Social Science(2), 2002, p. 31

Zhang, Wen Xian, The Jurisprudence,China University of Politics and Law Publication, 1993, p. 273

Zhang, Wu Sheng, Research on Problems of Reform in the Lower Courts, in: Review on Judicial Reform Vol. 2, China Judiciary Publication, 2001, p. 204

Appendices

Appendix-I (Questionnaire to the Parties)

Questionnaire 1

Part A. Court of First Instance

1. Time consumed from filing until settlement (dismissed or disposed)		
2. Time consumed for execution after judgment		
3. Does the claimant/claimed engage in a lawyer?	(Yes)	(No)
4. Type of the case (contract disputes, tort cases, or bankruptcy)		
5. Parties involved (individual, group, private, state-owned firms?)		
6. In case of retrial, how long does it take?		
7. Dispute Value		

Part B. Appellate Court

1. Time consumed from appeal until settlement		
2. Total time consumed from first filing until settlement		
3. Lawyer engaged?	(Yes)	(No)
4. Dispute Value		

Part C. Litigation Costs

1. Costs may be incurred according to the regulation of litigation cost (1989)
   a) Litigation fee
   b) Direct cost incurred, incl. collecting proof by the court, traveling costs, accommodation cost, food etc. relating to the case (especially when the court and the appellee/appellor are in different places)
   c) Economic loss caused when asset is frozen, under guarantee etc. (optional)
   d) Penalty incurred (by detaining in case of hurdling litigation)
   e) Other direct costs charged by the court according to the regulation of litigation costs (1989)

2. Costs not indicated in the regulation (1989)
   a) Lawyer's fee
   b) Other direct and indirect costs

Part D. Judicial costs (only for reference)

1. Costs of one judge in China (per year)
   a) Salary
   b) Welfare
   c) Costs of assistants, Secretary
   d) Housing
   e) Children's advantage in schooling
   f) Transportation (car, bus from the court)
   g) Pension
   h) Costs incurred in the court incl. building the building, maintenance, equipments, other material cost
   i) Other benefits

Cost per working hour will be also calculated based on the above calculation

2. Lawyer's cost (in 3 categories: 30, 40 and 50 years old))
   a) Cost of Secretary
   b) Costs of assistants
   c) Salary of a clerk
   d) Office set-up
   e) Traveling cost
   f) Expense when attending seminars

Part E Views to the Duration of the Court and Cost

1. What do you think about the duration of the court? ( ) very long ( ) long ( ) acceptable
2. What is your attitude towards litigation cost ( ) very high ( ) high ( ) acceptable
3. Can you recover litigation fees prepaid to the court in case of winning ( ) Yes ( ) No
4. What is your view on law enforcement ( ) very difficult ( ) difficult ( ) easy
5. Describe your experience in litigation.

Appendix-II (Questionnaire to the Courts)

Questionnaire 2

A. What is the main reason causing court delay? If you think that the listed item is the main reason, which affects the duration of the case, please place a cross in the square. You may choose several choices.

1. In the Process of Judgment
(1) Filing [ ]
(2) Pretrial Preparation [ ]
(3) Appearance and Hearing [ ]
(4) Meeting & Discussion of Collegial Panel [ ]
(5) Delivery of Court Orders/Decrees [ ]

2. Internal Factors
(1) Human Capital (Quality of Judges and their attitude towards judicial work) [ ]
(2) Waiting for Instruction from Higher Rank Official or Higher Court [ ]
(3) Waiting for the Decision of Collegial Panel and Trial Committee [ ]
(4) Signing of Legal Documents by President of the Court [ ]
(5) Other Reasons (budget, case management, court facilities and personnel autonomy etc) [ ]

3. External Reasons
(1) Delay in Providing Evidences by the Parties [ ]
(2) Difficulty in Delivery of Legal Documents [ ]
(3) Bad Cooperation from Lawyers [ ]
(4) Complication of Cases [ ]
(5) Intervention of Administrative Bodies [ ]

B. The Effect of *Regulation on Strict Implementation of Time Limit (2000)*, issued by the Supreme Court in 2000
1. Do you know the Regulation? [ ]
2. Do you think the Regulation has obvious effects to solve the problem of court delay?
(1) Very good effect [ ]
(2) Good effect [ ]
(3) It helps [ ]
(4) It does not have any effect in solving the problem of court delay. [ ]

2. What is your opinion regarding the implementation of the Regulation on Time Limit
(1) It is not easy [ ]
(2) Difficult [ ]
(3) Very Difficult [ ]

3. If you think it is difficult to implement the Regulation on Time Limit, what are the main difficulties? Please make a cross in the square. You may have multiple choices.

(1) The calculation on the time of filing and settlement [ ]
(2) The application for prolongation of time limit [ ]
(3) The assignment of cases in the event of appeal [ ]
(4) Enforcement of Court Orders/Decrees [ ]

4. What is your opinion towards court delay?

(1) Very serious before 2000 [ ]
(2) Still very serious [ ]
(3) Big improvement after the promulgation of Regulation on Time Limit [ ]

Appendix III (Judicial Statistics from 1988 to 2000)

Remarks:

- Sources from China Law Year Books with yearly filings and dispositions in the courts.
- The total number include pending cases of previous years.
- With respect to the enforcement of judgments, there is no statistics about filings, only the number of cases settled is available (since 1993).
- In this study, civil cases include the number of 'civil cases' and 'economic cases' as indicated in the tables.
- Cases under Judicial Supervision are retrial cases.

Judicial Statistics (1988)

Table 1988-1 Trial Cases, Appeal Cases and Retrial Cases (Judicial Supervision) by the People's Courts in 1988

Cases	Filing	Settled	Unsettled
Trial Cases	2290624	2226043	263268
Appeal Cases	160660	157118	24726
Judicial Supervision	112368	136164	38032
Total	2563652	2519325	326026

Table 1988- 2 Total Trial Cases in 1988

Cases	Filing	Percentage of total filing	Settled	Unsettled	Settlement Ratio (%)
Criminal	313306	13.68	312475	13573	96.09
Civil	1455130	63.53	1419056	166135	89.52
Economic	508965	22.22	481923	81588	85.52
Administrative	8573	0.37	8029	963	89.29
Traffic	4650	0.2	4560	1009	81.88
Total	2290624	100	2226043	263268	89.42

Table 1988- 3 Total Appeal Cases in 1988

Cases	Filing	No. of cases and the type of settlement						
		Settlement	Maintained	Reversed	Retrial	Withdrawal	Others	Unsettled
Criminal	46432	46430	33884	6603	3402	2160	381	2627
Civil	90430	87961	42400	20045	7664	5939	11643	17936
Economic	21311	20674	7863	5944	2554	976	3337	3968
Administrative	2356	2218	1573	371	152	71	51	172
Traffic	131	125	40	26	21	8	30	23
Total	160660	157408	85760	32989	13793	9154	15442	24726

Judicial Statistics (1989)

Table 1989-1 Trial Cases, Appeal Cases and Retrial Cases (Judicial Supervision) by the People's Courts in 1989

Cases	Filing	Settlement
Total	3209593	3182733
Trial Cases	2913515	2882103
Appeal Cases	196257	191132
Judicial Supervision	99821	109498

Table 1989-2 Total Trial Cases in 1989

Cases	Filing	Percentage of total filing	Settled	Unsettled	Settlement Ratio (%)
Criminal	392564	13.74	389597	16595	95.84
Civil	1815385	62.31	1808538	174255	91.21
Economic	690765	23.71	669443	103300	86.63
Administrative	9934	0.34	9742	1169	89.29
Maritime	4867	0.17	4783	1079	81.59
Total	2913515	100	2882103	296398	90.71

Table 1989-3 Total Appeal Cases in 1989

Cases	Filing	Settlement	No. of cases and the type of settlement				
			Maintained	Reversed	Retrial	Withdrawal	Others
Criminal	51758	51294	37657	7410	3344	2393	490
Civil	112500	109614	53393	25269	9547	7203	14202
Economic	28959	27216	10961	7684	3171	1133	4267
Administrative	2908	2888	1875	227	229	462	95
Traffic	132	120	52	31	15	5	17
Total	196257	191132	103938	40621	16306	11196	19071

Judicial Statistics (1990)

Table 1990-1 Trial Cases, Appeal Cases and Retrial Cases (Judicial Supervision) by the People's Courts in 1990

Cases	Filing	Settlement
Total	3211758	3216612
Trial Cases	2916774	2921806
Appeal Cases	213000	208109
Judicial Supervision	81984	86397

Table 1990-2 Total Trial Cases

Cases	Filing	Percentage of total filing	Settled	Unsettled	Settlement Ratio (%)
Criminal	459656	15.76	457552	16437	96.53
Civil	1851897	63.49	1849728	157602	92.15
Economic	588143	20.16	598317	79001	88.34
Administrative	13006	0.45	12040	2030	85.57
Maritime	4072	0.14	4169	890	82.41
Total	2916774	100	2921806	255960	91.95

Table 1990-3 Total Appeal Cases in 1990

Cases	Filing	Settlement	No. of cases and the type of settlement				
			Maintained	Reversed	Retrial	Withdrawal	Others
Criminal	57930	57048	41681	8579	3730	2508	550
Civil	116362	114401	54352	27550	9970	8662	13867
Economic	35103	33476	13176	9957	3909	1735	4699
Administrative	3431	3325	2192	662	258	102	111
Traffic	174	159	60	45	18	6	30
Total	213000	208409	111461	46793	17885	13013	19257

Judicial Statistics (1991)

Table 1991-1 Trial Cases, Appeal Cases and Retrial Cases (Judicial Supervision) by the People's Courts in 1991

Cases	Filing	Settlement	Unsettled
Trial Cases	290185	2950880	233673
Appeal Cases	229690	230864	32787
Judicial Supervision	83573	84538	22315
Total	3214948	3266282	288775

Table 1991-2 Total Trial Cases in 1991

Cases	Filing	Percentage of Filing	Settled	Unsettled	Settlement Ratio (%)
Criminal	427840	14.74	427607	18263	95.90
Civil	1880635	64.81	1910013	142334	93.06
Economic	566592	19.53	587148	70177	89.32
Administrative	25667	0.89	25202	2526	90.89
Maritime	951	0.03	910	373	70.93
Total	2901685	100	2950880	233673	92.66

Table 1991-3 Total Appeal Cases in 1991

Cases	Filing	Settlement	No. of cases and the types of settlement					
			Maintained	Reversed	Retrial	Withdrawal	Others	Unsettled
Criminal	56125	55817	40312	8728	3869	2260	648	4187
Civil	127113	128396	63487	30522	10474	10024	13889	21037
Economic	39467	39891	16007	12127	4345	2228	5184	7017
Administrative	6930	6708	4381	1385	543	224	175	515
Maritime	55	52	17	22	3	2	8	31
Total	229690	230864	124204	52784	19234	14738	19904	32787

Judicial Statistics (1992)

Table 1992-1 Trial Cases, Appeal Cases and Retrial Cases (Judicial Supervision) by the People's Courts in 1992

Cases	Filing	Settlement
Trial Cases	3051157	3049959
Appeal Cases	231907	236800
Judicial Supervision	81926	83226
Total	3364990	3369985

Table 1992-2 Total Trial Cases in 1992

Cases	Filing	Percentage of Filing	Settled	Unsettled	Ratio of settled cases (%)
Criminal	422991	13.86	424440	16459	96.67
Civil	1948786	63.88	1948949	141212	93.24
Economic	650601	21.32	648018	72286	89.96
Administrative	27125	0.89	27116	2520	91.5
Maritime	1654	0.05	1436	593	70.77
Total	3051157	100	3049959	233070	92.9

Table 1992-3 Total Appeal Cases in 1992

Cases	Filing	Settlement	No. of cases and the types of settlement						
			Maintained	Reversed	Retrial	Withdrawal	Return	Mediation	Others
Criminal	55484	55579	39402	9424	3897	2277	0	0	579
Civil	125096	129079	62271	28350	10405	10212	623	15507	1711
Economic	42931	43791	17225	11361	4525	2671	1355	5374	1280
Administrative	8334	8273	5333	1332	687	397	0	0	524
Maritime	62	78	37	15	12	5	3	4	2
Total	231907	236800	124268	50482	19526	15562	1981	20885	4096

Judicial Statistics (1993)

Table 1993-1 Trial Cases, Appeal Cases and Retrial Cases (Judicial Supervision) by the People's Courts in 1993

Cases	Filing	Settlement
Trial Cases	3414845	3406467
Appeal Cases	215408	219628
Judicial Supervision	69531	73121
Total	3699784	3699216

Table 1993-2 Total Trial Cases in 1993

Cases	Filing	Percentage of Filing	Settlement
Criminal	403267	11.81	403177
Civil	2089257	61.18	2091651
Economic	894410	26.19	883681
Administrative	27911	0.82	27958
Total	3414845	100	3406467

Table 1993-3 Total Appeal Cases in 1993

Cases	Filing	Settlement	No. of cases and the type of settlement					
			Maintained	Reversed	Retrial	Withdrawal	Mediation	Others
Criminal	46947	47602	33996	7382	3520	2066	0	638
Civil	114997	118638	56904	26115	9475	9267	14544	2333
Economic	46038	45804	18166	10967	3983	3087	5523	4078
Administrative	7426	7584	4859	1343	555	370	0	457
Total	215408	219628	113925	45807	17533	14790	20067	7506

Table 1993-4 Total Number of Judgments enforced in 1993

Total enforced cases	Civil	Economic	Administrative	Relating to criminal cases	Applied by administration	Others
912354	471844	314107	20580	10711	88147	6965

Judicial Statistics (1994)

Table 1994-1 Trial Cases, Appeal Cases and Retrial Cases (Judicial Supervision) by the People's Courts in 1994

Cases	Filing	Settlement
Trial Cases	3955475	3943095
Appeal Cases	241129	239938
Judicial Supervision	64377	67288
Total	4260981	4250321

Table 1994-2 Total Trial Cases in 1994

Cases	Filing	Percentage of Filing	Settlement
Criminal	482927	12.21	480914
Civil	2383764	60.26	2382174
Economic	1053701	26.64	1045440
Administrative	35083	0.89	34567
Total	3955475	100	3943095

Table 1994-3 Total Appeal Cases in 1994

Cases	Filing	Settlement	No. of cases and the type of settlement					
			Maintained	Reversed	Retrial	Withdrawal	Mediation	Others
Criminal	53161	52579	37819	7852	3810	2275	0	823
Civil	122099	123006	69855	26268	9248	10437	14682	2515
Economic	58170	56682	22479	12469	4461	4385	6490	6398
Administrative	7699	7672	4974	1196	573	429	0	500
Total	241129	239938	125127	47785	18092	17526	21172	10236

Table 1994-4 Total Number of Judgments enforced in 1994

Total enforced cases	Civil	Economic	Administrative	Relating to criminal cases	Applied by administration	Others
1085040	546683	357574	22800	11580	135355	11048

Judicial Statistics (1995)

Table 1995-1 Trial Cases, Appeal Cases and Retrial Cases (Judicial Supervision) by the People's Courts in 1995

Cases	Filing	Settlement
Trial Cases	4545676	4533551
Appeal Cases	272792	271741
Judicial Supervision	70885	70865
Total	4889353	4876157

Table 1995-2 Total Trial Cases in 1995

Cases	Filing	Percentage of Filing	Settlement
Criminal	495741	10.91	496082
Civil	2718533	59.80	2714665
Economic	1278806	28.13	1271434
Administrative	52596	1.16	51370
Total	4545676	100.00	4533551

Table 1995-3 Total Appeal Cases in 1995

Cases	Filing	Settlement	No. of cases and the type of settlement					
			Maintained	Reversed	Retrial	Withdrawal	Mediation	Others
Criminal	53576	53942	38786	7989	4140	2127	0	900
Civil	139298	138585	66759	29865	10865	11313	16418	3365
Economic	70224	69678	26211	15333	5687	5704	7667	9076
Administrative	9694	9536	6086	1408	676	658	0	708
Total	272792	271741	137842	54595	21368	19802	24085	14049

Table 1995-4 Total Number of Judgments enforced in 1995

Total enforced cases	Civil	Economic	Administrative	Relating to criminal cases	Applied by administration	Others
1337168	645421	450677	27510	13664	188584	11312

Judicial Statistics (1996)

Table 1996-1 Trial Cases, Appeal Cases and Retrial Cases (Judicial Supervision) by the People's Courts in 1996

Cases	Filing	Settlement
Trial Cases	5312580	5285171
Appeal Cases	323995	321962
Judicial Supervision	76094	75230
Total	5712669	5682363

Table 1996-2 Total Trial Cases in 1996

Cases	Filing	Percentage of Filing	Settlement
Criminal	618826	11.65	616676
Civil	3093995	58.24	3084464
Economic	1519793	28.61	1504494
Administrative	79966	1.5	79537
Total	5312580	100	5285171

Table 1996-3 Total Appeal Cases in 1996

Cases	Filing	Settlement	No. of cases and the type of settlement					
			Maintained	Reversed	Retrial	Withdrawal	Mediation	Others
Criminal	68038	67087	48948	9917	4614	2521	0	1087
Civil	159846	159702	77661	34787	12422	13122	17650	4060
Economic Dispute	84657	83808	31906	18307	6916	7331	8386	10962
Administrative	11454	11365	7206	1951	827	702	0	679
Total	323995	321962	165721	64962	24779	23676	26036	16788

Table 1996-4 Total Number of Judgments enforced in 1996

Total enforced cases	Civil	Economic	Administrative	Relating to criminal cases	Applied by administration	Others
1687790	788577	577970	31186	15934	256897	17226

Judicial Statistics (1997)

Table 1997-1 Trial Cases, Appeal Cases and Retrial Cases (Judicial Supervision) by the People's Courts in 1997

Cases	Filing	Settlement
Trial Cases	5288379	5249460
Appeal Cases	347651	340896
Judicial Supervision	86425	83512
Total	5722455	5673868

Table 1997-2 Total Trial Cases in 1997

Cases	Filing	Percentage of Filing	Settlement
Criminal	436894	8.26	440577
Civil	3277572	61.98	3242202
Economic	1483356	28.05	1478139
Administrative	90557	1.71	88542
Total	5288379	100	5249460

Table 1997-3 Total Appeal Cases in 1997

Cases	Filing	Settlement	No. of cases and the type of settlement					
			Maintained	Reversed	Retrial	Withdrawal	Mediation	Others
Criminal	64755	64548	44216	11957	4716	2427	0	1232
Civil	182766	177317	86129	39058	14552	15757	17664	4157
Economic	87376	86347	32596	19860	7646	8001	7799	10445
Administrative	12754	12684	7603	2105	937	1143	0	896
Total	347651	340896	170544	72980	27851	27328	25463	16730

Table 1997-4 Total Number of Judgments enforced in 1997

Total enforced cases	Civil	Economic	Administrative	Relating to criminal cases	Applied by administration	Others
1727439	823420	553882	40170	17991	264936	27040

Judicial Statistics (1998)

Table 1998-1 Trial Cases, Appeal Cases and Retrial Cases (Judicial Supervision) by the People's Courts in 1998

Cases	Filing	Settlement
First trial	5410798	5395039
Appeal Cases	380274	379206
Judicial Supervision	89687	90029
Total	5880759	5864274

Table 1998-2 Total Trial Cases in 1998

Cases	Filing	Percentage of Filing	Settlement
Criminal	482164	8.91	480374
Civil	3375069	62.38	3360028
Economic	1455215	26.89	1456247
Administrative	98350	1.82	98390
Total	5410798	100	5395039

Table 1998-3 Total Appeal Cases in 1998

Cases	Filing	Settlement	No. of cases and the type of settlement					
			Maintained	Reversed	Retrial	Withdrawal	Mediation	Others
Criminal	70263	70767	49603	11369	5603	2658	886	648
Civil	207186	204958	100865	44383	18825	17539	17620	5276
Economic	88495	89261	33372	20465	9148	8795	7328	10153
Administrative	14330	14220	7876	2446	1278	933	38	1649
Total	380274	379206	191716	78663	34854	29925	25872	18176

Table 1998-4 Total Number of Judgments enforced in 1998

Total enforced cases	Civil	Economic	Administrative	Criminal	Administrative – non-litigation	Arbitral	Legal documents	Others
2078038	961938	696710	44373	43771	297898	13233	6735	13380

Judicial Statistics in (1999)

Table 1999-1 Trial Cases, Appeal Cases and Retrial Cases (Judicial Supervision) by the People's Courts in 1999

Cases	Filing	Settlement
Trial Cases	5692434	5698705
Appeal Cases	438313	436804
Judicial Supervision	98765	96793
Total	6229512	6232302

Table 1999-2 Total Trial Cases in 1999

Cases	Filing	Percentage of total filing	Settlement
Criminal	540008	9.49	539335
Civil	3519244	61.82	3517324
Economic	1535613	26.98	1543287
Administrative	97569	1.71	98759
Total	5692434	100	5698705

Table 1999-3 Total Appeal Cases in 1999

Cases	Filing	Settlement	No. of cases and the type of settlement					
			Maintained	Reversed	Retrial	Withdrawal	Mediation	Others
Criminal	78862	78803	56086	11734	6026	3280	1088	589
Civil	246241	244550	124467	50435	21639	21399	19685	6925
Economic Dispute	95165	95379	36978	20203	9581	10336	7436	10845
Administrative	18405	18702	10222	2995	1743	1296	38	1778
Total	48313	436804	227753	85067	38989	36311	28247	20137

Table 1999-4 Total Number of Judgments enforced in 1999

Total enforced cases	Civil	Economic	Administrative	Criminal	Administrative - non-litigation	Arbitral	Others
2645341	1227192	899624	35819	58160	362863	30234	31449

Judicial Statistics (2000)

Table 2000-1 Trial Cases, Appeal Cases and Retrial Cases (Judicial Supervision) by the People's Courts in 2000

Cases	Filing	Settlement
Trial Cases	5356294	5380611
Appeal Cases	466827	469545
Judicial Supervision	95290	97909
Total	5918411	5948065

Table 2000-2 Total Trial Cases in 2000

Cases	Filing	Percentage of total filing	Settlement
Criminal	560432	10.46	560111
Civil	3412259	63.71	3418481
Economic	1297843	24.23	1315405
Administrative	85760	1.6	96614
Total	5356294	100	5380611

Table 2000-3 Total Appeal Cases in 2000

Cases	Filing	Settlement	No. of cases and the type of settlement					
			Maintained	Reversed	Retrial	Withdrawal	Mediation	Others
Criminal	87103	86619	61572	12792	6227	4190	1219	619
Civil	261800	86619	133114	54127	23652	24387	21210	8308
Economic Dispute	98271	98724	38789	20801	9955	10794	7225	11160
Administrative	19743	19404	10693	3060	1654	1296	580	2643
Total	466827	469545	244168	90780	41488	40667	29712	22730

Table 2000-4 Total Number of Judgments enforced cases in 2000

Total enforced cases	Civil	Economic	Administrative	Criminal	Administrative - non-litigation	Arbitral	Others
2639066	127977	844723	28811	63344	361961	43160	25090

FSC
www.fsc.org
MIX
Papier | Fördert gute Waldnutzung
FSC® C083411

Kolibri 360 GmbH
Ferdinand-Jühlke-Straße 7
99095 Erfurt, Deutschland
produktsicherheit@kolibri360.de